THE COMPLETE SIBERIAN HUSKY

Ch. Monadnock's King, Ch. Monadnock's Pando, and Mulpus Brooks the Roadmaster.

The Complete
SIBERIAN
HUSKY

by Lorna B. Demidoff
and Michael Jennings

FIRST EDITION
Third Printing – 1979

HOWELL BOOK HOUSE Inc.
230 Park Avenue
New York, N.Y. 10017

Copyright © 1978 by Howell Book House Inc.
All rights reserved.

Library of Congress Catalog Card No. 77-81705
ISBN 0-87605-314-2

Printed in U.S.A.

In Memory
CH. MONADNOCK'S AKELA
(1965–1975)

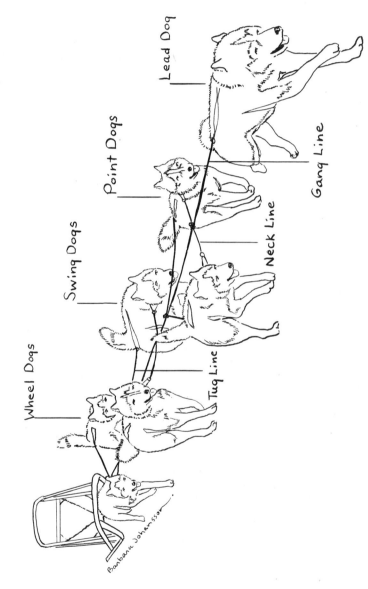

Drawing by Barbara Johansson illustrating terminology used for sled dog positions.

Contents

Lorna Demidoff, Leonhard Seppala, and "Short" Seeley at Laconia, 1960.

Lorna B. Demidoff (1950).

Michael Jennings.

The Authors:

LORNA B. DEMIDOFF has been identified with Siberian Huskies for over four decades. A charter member of the Siberian Husky Club of America, she has served as its president, and as its secretary-treasurer, and has now been named Honorary Lifetime Chairman of its Board.

Born in New York City in 1907, she has lived most of her life in New Hampshire. She first became interested in purebred dogs in 1930 when she attended the Laconia Sled Dog Derby and there saw Leonhard Seppala's team of Siberian Huskies. In 1931 she married Moseley Taylor, one of the founders of the New England Sled Dog Club, and was soon racing a team of her own. She became the first woman to win an official race, and remained active in the sport with the NESDC for over 25 years.

She began showing Siberians in the mid-30s, and her Monadnock Kennels has become one of the legendary kennels of the breed. Included in its honor roll is the first Siberian Husky to win Best in Show in the continental USA (bred, owned and handled by Lorna). In 1941, she married the then Prince Nicholas Alexander Lopouchine-Demidoff, who shares her interest in the dogs.

Mrs. Demidoff has been honored with lifetime honorary memberships of the board of the Cheshire and Ladies Dog Clubs, along with many other citations. Licensed by the American Kennel Club to judge all Working and most of the Sporting breeds, she has judged at virtually all the major shows in America and Canada, including many national Specialties.

MICHAEL JENNINGS' interest in the Siberian Husky began in 1966, while he was still in high school. Born in New Orleans, he spent a number of years in east Texas before moving with his family to Khuzistan Province, in southwestern Iran. There he trained and rode race horses, owned a mongoose, several gazelles and a number of dogs. A poet, he now lives with his wife in Chittenango, New York, where they raise, show and run their Demavand Siberians.

11

"Stew" Cochrane.—*Photo by Ron Testa*

Foreword

(The authors and publisher are deeply honored to have this Foreword by L. Stewart Cochrane. Mr. Cochrane is current delegate to the American Kennel Club for the Siberian Husky Club of America, and has served the breed as a past president of the SHCA, and as president for six terms of the Siberian Husky Club of Delaware Valley. He also presently holds office as Bench Show Chairman of the Kennel Club of Philadelphia, Vice Show Chairman of the Devon Dog Show Association, Vice President of the Chester Valley Kennel Club, Treasurer of the Penn Treaty Kennel Club, and has served as Vice President, Treasurer, and Director of the Pennsylvania Federation of Dog Clubs.)

CURRENTLY 14th in popularity as based on AKC registrations, the Siberian Husky is exceptional among the top breeds in that it happily still has active in its midst some of those who were part of its early development in this country. This book is one dividend of that good fortune.

No one has been more influential in the progress of the Siberian Husky than Lorna Demidoff. She first came to know and love the breed as a racing sled dog, and was the first woman ever to win a sled dog race. She is a founding member of the Siberian Husky Club of America and was on the committee that drew up the 1938 standard. Her Monadnock Kennels stood as the bulwark of the breed for over three decades—not only in the record-establishing dogs it itself produced, but also in the fountainhead it became for other kennels. And today Lorna remains active as one of our most authoritative and respected judges.

In the opportunity that it gives us to see the breed through her eyes, and to know and understand it in the light of her unmatched experience, THE COMPLETE SIBERIAN HUSKY provides a real privilege to the reader.

13

It is well, too, that Lorna has chosen to do her book in collaboration with Michael Jennings. Not only does he bring an academic capability and a fresh enthusiasm for the breed to the writing, but his third person viewpoint helps assure that none of the Monadnock story is lost through Lorna's innate modesty. Together, with the acknowledged cooperation and research of such respected hands as Peggy Koehler, Kathleen Kanzler, Robert Crane, Elizabeth Nansen, Lorna Coppinger, Lee Muller, Anna Mae Forsberg, Alice Watt, Betsy Korbonski and Rachel Page Elliott, plus the celebrated conformation drawings by Barbara Johansson, they have here given us a book on the Siberian Husky that no enthusiast—novice or oldtimer—will want to be without.

As an officer of the Siberian Husky Club of America, I share with many the pride in the zest and zoom with which the breed has taken hold. But we are all well aware that popularity has its dangers, too. We must stay alert to keeping the Siberian Husky the great dog he has been and is.

In this, THE COMPLETE SIBERIAN HUSKY should prove invaluable. It is an old truth that to fully appreciate the present, we must look to the past. Today's breeders are reaping the rewards of the wisdom and dedication of Short Seeley, Lorna Demidoff and the other great early breeders whose stories are told in this book—all of whom bred for dogs as capable for the sled as for the show ring.

In giving us this first-hand look at the beginnings, in preserving the pedigrees of the influential dogs from whom so many of today's dogs trace, and in its treasure of irreplaceable historic pictures—THE COMPLETE SIBERIAN HUSKY provides us with an appreciation and understanding of the Siberian Husky beyond anything we have ever had before.

Important, too, is that this is an "honest" book. While fully celebrating the qualities that make the Siberian Husky a very special dog within its own sphere, it does not pretend that it is a breed for all owners and all purposes. For example, it cautions that the breed is generally too democratic in its affection to be an ideal watch dog, and warns that Siberian Husky puppies are born with an insatiable desire to run. At the same time, the book's fascinating coverage of the Siberian Husky as a sled dog is sure to inspire appreciation of the breed's true metier.

To the long list of accomplishments for which the Siberian Husky fancy is indebted to Lorna Demidoff we add THE COMPLETE SIBERIAN HUSKY. Our salute to Lorna and Mike for a job extremely well done.

—L. STEWART COCHRANE

Authors' Note

It WILL be quickly seen that this book's emphasis is upon the historical.

There are a number of reasons we have chosen this approach. For one, it is the most cohesive. For in recent years there has been such an upsurge of the breed that it would be impossible, in a book of this kind, to note every individual or kennels that has made a significant contribution.

But more important, it is our belief that not enough is known about the breed before 1960. Since the breed has only been on this continent some sixty or so years, there will never again be the opportunity to distill the available information concerning these formative years that the present offers. In another ten years, for example, it will probably be impossible to present—as we have here—some thirty pedigrees with realization that the geneology of almost any contemporary Siberian can be traced right back to the original imports.

Also implicit in our approach is the belief that there is probably no other way, and certainly no better way, to come to an understanding of the Siberian of today than by gaining insight into what he has been in the past. And certainly no breed has had so colorful and intriguing a past, or made such an impact on three continents, as has the breed that we today call the Siberian Husky.

— Lorna B. Demidoff
Michael Jennings

Leonhard Seppala in Alaska.

1

The Siberian in Alaska

GOLD was first discovered in Alaska in 1880 near the present site of Juneau. But it was not until 1896, when prospectors from the Juneau area struck gold in the Klondike region of the neighboring Yukon Territory, that the gold rush, as such, really began. With this strike, thousands from all over the world poured into the Yukon and Alaskan Territories. Some found gold, but most didn't. The rush did not last long and the last major strike was made in Fairbanks in 1902. During the peak of the rush luckier prospectors might dig or pan as much as $5000 worth of gold dust in just a few days. But with eggs selling at a dollar apiece, few kept their hard-earned diggings long. Often the richest man in town was the "swamper" whose duty, or privilege, it was to sweep the sawdust, rich with gold dust from carelessly handled pokes, from the barroom floor.

But if few of the thousands of new inhabitants shared in the newly found wealth, all shared in the hardships. And foremost among these, probably greater than the problems of simple co-habitation, or crossing the Rockies, or a run of bad luck, was the severe, treacherous and almost constant cold. Many died from it and more left because of it. But as the fervor of the rush subsided and life in the mining towns took on the almost staid qualities of well regulated businesses, those who stayed came to depend, like their Indian and Eskimo predecessors, upon the sled dog for survival.

Nowhere was this more the case than in a small settlement on a spit of land jutting into Norton Sound. By an odd quirk of fate appropriate to a boom town, the words "No Name," scrawled on a map by a clerk in the Territorial Land Office, had been misread and the town came to be called Nome. Nome entered the ranks of boom towns when, in 1899, gold was discovered in nearby Daniels Creek. Situated as it was on a narrow peninsula with room for only a single main street along its length, the sudden explosion in population in 1900 created a "tent city" all along the frozen beach. With ice shutting off all communication by sea for the greater part of the year, Nome residents became

Start of first team in first All Alaska Sweepstakes, 1908.

completely dependent upon the only other means of transportation to the outside world—dog team. Consequently, it has been estimated that at the turn of the century there were probably more dogs per capita in the town of Nome than anywhere else in the world.

Like the inhabitants themselves, these dogs were a varied lot. Some were native dogs—thick-coated, erect-eared, arctic types; others showed their more southern heritage—flat-coated, lop-eared dogs who had either migrated north with their owners or, as was probably more commonly the case, had been shanghaied and shipped north for profit. Generally they were large, brawny, fierce dogs, and, like the inhabitants themselves, the ones who survived were accustomed to hard work, severe cold and relatively little food.

Since life virtually depended upon these dogs, a good one was not only a possession of great value but an object of immense pride and prestige as well. It is not surprising, then, that at night—when the men gathered around the pot-bellied stove of a local saloon—the topic of conversation was often dogs. And as the night progressed and the tales grew taller, the feats of this leader or that leader, or the speed of one or another team, took on marvelous proportions. And with each man extolling the virtues of his team while pointing out the weaknesses of his neighbor's, the debates grew increasingly heated. Some teams were fast for short distances, while others had more stamina; some could nose into a blizzard, while others could run well with a tail-wind; some hated breaking trail in deep snow; others couldn't take ice glare. And so the disputes continued.

Finally, Allan "Scotty" Allan, who was to become one of the most popular figures in Alaskan history, proposed that they run a race to prove once and for all just who did have the best team. Although Scotty had made a fortune in the gold fields, he had lost it all with the sinking of a steamer he had bought and was at this time employed as the bookkeeper for the Darling and Dean Hardware Merchants. An excellent dog driver himself, it was, in fact, his children's habit of "racing" their dogs that inspired him to suggest this idea to the dog drivers of Nome.

It became immediately apparent, however, that this could not be just an ordinary race. In order to prove anything it would have to be a big event, have public interest and support, be well organized with machinery to make and enforce rules, and be a fair test of the capabilities of dogs and drivers alike. After months of discussion, the Nome Kennel Club was formed in 1907 in order to organize and sponsor the event. Albert Fink, a lawyer, was its first president and helped in the drafting of the rules. Basically they were as follows:

— All drivers had to be members of the Nome Kennel Club.
— All dogs had to be registered with the Club.
— A driver could have as many dogs on a team as he wanted, but all who started had to be brought back, either in harness or on the sled, and all dogs would be specially marked at the start of the race to prevent substitutions along the trail.

19

— There could be no ''pacing'' or team work of any kind. When two teams traveling in the same direction came in close proximity, the one behind would be given the right to pass and should be given any assistance necessary in passing by the forward driver. This rule, however, would not be considered in effect during the last leg of the homeward stretch.

In addition to these rules, there was a long list of technicalities.

But it was the laying out of the course, itself, that was the prime consideration. For if the race was indeed to prove which was the best team, the course would have to test every aspect of the dogs' and drivers' capabilities. Finally a course from Nome to Candle and return was decided upon, a distance of 408 miles that included extremely varied driving conditions. There was sea ice, tundra, mountains, timber, glaciers and even one valley that was almost always engulfed in a blizzard, no matter how fair the weather elsewhere.

It was decided that the race should be held in April when climatic conditions were most ideal. In order to get dogs and drivers in proper condition, preliminary races were held all winter, starting in October with a seven mile race and working up to 75 miles just prior to the proposed date. Such intensity of focus naturally resulted in a re-evaluation of the entire sled dog scene. Special enriched diets were fed and dogs were weighed daily. Drivers gave considerable attention to the condition of their dogs' feet, toughening pads against sharp ice. Innovations, like flank protectors for short-coated dogs and green netting or goggles for protection against snow-blindness, were tried. Sleds were made lighter, and lines and harnesses were improved. Thus the lot of sled dogs in general was vastly improved, and the rate of progress in driving techniques accelerated greatly.

The All Alaska Sweepstakes

The first All Alaska Sweepstakes was held in 1908 and was more or less in the nature of an experiment. In this race and in the 1909 race, the usual heavy basket sled was still used. Subsequently a lighter racing sled was developed and used. Starting procedures also underwent some refinement in these early years of the race. In the 1908 race, starts were spaced at two hour intervals and each team's time was calculated from the time it started. But with weather and trail conditions changing quickly along the course, it was found that such long intervals between starts could unduly influence the outcome of the race. Some teams might have fair weather for the major part of their run while others might run into nothing but blizzard conditions. Gradually, then, the interval between starts was decreased until 1913, from which time teams were started at one minute intervals and all were considered to have started at the same time.

Winners, first All Alaska Sweepstakes, 1908. Albert Fink, owner; John Hegness, driver.

Winners, second All Alaska Sweepstakes, 1909. J. Berger, owner; "Scotty" Allan, driver.

Winners, third All Alaska Sweepstakes, 1910. Col. Ramsay, owner; John Johnson, driver.

Winners, fourth All Alaska Sweepstakes, 1911. Allan and Darling, owners; "Scotty" Allan, driver.

Winners, fifth All Alaska Sweepstakes, 1912. Allan and Darling, owners; "Scotty" Allan, driver.

Winners, sixth All Alaska Sweepstakes, 1913. Bowen and Dalzene, owners; Fay Dalzene, driver.

Winners, seventh All Alaska Sweepstakes, 1914. John Johnson, owner and driver.

Winners, eighth All Alaska Sweepstakes, 1915. Leonhard Seppala, owner and driver.

Winners, ninth All Alaska Sweepstakes, 1916. Leonhard Seppala, owner and driver.

"Scotty" Allan, veteran of Alaskan dog racing, with famous leader "Baldy of Nome."

Trophy cup of the
All Alaska Sweepstakes.

John Johnson, the "Iron Man," with two of his lead dogs. Kolma, the most notable, is at left.

The 1908 All Alaska Sweepstakes was won by the team owned by the club's president, Albert Fink, and driven by John Hegness. The event itself turned out to be more successful than its organizers could possibly have hoped. It was THE event of the year as far as Nome residents were concerned, and public opinion demanded that it become an annual affair. Not only did the race provide an excuse for a four day holiday, with schools closing, businesses all but shutting down and even the election of a "Queen of the Sweepstakes," it also provided an opportunity for that favorite of frontier pastimes — gambling.

In fact, it was this last nerve-racking aspect of the race that probably accounts for its immense popularity. The course ran along a telephone line which allowed constant reports on the progress of the teams to be sent back to bettors in Nome. There, assembled in the Board of Trade Saloon on Front Street, the gamblers watched progress reports on each team as they were put up on a large board. The unique thing about the betting was that the books remained open until the first team crossed the finish line. This meant that the odds were perpetually changing; as one or another favorite fell behind, hedging bets could be placed, and, consequently, fortunes could be won or lost in just a few days. In addition, weather and trail conditions could change so rapidly that even the fastest, most experienced teams could be beaten by slower ones if luck was against them. Consequently few of the gamblers dared leave the saloon during the entire four days of the race. Food was brought in to them and, at the end of the race, many of the bleary-eyed men emerging from the saloon seemed considerably worse for wear than the drivers themselves. So popular, in fact, was this form of entertainment that before the start of the Second All Alaska Sweepstakes in 1909, there was already more than $100,000 on the books.

This race also saw the entrance of an unknown quantity. During the preceeding summer of 1908, a Russian fur trader named William Goosak had arrived in Nome with a team of dogs from Siberia that were substantially different in size, disposition and appearance from the local dogs. Whereas the native dogs were large, rangy, fierce, often wolf-like dogs, prone to fighting and giving the impression of great strength, these Siberian dogs were compact, small, docile and rather more fox-like than wolf-like in appearance. Although the dog fanciers of Nome found the attractiveness and amiable dispositions of these dogs appealing, the suggestion that they be entered in the sweepstakes to compete against the larger and apparently much tougher native dogs was not taken seriously. The oddsmakers, themselves, used the assessing teams largely on the basis of leg length, hardly gave the team a second thought, since the little dogs had considerably less leg than any other entry. Despite this unreceptiveness, however, Goosak did manage to persuade a man named Thurstrup to drive the team. So, on a cold, bleak morning in April, 1909, the first team of Siberian Huskies to be seen on the North American Continent loped out of the town of Nome and into the annals of history.

They did not win the race, however, largely because of a poor strategical maneuver on the part of their driver, Thurstrup. Much of the success of a team in a race of this length depended not only upon the actual driving skill of the driver, but upon his ability to gauge the speed and endurance of his dogs; and each driver painstakingly worked out a pre-race strategy based upon arduous practice. Would he drive his dogs eight hours and rest six? If he saw a chance to overtake an opponent, would he risk cutting short his dogs' rest period? Every driver tried to decide these questions well in advance of the race, and caches of food and supplies were hidden along the trail at the anticipated rest stations.

But even the best laid plans were dependent upon such things as weather and injuries. As it happened, a blizzard struck Nome just as the race was starting, and of the 14 teams that started only three were able to keep going. These included the favorite, Scotty Allan, driving his mixed-breed team; Percy Blatchford, driving Allan's second string team; and Thurstrup, driving Goosak's Siberians.

As the little Siberians managed to stay only slightly behind Allan on the way to Candle, and as reports of this reached Nome, those who had bet heavily on Allan began to grow anxious. Consequently, when Allan reached Candle, he received urgent calls urging him to shorten his proposed seven hour rest stop and to start on the home stretch as quickly as possible. But Allan refused to risk the consequences of such action and stayed in Candle until he felt his team was sufficiently rested.

Arriving in Candle shortly after Allan, Thurstrup did not display the same self-control. Checking in with the officials there, he immediately started out again, and although he led the race for the next hundred miles, the lack of rest for himself and his dogs cost him the race, as both Allan and Blatchford managed to overtake him before the last quarter mark was reached.

Allan won the race with Blatchford taking second and Thurstrup third. But even a third place finish was enough to convince the dog fanciers of Nome of the calibre of the Siberians. Not only had they shown their speed and endurance, but all who had seen them had been struck by their remarkable manageability.

The previous spring a young Scotsman named Fox Maule Ramsay, second son of the Earl of Dalhousie and a graduate of Oxford University, had arrived in Nome with his two uncles, Colonel Charles Ramsay and Colonel Weatherly Stuart, the family having invested money in the Nome goldfields. Being young, Ramsay quickly took to the life of the North, especially dog driving, and in 1909 he drove a team in the Sweepstakes but did not place. But after seeing the Siberians in action, and at the advice of Ivor Olsen, a man familiar with Siberia, Ramsay chartered a schooner in the summer of 1909, paying what for those days was the not inconsiderable price of $2500, and crossed the

Bering Sea to Siberia. He returned with some seventy Siberian Huskies, obtained from the small settlement of Markova on the Anadyr River.

From these dogs Ramsay entered three teams in the 1910 All Alaska Sweepstakes, one for himself and one for each of his uncles. The team entered in the name of Colonel Charles Ramsay and driven by John "Iron Man" Johnson took first place with an elapsed time of 74 hours, 14 minutes, 37 seconds, a time that in the history of the race was never equaled. Ramsay, himself, driving his own team, took second, and the third team of Siberians, driven by Charles Johnson, finished fourth.

During the next few years luck seems to have been against the Siberian entries. Perhaps it was more than luck since it appears that, at least on one occasion, the dogs on John Johnson's team were doped. Apparently so much money had been bet on him that had he won, it would have broken the gambling ring. No one knew exactly what had happened, but Johnson claimed that on a certain part of the trail his dogs kept picking up what appeared to be small pieces of meat. Soon afterward they became drowsy and finally could not be roused. Other people claimed that he had simply thrown the race. At any rate the races of 1911 and 1912 went to Scotty Allan's team of cross-breeds, with a Siberian entry driven by Charles Johnson taking third in both races. The race of 1913 went to Fay Delzene, who also drove dogs of mixed breeding, with John Johnson and his Siberians managing to capture second place. Finally in 1914, the "Iron Man" again brought the Siberians in first.

Johnson left Nome shortly after this race to go to California, but although his performances had been somewhat erratic, he had proven the superiority of the Siberian on at least two occasions. It now only remained for someone to take sufficient interest in the little dogs to further their cause.

Leonhard Seppala

Arriving in Nome around 1900, Leonhard Seppala was better prepared than most to meet the hardships of this new country. Born in the fishing village of Skjervoy, Norway, some 250 miles north of the Arctic Circle, he had first faced the perils and hardships of an arctic fisherman's life at the age of eleven. During the summer months he had worked with his father as a blacksmith, and with the idea of eventually taking over his father's business, he had completed his apprenticeship in that trade in the town of Christiana. The constant hard work coupled with an avid interest in sports helped Leonhard to develop into a lean, sturdy young man, and, although extremely small, he was both an expert skier and a proficient wrestler.

The idea of taking over his father's business and settling into the traditional life of Skjervoy lost its appeal, however, with the sudden death of his childhood sweetheart and fiancee. With her death, life in Norway suddenly seemed bleak and repetitive to the young man, and when an old friend, Jafet

Lindeburg, returned from the Alaskan goldfields with accounts of a new life and unheard of wealth, Seppala decided to emigrate. Once in Nome, he worked at various jobs in and around the mines. He also tried prospecting, when opportunity and funds permitted, but never struck pay dirt. But like most long-time residents of the peninsula, he acquired the art of dog driving, and, like the rest of the community, became an avid follower of the new and rapidly growing sport of sled dog racing.

Until the first All Alaska Sweepstakes in 1908, skiing had been the major sport in the area, and Seppala was among the best. But with the introduction of sled dog racing, the public's attention switched rapidly. Seppala, himself, had never considered himself a particularly expert dog driver, and when a friend suggested that he enter one of the small races that were held throughout the year in preparation for the Sweepstakes, Seppala thought he was joking. At this time, Seppala owned a team of mixed-breed freighting dogs which he had never thought as racing dogs. But his love of sporting events, along with his friend's persuasiveness, finally overcame his initial timidity, and he entered the Moose Burden Handicap race.

As it happened, it was a buzzard who decided the outcome of the race and, in doing so, probably changed the history of sled dog racing. Seppala had no real thought of winning the race, and when one of the faster teams pulled up behind him, he was about to pull over to let the other team by when his own team gave a sudden burst of speed. Looking ahead, Seppala saw a buzzard on the trail. And as his team gave chase, the buzzard flew up and settled again further along the trail. This kept up for about four miles until the buzzard grew tired of the game. But the extra speed had been enough, and when Seppala looked back, his competitor was no longer in sight. Crossing the finish line, no one was more surprised than Seppala when he learned that he had actually won the race. He knew the win had been a fluke, but the sensation of victory in this new sport was addictive, and so Leonhard Seppala, the skier, became Leonhard Seppala, the dog racer.

But he was not really in the big leagues yet, and in the years that followed, the teams of John Johnson, Scotty Allan and Fay Delzene were still the teams to be reckoned with in the Sweepstakes.

In 1913, however, Jafet Lindeburg, having collected the best of what could be found of the first Siberian imports and their offspring, asked Seppala if he would take charge of raising and training the young dogs. There were about 15 dogs in all, mostly puppies and bitches, and it was intended that they be presented as a gift to Captain Roald Amundsen for his proposed expedition to the North Pole the following year. Fortunately for Seppala and for the reputation of the Siberians, Amundsen had to cancel his expedition at the outbreak of World War I, and Seppala managed to keep possession of the dogs.

But the dogs were very young, the lead dog Suggen being the only experienced one on the team. So, when the Nome Kennel Club along with Scotty Allan suggested that the teams be entered in the seventh All Alaska Sweepstakes in 1914, Seppala was extremely dubious. He acquiesced at the last moment, however, and entered the race without ever having been over the course. This turned out to be a mistake, for as soon as the race began, a blizzard started and Seppala and his team took a wrong turn and became lost. After almost toppling over a cliff several hundred feet high in the blinding squall, Seppala finally managed to make it back to the trail. But the dogs feet were badly bleeding and they were exhausted. Consequently he was forced to withdraw from the race.

Throughout the following winter, however, Seppala and his team trained as never before. In order to subsidize the training, Seppala began hauling freight and passengers all over Alaska, and by the start of the eighth All Alaska Sweepstakes in 1915, his team was in excellent condition. He had been careful to train far out of town so that no one had any idea of the speed of his team. This fact, coupled with his ignominious withdrawal the year before, made him the long shot of the race.

Nevertheless, Seppala won the race with ease. His nearest rival was Scotty Allan, and Seppala, expecting a homestretch battle with Allan, had intentionally "saved" his Siberians for just such an encounter. But by Cape Nome, 13 miles from the finish, Seppala was a full hour ahead of Allan and managed to win "going away." Seppala's wife, Constance, had been elected Queen of the Sweepstakes that year, and as the cannon at Fort Davis boomed, and the whistles of the power station and fire stations shrieked to announce the winner, she was the first out to greet him.

Seppala won the next two Sweepstakes in 1916 and 1917 with the same ease. After 1917, the lack of competiton for him and the increase in the war effort caused the race to be discontinued. And so, what was perhaps the most spectacular chapter in the history of sled dog racing came to a close.

But in the years that followed Seppala went on to prove the versatility of his little dogs, winning many of the shorter races and breaking many records in the process. In doing so he proved his contention that, with proper training, the Siberian could be as successful in races of medium distances as it had been in the gruelling Sweepstakes races. He won these races, not only in Alaska, but in Canada and New England as well; wherever he went, "the little man with his little dogs," as they came to be called, won the admiration and affection of all. What seemed to astound people most was the willingness of the dogs to work and Seppala's uncanny ability to instill this desire in them. One discouraged rival in New England described it this way:

> That man is superhuman. He passed me every day of the race, and I wasn't loafing any. I couldn't see that he drove his dogs. He just clucked to them every now and then, and they would lay into their collars harder than I've ever seen dogs do before. Something came out of him and went into those dogs with that clucking. You've heard of some men who hold supernatural control over others. Hypnotism, I guess you call it. I suppose it's just as likely to work on dogs. Seppala certainly has it if anyone has.

A fact in which Seppala took great pride was that in all the years he raced, he never used a whip on a dog. Only once was he ever called upon to even crack his whip, and that was simply to get the dogs up quickly after a rest stop in the 1915 All Alaska Sweepstakes.

Times for the
All Alaska Sweepstakes

Race	Winning Driver	Breed of Dog	Elapsed hourly time
1908	John Hagness	Mixed malemute	3.51 miles per hour
1909	A. A. Allan	Mixed malemute	4.97
1910	John Johnson	Siberian	5.58
1911	A. A. Allan	Mixed malemute	5.05
1912	A. A. Allan	Mixed malemute	4.66
1913	Fay Delzene	Mixed malemute	5.39
1914	John Johnson	Siberian	5.04
1915	Leonhard Seppala	Siberian	5.18
1916	Leonhard Seppala	Siberian	5.06
1917	Leonhard Seppala	Siberian	

Siberian Entries

Race	Place	Driver	Elapsed hourly time
1908	No entry		
1909	3rd	Thurstrup	4.54 miles per hour
1910	1st	John Johnson	5.58
	2nd	Fox Ramsey	5.34
1911	3rd	Charles Johnson	4.80
1912	3rd	Charles Johnson	4.59
1913	2nd	John Johnson	5.28
1914	1st	John Johnson	5.04
1915	1st	Leonhard Seppala	5.18
1916	1st	Leonhard Seppala	5.06
1917	1st	Leonhard Seppala	

Not all of Seppala's runs, however, were in the nature of sporting events, and often his most spectacular were not.

From an early age, Seppala seems to have been endowed with those qualities of courage and presence of mind that prove useful in times of crisis. At

Leonhard Seppala.

the age of nine, he dragged an older and much larger playmate from a fire. Later, during a storm, he helped his father rescue a boatload of drowning fishermen from the icy Arctic Ocean. Within his first few years in Alaska, he pursued and caught a man who was attempting to kidnap a young woman. Being a superior dog driver, he had managed to catch up with the man even thought the latter had a considerable headstart. Once having caught up, Seppala, although unarmed, managed to disarm the man and return the girl to Nome.

On another occasion, shortly after winning the All Alaska Sweepstakes in 1916, Seppala, arriving in Dime Creek after making a forty mile run, learned that a friend and fellow Sweepstakes racer named Bobby Brown had been badly mangled in a sawmill accident. The nearest hospital was in Candle, 62 miles away, and the townspeople, hearing that Seppala was in the area, rushed out to implore him to make the trip. It was already one o'clock and his dogs were tired. Besides Seppala already had one passenger and was unfamiliar with the trail. Pointing out these facts, Seppala, although stating that he was willing to try, suggested that their best driver and a fresh team of dogs could probably make better time. The townspeople, however, were determined that Seppala was the best man to make the drive. They did agree to send along their best driver with a fresh team to act as guide and to take the other passenger. And so the two teams left for Candle.

31

It became immediately apparent, however, that the other team could not keep up, even when Seppala took the other passenger back onto his sled. At this point, Bobby Brown, who was still conscious, told Seppala that if he were kept informed of the passing landmarks, he could guide them to Candle. So the other team turned back and Seppala, carrying two passengers, continued on to Candle, arriving around eleven o'clock that night. His team had covered 102 miles in one day with sometimes two and sometimes three men on the sled. In all of Seppala's experience, he had never heard of a team making as long a drive with such a load in one day and in one drive. Unfortunately, Bobby Brown died three days later.

Seppala and the Historic Serum Drive

But it was in 1925, when diphtheria threatened to decimate the population of Nome, that Seppala and his Siberians gained international acclaim. It was in January of that year that the first child died of the disease, and soon others were affected. The existing supply of antitoxin in Nome at the time was small, and as the disease spread, it was quickly used up. The nearest available supply of the antitoxin was in Anchorage, 955 miles away. It could be transported by rail as far as Nenana, 297 miles north of Anchorage, but no further. The only two planes in Alaska were dismantled and sitting in Fairbanks with no one to fly them, since the only three pilots in the territory were away for the winter. The nearest operable plane was in Seattle and there was not time to bring it north. This meant that the only means of transporting the serum the remaining 658 miles from Nenana to Nome was by dog team. The trip was an arduous one in any season, but in the middle of winter, it was especially so. In the best weather, the U.S. mail teams took 25 days to cover the distance.

Seppala's plan was to drop some of the dogs off along the way at various Eskimo villages where they could be cared for and rested for the return trip. By dropping off a total of twelve along the way, he planned to reach Nulato, where he was to meet the team coming from the other direction, with eight. This would be a sufficient number, he calculated, since he had been informed that the package containing the serum was very light.

But after Seppala passed out of telephone communication with Nome, the epidemic increased so alarmingly that it was decided to speed up the transportation of the serum by running shorter relays night and day from the other direction. Thus, toward the end of the fourth day, as Seppala and his team were just coming in sight of the village of Shaktolik, they met the driver with the serum. Seppala had only traveled 170 miles since leaving Nome, while expecting to travel 300. Consequently, he had almost passed the driver with a word of greeting when he made out the words, "Serum—turn back." Although this would make his total journey shorter, Seppala had just covered the worst 43 miles over the ice of Norton Sound from Issac's Point to Shaktolik, and now, with night approaching and a high wind in their faces, they would have to make it back over the ice. On this part of the journey there was the ever-present danger of the ice breaking off and drifting out into the Bering Sea. Many men had been lost in this way, and with the high wind, the chances of such an occurence were greater. Nevertheless Seppala reached Issac's Point, making the team's total mileage for that day nearly ninety miles. The next day, on the advice of an old Eskimo, Seppala drove the team closer into shore. Even so, at one point, they passed only a few feet from open water where the trail they had traveled the day before had drifted out to sea. Nevertheless, that afternoon they reached the village of Cheenik where the next relay team took over.

The last relay team, driven by Gunnar Kasson, reached Nome at 5:30 on the morning of February 2, 1925, the entire trip of 658 miles from Nenana to Nome having been made in just five and one-half days. And of the 650 miles, Leonhard Seppala and his team had gone 340 miles, while no other relay had done more than 53.

So impressive, in fact, had been the efforts of dogs and drivers in averting the diphtheria epidemic, that Senator Dill of the state of Washington introduced a resolution in Congress that made the story of the serum drive part of the Congressional Record. One sentence of this account reads, "Men had thought that the limit of speed and endurance had been reached in the grueling races of Alaska, but a race for sport and money proved to have far less stimulus than this contest, in which humanity was the urge and life was the prize."

After the serum drive, Seppala traveled extensively throughout the United States and Canada, winning races wherever he went and providing the foundation stock for many of the early Siberian kennels in both countries. The record he compiled as a racer is undeniable. He was not only the winner of the All Alaska Sweepstakes in 1915, 1916 and 1917, but also won the Yukon Dog Derby twice, the Bordon Marathon four times, the Ruby Derby, the New England Point to Point race three times, the Eastern International in Quebec, the Lake Placid race twice, the Poland Spring race in Maine three times, and the Solomon Burden race twice. In many of these he set records, some of which stand to this day.

But as deserving as he is of the title of "the world's greatest dog driver," Seppala's primary concern was not simply that of personal glory. Settling late in his life in Seattle, Washington where he helped in the breeding and maintenance of Earl Snodie's Bow Lake Kennels, he once remarked that, to him his greatest accomplishments had been in furthering the cause of the Siberian dogs he had come to know and love, and which it had been his honor to drive for so many years, and to have bettered the treatment of sled dogs in general.

He died in 1967 in Seattle. In old age he remained what he had always been: a quiet, unassuming, humorous man, always somewhat surprised but shyly pleased when someone remembered him.

Togo

Many, if not most, breeds have that one specimen which, for one reason or another, attains the status of legend, and against which all who come after are held up for comparison. And as one rolls back the generations of Siberians, past this year's Best in Show winner and last year's top producer or top lead dog, always out of the white frozen landscape of the past there looms Togo: small, dark, compact, oblivious of the praises that have been heaped upon him, irreverent, foxy, and, except for that certain poise and the confident response to command, like a true Siberian, unabashedly disreputable.

Togo was born in Seppala's kennels in Little Creek, Alaska, probably in 1915 or 1916. Named after the famous Japanese admiral, he was sired by Seppala's lead dog Suggen, who led the Siberian team to loss and then to victory in the Sweepstakes races of 1914 and 1915.* His dam was a bitch named Dolly. He was the only puppy in the litter and, according to Seppala, was lonely, sometimes sullen and often mischievous. He first belonged to a man named Victor Anderson, but when he proved to be too much of a bother, Anderson returned him to Seppala at age of about six months. Seppala, in turn, gave the puppy to a woman who wanted a pet. But for all the lavish attention he received at this new home, Togo repeatedly broke his chain or jumped out the window and returned to Little Creek. Finally succumbing to the inevitable, Seppala took the little dog back and decided to keep him.

Thrilled to be back in the only environment that he apparently enjoyed, Togo roamed the surrounding tundra at will or ran loose beside the team during their daily run. This latter activity seemed to have special appeal to the puppy but soon became annoying to Seppala, since Togo loved nothing better than to come charging past the team and, watching his chance, take a nip at one or another of the dogs' ears and get away quickly.

Accordingly, when Seppala was planning a trip to Dime Creek in November, he left Togo in the large corral with a seven-foot wire fence with instructions to the kennel hand that the puppy was not to be released until a couple of days after the team had gone. Togo, quite untypically, showed no outward sign of disappointment at being left. That night, however, Togo made a leap for it and almost made it. A rear leg, however, caught in the wire and when the kennel boss came out to see what was causing the commotion he found the little dog hanging upside down on the outside of the fence with a severe gash in his leg. But the dog's only concern seems to have been to catch up with the team, and when he was cut down he quickly disappeared into the night.

Seppala had camped at Solomon that night. When he started out the next morning the team began pulling with unusual speed, and Seppala decided that

---

* This is based upon Seppala's account of his dogs in the book, *Seppala, an Alaskan Dog Driver*, by Elizabeth Ricker, but there is some evidence that Seppala's lead dog in 1915 may have been a cross-breed named Russky.

Togo, leader in the serum drive.

they must have picked up the scent of reindeer. As the sun rose and the wind died Seppala saw what appeared to be a fox on the trail ahead. Soon, scarcely believing his eyes, he realized that it was Togo. At this point the puppy charged the team, nipping the leader on the ear as he passed and succeeded in creating havoc for the rest of the day. Having bandaged his leg as best he could, Seppala decided the next day that there was nothing to do with the eight-month-old trouble maker but to try him in harness with the rest of the dogs. As is customary with new dogs, he was hitched far back in the team so that Seppala could keep an eye on him. Once in harness, however, Togo started off like a veteran, as if this was just the chance he had been waiting for. And as the day proceeded and he continued to work harder than any of the adults, he was gradually promoted forward until, at the end of the day, he was actually sharing the lead position with Seppala's experienced lead dog.

Needless to say, Seppala could hardly believe what he was seeing. Here was an eight-month-old puppy who had never been in harness and who had an injured leg, but who, in his first day on the trail, had travelled 75 miles and pulled in ahead of the seasoned team. From that day on it was Togo who was the favorite and could always be depended upon.

Even in maturity Togo weighed only 48 pounds. But as the years rolled on, his strength, speed and endurance became legendary throughout Alaska, and his reputation as a lead dog was rivaled only by that of Kolma, John "Iron Man" Johnson's famous lead dog who led the record-setting team of Siberians in the All Alaska Sweepstakes in 1910.

At left, Leonhard Seppala with Togo at Poland Spring, Maine, 1929. Below, 31 years later, Mr. Seppala with Ralph Morrill visits Togo in his preserved state at Peabody Museum of Yale University.

It is somewhat uncertain exactly when Togo became the full-fledged leader of Seppala's team. His first major race was probably the 1918 Borden Marathon. It is certain that he was the leader in most of the races subsequent to the Sweepstakes and that during his years as leader he earned the title of the "world's most traveled dog," logging, by Seppala's estimation, approximately 5,000 miles during his career.

In 1925 it was Togo whom Seppala counted on to lead the team on the Serum Drive. And during that run, according to Seppala, the famous leader worked harder and better than ever. But the miles had taken their toll, and the Serum Drive was the last long run the old dog made. Since he had logged 340 miles in the interest of the serum, and since the run had left him permanently lame, it is not surprising that many were dismayed when reporters from the States gave the greatest publicity to a dog named Balto, one of the second string dogs that Seppala had left behind with his scrub team and whom Gunnar Kasson had used to relay the serum the last fifty miles into Nome. Impressed with the romantic ring of his name, reporters had simply given Balto Togo's record as a lead dog and thus publicized him as "the greatest racing leader in Alaska." Consequently, the statue that was erected in Central Park, New York, to commemorate the event bears the name Balto instead of Togo.

Fortunately fame is not a canine aspiration, and Togo lived out the remainder of his life with all the comforts and attention that he deserved. While traveling in the States, Seppala presented him as a gift to Mrs. Elizabeth Ricker, feeling that the easier life in her kennel was more suited to his age. It was at her kennel in Poland Spring, Maine that he died on December 5, 1929.

Togo's body was taken to the Peabody Museum at Yale University where Ralph C. Morrill prepared him for exhibition with other famous dogs in the Whitney Collection. Subsequently he was moved to the Shelbourne Museum near Burlington, Vermont, where each summer Siberian fanciers from all over the country come to pay their respects to the dog that, more than any other, has come to symbolize the words on Balto's statue in Central Park, New York. They read:

> *Dedicated to the indomitable spirit of the sled dogs*
> *that relayed antitoxin six hundred miles over rough*
> *ice across treacherous waters through arctic*
> *blizzards from Nenana to the relief of stricken Nome*
> *in the Winter of 1925.*
>
> *Endurance*
>
>   *Fidelity*
>
>   *Intelligence*

Millie Turner's and Harry Wheeler's teams combined, at St. Jovite.

2

Origin of the Siberian Husky

THE BREED that is today recognized by the American Kennel Club as the Siberian Husky has evolved directly from these early imports to Alaska and from one other importation directly to New England. The first of these imports was, of course, that of William Goosak, the fur trader. These dogs came from Markovo, one of several fairs along the Anadyr River where a dog-breeding people known as the Chukchi came to sell or trade their dogs. Impressed with the performance of these dogs in the 1909 All Alaska Sweepstakes, William Madsen acquired them from Goosak along with their first litter of pups whelped on November 29, 1908, and returned to buy 14 more Chukchi dogs. In turn, all of these dogs were acquired eventually by John Johnson and combined with the dogs that Fox Maule Ramsey and Iver Olsen bought in 1909, also at the Markovo Fair.

As we have seen many of the best of these dogs were gathered together in Nome by Jafet Lindeberg as an intended gift to Roald Amundsen for his proposed ''dash to the pole.'' When Amundsen's expedition was canceled, these dogs went to Leonhard Seppala, and, together with the direct imports to New England by Olaf Swenson in 1930, formed the foundation of what is known today as the Siberian Husky.

Therefore, in order to trace the development of this remarkable breed that almost overnight captured the interest of sled dog fanciers throughout the North American continent, it is necessary to look far back into the arctic past at a culture so ancient as to remain obscure even to the most ardent researchers and at a people so adapted to the climatic and political severity of their culture as to have earned the appellation ''the Apaches of Siberia.'' These were the Chukchi people of Northeastern Siberia.

When and where the first symbiotic relationship between men and wolves or men and jackals developed is unknown. How long this relationship lasted before the process of domestication began is also a matter of conjecture. We know that the dog has served man in a vital capacity in both hunting and herding cultures for hundreds, and in some cases thousands, of years. In no instance, however, has the dog been any more crucial to survival than in the sled dog cultures of the far north, and probably never has he held such a sustained and integral position in the entire economic, spiritual, and political structure of a culture as in the case of the Chukchi.

The Chukchi Sled Dog

It is, of course, impossible to prove definitively that the Siberian Husky of today, as recognized by the American Kennel Club, has evolved in a state of absolute purity from the Chukchi sled dog, or that this strain had itself remained pure from some three thousand years prior to the time the first dogs were exported to Alaska. On the other hand, since there have been various arguments in the past disputing the relative purity of these dogs, it is necessary to note some of the causes of the confusion.

In the first place, the Chukchi culture was basically a Stone Age culture. They kept no written records. For accounts of their dogs, then, we must rely upon the accounts of early explorers and traders. These accounts are often highly questionable, since these men were seldom particularly knowledgeable either about dogs or the Chukchi. Most failed to realize, for instance, that only a minority of the Chukchi people actually bred dogs as a way of life, and that these lived only along the Arctic and Pacific coasts in a reservation that was off limits to all Russians from 1837 until 1917. The reindeer-herding Chukchi, who lived inland and along the rivers, sometimes had dogs, but these usually were mongrels. A dog seen in a village of mixed Russian and Chukchi inhabitants unfortunately is often described as a Chukchi dog.

The disparities in these descriptions are often used as evidence to support the contention that the Chukchi were in fact not breeding any consistent strain of dogs. The misunderstanding lies in the fact that although many of these dogs were bred and lived in *bona fide* Chukchi villages, they were not the Chukchi dogs of legend. In recent history, many Arctic peoples have bred and sold dogs to outsiders in order to avoid starvation. The "Reindeer Herding" Chukchi, as distinct from the "Dog Breeding" Chukchi, have resorted to this means of survival from time to time, even though they knew little or nothing about dogs, and even though keeping large numbers of dogs is basically incompatible with keeping reindeer, since the sled dogs would kill the reindeer.

All the evidence indicates that the true Chukchi dog remained pure until the present century only along the Arctic coast within 400 miles of the tip of Asia opposite Alaska and along the Pacific within 300 miles of this tip. In much of the Chukchi homeland, both former and present, in which the majority of observations available in English were made, the purebred Chukchi

40

dogs had been replaced by those of other native peoples and those of the dominant Russian culture. This is particularly true in the Kolyma region, where there have been no dog-breeding Chukchi for centuries, but which persists in Western literature as the alleged source of the purebred Chukchi sled dog.

This brings us to a second problem in tracing the history of the Chukchi dog. The bulk of information is written in Russian, much of which is not available outside the Soviet Union. What little has found its way into English has done so more or less by chance.

The greatest obstacle in tracing the relative purity of these dogs, however, is the fact that it has been the official Soviet policy to discredit all isolated native breeds and to deny not only their purity but their functional value as well. In the 1930s, the Soviets, recognizing the impracticability of mechanized transport in the remoter areas of Siberia at the time, tried to promote the value of sled dogs by systematizing their breeding. This was done by discarding the earlier ethnic classifications of northern breeds by Shirinskiy-Shikhmatov and adopting a functional categorization in 1934 designed to maximize the value of the dog as a tool of economic production.

In 1934, the Soviets divided their northern breeds, then known collectively as Laikas, into four basic types. These were the sled dog, the big game hunting dog, the reindeer herding dog, and the small game hunting dog. Standards for each were established in Leningrad over a three year period by averaging the measurements of 400 "representative" dogs. The standard for the sled dog was obtained by measuring 33 almost randomly selected sled dogs, not a single one of which came from eastern Siberia. The Chukchi dogs were specifically excluded from the sample because these dogs were considered far too small for the expected freighting requirements of the future Soviet Arctic economy.

In 1947, the All-Russian Cynological Congress disestablished both the sled dog and the reindeer-herding dog (the AKC Samoyed), and grouped the two Arctic hunting types of dogs into four artificial breeds of "laikas": the Karelo-Finnish, Russo-European, West Siberian, and East Siberian. Each was a composite of three or more native hunting breeds indigenous to its area.

In 1967, the Soviet government embarked in earnest on a widely publicized and intensely debated campaign to forbid the breeding of any Arctic dogs other than the four artificially created and officially recognized hunting breeds. By this time all the natural breeds of sled dogs in Siberia, which the native people had developed over hundreds of years, had already been replaced by the single large Northeast Siberian Draft Dog. And this standard sled dog was itself viewed as a relic of the early Soviet period with no long-range economic future. This is why no sled dogs or Samoyeds have ever been admitted to any Soviet dog shows and probably never will be.

Since the Soviets, however, had artificially created the only recognized breed of sled dog in Siberia, they could well claim that this dog is the only legitimate "Siberian Husky." And, indeed, they did recently in effect deny that

41

the AKC Siberian Husky is a legitimate breed of Siberian sled dog. The Department of Nature Preservation of the USSR Ministry of Agriculture, through the Embassy of the USSR in Bern, Switzerland, suggested in 1971 that the AKC Siberian Husky either must be degenerated from the Northeast Siberian Draft Dog or else be descended from more southerly hunting breeds. In the Soviet Union, the Siberian Chukchi Sled Dog has joined the ranks of those who officially never existed.

Even before this systematic attempt to discredit and destroy the dogs bred by small isolated tribes in Siberia and to promote the Leningrad amalgamation, evidence indicates that there were only three kinds of sled dogs in Siberia whose breeding can be considered pure. The oldest kind, and the only true sled dog breeds, were kept by the four paleo-Asiatic tribes located along the Pacific Ocean: from south to north, the Nivki (Gilyak), Itelmen (later cross-bred to become the Kamchadal), the Koryak, and the Chukchi. The second kind of Siberian sled dog is a combined hunting/draft dog, of which there were only two breeds, both from interior Siberia. These were developed by the only other major paleo-Asiatic tribe, the Yukagir, and by the Uralic Ostyak. The Ostyak dog looked surprisingly like a Siberian Chukchi Sled Dog and forms the base of the officially recognized hunting breed known as the East Siberian Laika. The third kind of Siberian sled dog is the combined herding/draft dog, of which only one pure breed ever existed, the Samoyed sled dog. Each of these seven breeds of dog developed in different conditions of snowcover, temperature, terrain, and hunting requirements, and each was unique in performance capabilities, except that the Koryak was almost identical to the Chukchi dog.

The conformations of these seven breeds of sled dog native to Siberia reflect their basic use. The smallest are the true sled dogs, which are distinguished by their relatively short coupling producing a length not much greater than the height. The southernmost of these, the Nivki, was developed to pull sleds fast through deep snow between the year-round villages on the Amur River and the winter sea-mammal hunting grounds 100 miles away on the island of Sakhalin. This dog had long, thin legs but maintained the ''square'' proportions of height to length typical of true sled dog breeds.

The largest of the purebred sled dogs are the hunting/draft dogs, because they were originally developed so that one, or at most two, could pull the hunter's game-laden sled. It was these dogs, many of which stood 33 inches at the withers, which formed the basic stock of the Russian mixed breeds. These dogs were noted for their great size, strength, and long coupling. Although they were not originally bred as a form of human transportation, these hunting/draft dogs formed the basis of the official Soviet sled dog.

Similar to the true sled dogs in size and conformation is the Samoyed sled dog, which indeed may have a Chukchi sled dog heritage resulting from a Chukchi migration almost 300 years ago from the Kolyma region to the Taymyr tundra of the Nganasan-Samoyeds. This 22-inch combined sled dog/

herding dog is to be distinguished from the probably older Samoyed herding dog, the short haired Loparskiy dog or Finnehund, which stands only 18 inches tall and is maintained as a pure breed by the same Samoyed owners who still breed the true Samoyed recognized by the American Kennel Club.

In contrast to these sled dogs, the pure hunting dogs and combined herding/hunting dogs of the Altaic tribes that had pushed north to the Arctic by the time the Russian pioneers had penetrated Siberia were very small spitz-like dogs. These shared the fate of many of the purebred sled dogs in the Russian settlements when they were crossed with Russian mixed breeds and with southern hunting dogs from European Russia. The resulting mongrels occasioned a comedy of misintepretations culminating finally in a conclusion that these small mixed hunting dogs formed the origin of the dog recognized by the AKC as the Siberian Husky.

Climatic Influence

Regardless of the various barriers obscuring the geneology of today's Siberian Husky, there is nevertheless sufficient data available to make it appear more than probable that this breed descends directly from the ancient Chukchi sled dog. And to appreciate the evolution of this remarkable breed, it is necessary to have a basic understanding of the forces, both climatic and political, that were involved.

It is also necessary to have some notion of the depth of Arctic time. Although in the popular mode of thinking Arctic culture is only as old or slightly older than its first European explorers, this is far from factual. Recent excavations and scholarship have not only shown that man has inhabited Arctic environments for at least half a million years, but have further ascertained that the Arctic has not always been as bleak an environment as it is today. In fact, while glaciers ground south as far as Kentucky and Antarctic-type blizzards swept much of the United States, an oasis remained in the Far North. The Russian Arctic in Siberia, which is the size of all North America, remained 80% unglaciated and provided what was probably one of the richest hunting grounds anywhere in the world, hunting grounds which were inhabited by the mutual ancestors of the Chukchi and the Eskimos.

This primal garden, known as Beringia, was a low flat plain stretching 1000 miles north to south and connecting Asia and America. It extended far out into what is now the Arctic and northern Pacific Oceans and was an immense grazing ground for the Siberian mammoth and American mastodon who browsed on the lush Arctic willows, immune to all attack except by man and the giant dire wolf.

Ten thousand years ago, melting ice masses caused the oceans to rise hundreds of feet and flood all except the Beringian uplands, which now remain as Alaska and the Chukchi Peninsula. But it was not until 3000 years ago that the present cold period set in, necessitating a sled dog culture as we know it. Any varieties of sled dogs that developed along the shores of Beringia in the Arctic and Pacific Oceans during the ice age more than 10,000 years ago probably differed substantially from those that evolved during the warmer period which reached its height from 6500–2200 B.C. And these post-glacial sled dogs, who probably doubled as hunting dogs, in turn undoubtedly differed greatly from the modern Chukchi sled dog that developed in response to the changed hunting conditions of the cold climate that followed.

Hunting conditions on land have probably remained substantially unchanged in the Soviet Arctic for the past 20,000 years. On the other hand, hunting conditions in the seas along the Chukchi Peninsula have changed drastically, since the length of the ice-free season determines the migration patterns of all the animals inhabiting Arctic waters. As the present cold period set in about 1,000 B.C., it was hardest on the Chukchi for they inhabited the western side of the Bering Strait, the side always poorer in food supplies because the upwelling of water toward the Alaskan coast helped maintain a rich diet for the Alaskan sea-mammals even in the coldest years. Furthermore, the growing ice-shelves not only put the walrus and other rookeries out of reach of the shore-bound Arctic Chukchi, it also caused a mass shift of the rookeries to the Aleutians which had no build-up of shelf ice. As so often happens in ecological crises, the process of deterioration fed on itself and the final consumer in the food chain, the Chukchi themselves, were hurt worst of all.

In response to these harsh conditions, the Eskimos on the east of the Bering Strait developed the kayak and harpoon toggle and took to the open sea to hunt a brand new source of food, the humpback whale. Meanwhile, in the west, the Chukchi developed a culture based on a long distance sled dog. Because a series of wars with the Eskimos over the control of the Bering Strait gradually pushed the Chukchi back to poorer and poorer hunting grounds, they were forced to develop this far ranging, low energy consuming breed of dog to its highest perfection in order to survive. They could not become nomadic land hunters, as some non-dog-breeding Arctic tribes may have done, because the life of the nomad is totally incompatible with the breeding of sled dogs, and, by this point, the sled dog had become sufficiently entrenched in the Chukchi life style and religion to make the tribe unwilling to give it up. In fact, the need now to store food for even longer periods of time to feed their dogs further consolidated the Chukchi in their permanent villages along the Arctic coast.

This refusal to give up a tool once it had proved useful is part of a phenomenon called "Arctic lag," a peculiar characteristic of Arctic cultures. New tools or animal species become permanent innovations only rarely, and once a tool, like a sled dog, is established, it tends to survive unchanged for thousands of years until a major outside force, such as a change of climate, intrudes.

The beginnings of the modern Chukchi sled dog can thus be traced back

Seppala at the finish of a Laconia race. Mrs. Elizabeth Ricker (Nansen) is pictured on the runners.

Seppala in Fairbanks, Alaska, 1946.

Millie Turner, Lillian Bowles, Lorna Taylor (Demidoff) and Clara Read.

Lorna Taylor with Burka of Seppala and Sapsuk of Seppala, 1938.

46

3000 years to the beginnings of the uniquely harsh hunting conditions and climate where the Chukchi had always lived. Their sled dog allowed them to cover the enormous distances necessary over the ice pack in order to hunt the sea mammals upon which their survival depended. To say that for this purpose they consciously evolved a pure breed of dog, in the modern sense, is, of course, ridiculous. However, the uniquely severe conditions no doubt hastened the process of natural selection and caused the breed rapidly to evolve to its highest perfection, a hunting tool which Soviet archeologists compare to the simultaneous invention by the Eskimos of the kayak and the harpoon toggle. And, like other forms of adaptation to the delicate balance of Arctic life, the Chukchi dog remained relatively unchanged for thousands of years until some of the last purebred descendants were imported to America less than a century ago.

Political Pressures

The purity of the Chukchi sled dog in Siberia up until the time of the modern exports to Alaska resulted directly from the Chukchi's unique success in maintaining political and cultural independence in the face of almost constant harassment by European invaders. Alone among all the native Siberian peoples, the Chukchi survived 300 years of alternating Russian policies of warfare and friendship.

The policies of warfare were designed to destroy and entirely eliminate the Chukchi, but their effect was merely to strengthen Chukchi society and to improve the quality of the Chukchi sled dog by placing additional demands on it as a means of achieving superior mobility in extended guerilla campaigns. The more successful policies of "friendship" were designed to assimilate the Chukchi, and their ultimate effect, particularly under the Soviets during the past half century, was to raise the Chukchi standard of living and thus destroy both their traditional independence and the harsh laws of natural selection that had originally produced and maintained the Chukchi sled dog.

Because of Russia's desire to annex Siberia in order to monopolize the fur trade in that region and get an edge on the other European powers in the conquest of Japan and America, a long series of wars ensued throughout the 1700s between the Russians and the native tribes. These wars eventually resulted in the complete subjugation of all but the Chukchi. The causes of the Chukchi victory against Tsarist Russia have long been debated in both pre-revolutionary and Soviet literature, since it represents the first successful liberation war in modern times against colonial oppressors.

This victory, or more accurately this standoff, was nevertheless at incredible expense to the Chukchi. In the year 1731, the rest of the Siberian tribes having been fairly well subjugated, the Russian, Nizhnegorod, led an expedition of 230 Russians and 200 Koryak and Yukagir hirelings against the Chukchi who lived in the small villages along the Anadyr River and Pacific coast. Their mission was to kill all the Chukchi they could find. When 700 Chukchi finally made a stand on May 9, 450 Chukchi men were killed and 150 women and children taken prisoner. Only two Russians were killed. A month later, on June 29, the entire Chukchi nation of 10,000 men, women and children assembled to mount an attack on the Russian invaders. The results were 300 Chukchi dead and not a single Russian casualty. This was the all-time low point of the Chukchi fortunes.

Although the Chukchi were always defeated in pitched battle, these defeats merely increased their unique determination to risk their physical survival as a people in order to maintain their independence and politico/cultural integrity. They succeeded in constantly harassing the Russians in guerilla skirmishes, because both their dog teams and reindeer cavalry could easily outdistance their Russian pursuers. When pressed, the dog-breeding Chukchi would simply move the population of an entire village out over the ice to hunt seal until the Russians had gone. One village of Arctic coast Chukchi was officially destroyed when its inhabitants abandoned their winter dogfood stores of frozen walrus and disappeared out over the Arctic pack ice. Six months later, just before ice breakup, the entire village returned in better shape than before.

Finally, after repeated efforts to harass and punish the Chukchi into submission had failed, the Russian Senate in Moscow on February 3, 1742, declared a policy of all-out and systematic genocide against the Chukchi nation. For this purpose, the best Cossack fighters were assembled from all over Siberia. All Chukchi men were to be killed and the women and children captured and distributed throughout the Yakutsk Province around various Russian strongholds where it was believed they would forget their independence and become Christians. Accordingly, the Russian commander, Pavlutskiy, embarked with 400 of the best fighters in Siberia on February 4, 1744, but succeeded only in chasing the Chukchi out into the Bering Straits where they loaded their dog teams into skin boats and disappeared, probably to their trading partners, the Alaskan Eskimos. When Pavlutskiy tried again on June 25th, after the ice had broken up, the Chukchi waited on shore until he approached and then paddled safely back and forth just out of gunshot range.

The next winter, Pavlutskiy did manage to surprise the Chukchi villages of the Chuan River region on the Arctic coast and killed all the men. He failed, however, to take any women or children captive, as required by the decree of the Russian Senate, because the Chukchi women killed their most prized possessions, their dogs, then their children, and then all committed suicide, thereby gaining a high place in the Chukchi heaven.

Finally, on March 14, 1747, rather like the American General George Armstrong Custer, Pavlutskiy tried to save his waning military reputation by charging into what proved to be a cleverly conceived Chukchi trap. Until this point the Chukchi, armed only with spears, had stood little chance against the well armed Cossacks. On this occasion, however, by luring Pavlutskiy and his men up a narrow ravine, the Chukchi warriors managed to totally overwhelm the Russian force before the Russians had time to reload. Pavlutskiy and his senior officers were killed and the remainder of his force survived only by retreating to a makeshift fortress of dog sleds. During the battle the Chukchi managed to capture 16 guns and some sympathetic Russian serfs to give instruction on their use.

This Battle of the Orlovoy, which took place next to the mouth of the Or lovoy River near Fort Anadyrskiy (below modern-day Markovo), marked the real end of the war against the Chukchi. Although both the Chukchi and the Russians mounted occasional attacks against each other, each confrontation merely demonstrated that the Chukchi were rapidly mastering the art of modern warfare.

Accordingly, the Russians switched their policies and decided that the most effective weapon against the Chukchis would be simply to stay out of their way until they would seek peaceful trading relations of their own accord. The switch paid off. The elimination of the threat to their integrity as a people caused the rapid dissolution of the, by then, Spartan-like and highly unified government of the Chukchi and resulted, finally, on February 1, 1792, in a request by the peaceful reindeer Chukchi for the reestablishment of Russian trading posts within the Chukchi domain.

Although the Russian government formally annexed all of the Chukchi Peninsula in 1789, the Russians never again tried to impose direct control over the Chukchi people, and in 1837 a treaty was signed that guaranteed the Chukchi complete political independence within the Russian Empire. It furthermore exempted the Chukchi from taxation and forbade Russians from living in the Chukchi region. In return, the Chukchi agreed to give a nominal tribute to the Russian government in recognition of exclusive Russian (as distinct from any other European) sovereignty over their land.

The Last of the Purebreds

The political autonomy afforded by this treaty allowed the Chukchi complete cultural independence. Thus, for 300 years the Chukchi, and to a certain extent the Samoyedic tribes, remained completely out of the reach of European influence. Throughout the 18th century, the Chukchi, Koryaks, and what was left of the Itelmen on the Kamchatka Peninsula, hunted exactly as they always had. In this endeavor, they remained completely in the Stone Age, subject to the same harsh laws of natural selection that had formed their own society and maintained the genetic superiority of their dogs for 3,000 years. As a result of the military standoff and the 1837 Treaty, according to modern Soviet historians, Chukchi culture and social life, including the use and preservation of their sled dogs, remained completely unchanged from the 17th at least up until the middle of the 19th century.

This isolation also insured the preservation of the very distinct type of sled dog developed by the Chukchi. Size, for instance, was no object among the Chukchi breeders. In fact, bred to pull light loads at moderate speeds over incredible distances on relatively little food, these dogs were the smallest of all the native sled dogs. Consequently, because they lacked either the sprinting capacity or heavy freighting ability of one or another of the other native breeds, they were considered the poorest of all such breeds by the majority of Russian observers. This was largely because, unlike many of the other tribes who prided themselves on their small teams of powerful dogs, the Chukchi minimized the load per dog by using large teams. Of course, the other tribes' dogs were not well-trained enough to work effectively in teams of more than six to eight dogs. In contrast, one observer noted that the Chukchi, "going on a long journey borrow from their friends and relatives as many dogs as they can, and thus have teams of from sixteen to eighteen dogs. Even double teams of more than twenty dogs are used."

Even though these dogs were generally considered the poorest by Russian commentators, their superiority to all other breeds in distances exceeding 100 miles was readily acknowledged. Some of the best Chukchi dogs were those of the dog-breeding Chukchi along the Arctic Coast that made the run at the end of winter from the annual Anuy Fair near the Kolyma River to beat the ocean-going fur traders to Alaska before ice-breakup. These dogs were sometimes known as Kolyma dogs, but should be distinguished from the larger, rangier sled dogs bred by the Russians in the Kolyma Valley. The Kolyma/Chukchi dogs excelled in distance races.

The most famous race was a challenge match in 1869 between the fastest Russian sled dog team, owned by a Russian officer, Anatovskiy, and a team assembled by a native from the fastest Chukchi dogs. A local merchant, Baramagin, paid the native to assemble the team and train it for a year just for this race. Starting at the Anuy marketplace, the Chukchi team covered the 150 miles to Nizhne-Kolymsk on a good surface in 15 hours, arriving one hour ahead of the best Russian team in all Siberia. These times, according to one commentator, Bogoraz, were the fastest "that Siberian dogs have been known to exhibit over long distances."

Unfortunately, because few of the early Russian observers were permitted in the territory of the dog-breeding Chukchi or took particular interest in these dogs, we have few descriptions. An exploration party, however, did measure ten male dogs from the Chukotsk Peninsula in 1930. These averaged 22 inches at the withers but ranged from 20 to 24 inches. They were short-coupled, averaging only 23.1 inches, as compared to 27 inches required for the "standard" sled dog. Also there is one description of the Kolyma/Chukchi dog from the Arctic Coast near Alaska in 1902 as having "relatively short and thick legs, an exceptionally deep and well-developed chest, and short, thick hair." The wolf-like appearance, like that of all Arctic breeds, was also noted. Far too much has been made, however, of the wolf heritage. Although the

Chukchi reportedly cross-bred their dogs with wolves, both accidentally and experimentally, the resulting pups generally lacked the obedience qualities of their purebreds.

Although it would be ridiculous to assume the Chukchi breeding program resulted from any concept of line breeding, the customs of the dog-breeding Chukchi nevertheless effected a breeding program that would be hard to match today. During the summer months all the dogs were allowed to run free, hunting their own food and returning sleek and fat at the sign of first snow. During the rest of the year, which included the heat seasons of the bitches, all the dogs, except the lead-dogs and other obedient dogs that had been taught not to steal food, were tied up. The well-trained dogs were tied up only for a couple of days before a long trip in order to conserve energy. Any new dogs acquired by a village required at least two or three days before they were accepted by the pack and had to be watched carefully for their safety. This assured a certain kind of line-breeding and in-breeding since the free-running lead dogs controlled the breeding of the bitches.

During periods of famine many dogs died, although observers noted that, at least in the Anadyr Region, those that died were usually killed by the natives to prevent them from suffering during the last weeks of starvation. And it is probable that the natives would not kill their best dogs since they were always careful to maintain their best for breeding stock. In fact, so high a premium was placed on these dogs that, according to one report, in 1822 when famine and the accompanying distemper threatened to destroy the entire pack of the westernmost Arctic Coastal Chukchi, a Chukchi woman managed to keep the line from dying out by nursing two pups at her own breast.

The bitches were selected by the simple method of killing all but the most promising at birth or as young pups, those that the women, who were largely in charge of such matters, wanted to keep for breeding. The males were selected only after several months in harness. At the age of one year, or after the first winter in harness, whichever came first, all males were gelded to keep fat on them and make them more tractable as team dogs. The leaders and particularly strong dogs, however, were left ungelded to be used for breeding. The majority of these dogs usually belonged to the village leader who could afford to maintain dogs primarily for breeding.

Among the Samoyed peoples, the bitches were tied up when in heat and excused from work in order to prevent indiscriminate breeding. This was unnecessary among the Chukchi because the bitches were tied up during their heat anyway, and the only ungelded dogs having access to them were the ones selected precisely for breeding. Bitches in whelp were never permitted to work on a team. This "down-time" of the bitches was, in fact, one of the principal reasons why the Chukchi preferred to keep a ratio of only one bitch to every seven males.

The American sled dog expert, Olaf Swenson, noted from his years of observation in the Chukchi region that the best dogs were not produced by conscious selective breeding, but resulted from selection among many pups based entirely upon performance. Nevertheless the practices of the traditional Chukchi villages produced a "dog breeding ecology" that probably could not be surpassed or even equaled in the best modern dog-breeding circles. And, contrary to early Russian observations, the perpetuation of these pure native breeds was in no way threatened by the mere presence of outside dogs in the Russian villages visited by the Chukchi teams.

The introduction of outside dogs, in fact, was common along the trade route from Gizhaga north from Kamchatka 500 miles to Markovo in the heart of the Anadyr District for more than a century before Russian observers noted a distinct breed of dog being bred by the dog-breeding Chukchi who visited this trade center. One of the most common of these outside dogs was a collie-like dog with a long shaggy coat. This dog resulted from crossing the original, large dog of the Itelman with smaller dogs imported by the Russians. A group of these dogs were, in fact, imported to run in the All-Alaska Sweepstakes, and one of them, Russky, actually served as one of Seppala's best lead dogs. These collie-like dogs were bob-tailed, were very probably neutered before export and, at any rate, according to Seppala, were never used for breeding.

Today it would probably be impossible to find a purebred Chukchi sled dog anywhere in Siberia. The last of these dogs succumbed to the ravages of collectivization during the 1920s on the Pacific Coast and during the 1930s along the Arctic Coast. In order more readily to synthesise the native tribes by breaking down old tribal hierarchies, the Soviets managed to either starve or kill the village leaders, known as *kulaks*, since these men were always the richest in the villages. What the authorities, who were simultaneously perplexed by the grave decline in the quality of local dogs, failed to realize was that these kulaks were wealthy primarily because they kept and saw to the breeding of the best dogs in the villages, thus ensuring successful hunting.

Witnessing the decline of the native breeds, the Soviet administration, on the recommendation of various fact-finding missions into the territory, launched a large-scale program of collectivized breeding based on the standard of the "Leningrad factory breed." The final blow was the establishment, in 1935, of a political indoctrination center on the Arctic Coast at Chaun with traveling teams of political activists and a "nursery for the breeding of pedigreed dogs." By the late 1930s all major Chukchi villages had permanent Russian residents to oversee the implementation of Soviet modernization programs.

The Last Exportation to America

These programs, however, probably did not seriously affect the last holdouts among the Chukchi villages until almost one hundred years after the Treaty of 1837 had recognized the Chukchi lands as a semi-autonomous country within the Russian Empire. This is significant because the fourth and last group of purebred Chukchi sled dogs exported to America were selected in 1929 from the Chukchi villages near the North Cape on the Arctic Coast of Siberia to form the personal team of Arctic trader, Olaf Swenson.

Swenson had spent most of his life establishing a legendary reputation as a friend of the Chukchi and as a connoisseur of their purebred sled dogs, and he managed to ship four of the best Arctic Coast Chukchi dogs in the summer of 1930 directly to the East Coast of America. The most famous of these dogs, Kreevanka and Tserko, started their contributions to modern AKC Siberian Husky pedigrees, first at Mrs. Elizabeth Ricker's Poland Spring Kennels in Maine and later at Harry Wheeler's Grey Rocks Inn at St. Jovite, thirty miles north of Montreal. The others, Laika's Bilka and Volchok, went to Mrs. Ricker and were interbred with the Siberians that Leonard Seppala had brought south with him from Alaska.

Swenson had spent a quarter of a century working especially with the Chukchis because he said he had developed a special fondness for them as a people. He was the last contact of the Chukchi with the outside world, because he had obtained an exclusive five-year contract with the Soviet government in 1926 to bring supplies into Siberia and take out furs collected by the Soviet government from the natives. Swenson knew sled dogs as well as, if not better than, anyone in the Arctic at the time, and he had no use at all for mixed breeds.

After his ship became locked in the ice near Cape North in the center of the Arctic Coast Chukchi area in October, 1929, Swenson achieved fame by escaping overland 4500 miles to the Trans-Siberian railroad at Irkutsk just north of Mongolia. He set out on this trip with a Chukchi dog team which was returned to his ice-bound ship from the Kolyma River and then picked up the following spring for export to New England.

Although Swenson paid no attention to the markings of his dogs, he was a master in judging both conformation and behavioral characteristics or "attitude." He commented that, "I have paid as high as $150. each for good dogs and found them hard to find, whereas I could have bought all the ordinary animals I wanted for $10. apiece." He spoke of the innate dignity of a good Chukchi working dog and of the close personal and lifelong relationship between these dogs and their master, contrasting it with the cruel treatment of dogs suffered in most other tribes. The loyalty of the Siberians to their master even today is so great that many Alaskan drivers will not buy a Siberian Husky, because once he is taken from his original master he may never run well again.

The key to the close personal relationship observed by Swenson between the Chukchi dogs and their master no doubt is the role of the dog in the Chukchi religion. Swenson corroborates earlier observations that the Chukchi had a highly sophisticated and monotheistic religion, and he emphasizes the central importance of a divine man who was perfect and ascended to heaven in order to give the Chukchi good hunting and a good death. This religion required strict moral behavior and was so strongly adhered to that during the first two centuries of Christian missionary efforts not a single Chukchi was converted. The Chukchi believed that the gates of heaven were guarded by their Chukchi dogs, and that any Chukchi who mistreated a dog would never get past this dog on the way to heaven.

The Chukchi dogs, unlike those of almost all other Arctic tribes, often slept in the snow houses as cushions for the Chukchi children at night. No doubt, the older women, who were so influential in picking the puppy bitches to carry on the breed, placed importance on good personality in their dogs so they would be well suited to harmonious communal living. The affection of the bitches, together with the qualities of obedience and intelligence that determined which male dogs would be used for breeding, combined to produce the personality traits for which the AKC Siberian Husky is still well known.

Swenson devotes an entire chapter in his book, *Northwest of the World: Forty Years Trading and Hunting in Northern Siberia*, to one dog, and the story of his efforts over a period of two years to buy this dog, named Bilkov (Snowball), at almost any price. After he finally gave up, the dog's master one day gave him Bilkov as a present and was insulted when Swenson wanted to pay for him. Such was the inherent dignity of the Chukchi. And of their dogs, he wrote:

A working dog in Siberia has none of the insipid, fawning tricks of the pet house dog. He has a dignity which is frequently unapproachable, and Bilkov had this to a high degree . . . . When I started out to work with the dog, . . . for six months he was the worst dog I had ever known. He simply refused to accept me as his boss and constantly took matters in his own hands. Finally, however, he gave up the struggle and from then on until the day he died several years later he was the best dog I had even seen in any man's team. When we were on the trail, with Bilkov leading, there was never any trouble. I could put into the team the most stubborn fool cur in the world, the kind of dog who will tangle the whole team by refusing to follow the leader, but when the leader was Bilkov, he had only to take command, go to the right or to the left, and every dog in the team would follow him, so that they acted and looked like one unit.

Further on Swenson states:

It is absolutely impossible to place a price on a good dog, especially if he is a leader. Buying one is almost like buying a human being who is going to undertake a joint venture with you. You know that before your trip is over the dog may have saved your life by his intelligence, instinct and courage. It is he and his team who will often lead you through a snowstorm when every guide which you have has failed. Many a time when I have been on the trail, fighting my way back to camp through blinding, driving snow, I have turned the job completely over to the dogs; they could smell the way back to camp, pick up an old trail which even a native would be unable to find, and bring me safely in. Sometimes, when you are traveling on ice and the sled breaks through, a good leader who minds instantly and accurately, will get you out without difficulty, whereas a poor one will simply increase your hazard and, likely as not, send you to your death. This is the kind of dependability on which it is impossible to place any market value. You try to find the animals you want, that you can believe in and depend upon, and once you have found them, you buy them (if you can) for whatever price you can arrange.

We are fortunate that the last of the purebred Chukchi dogs exported as foundation stock for the present day Siberian Husky were selected by a man who both knew and appreciated them and could obtain the best.

Champions Belka, Panda, Kira—pictured in 1947.

Moseley's Taylor's team at Laconia, 1930–31; driver, Roger Haines.

Seppala Siberians at St. Jovite, 1932; driver, Harry Wheeler.

56

3

The Early Siberian
in New England

IRONICALLY, activities that in one part of the world constitute
a grueling way of life, can—in another part and under different circumstances—become a matter of pleasure and sport. Such became the case when,
in 1922, the Brown Paper Company of Berlin, New Hampshire, sponsored a
three-day, point to point sled dog race covering 123 miles. The winner of this
first International Race was Arthur Walden of Wonalancet, New Hampshire,
driving a single hitch of nine dogs with his famous dog, Chinook, on lead.

Walden had become interested in sled dogs while prospecting in Alaska,
and had returned to Wonalancet Farm (which his wife ran as an inn) determined to establish a line of sled dogs based upon Chinook, his large, yellow,
mixed-breed dog. Chinook was bred to a number of bitches including a large
German Shepherd Dog named Erica. From these breedings, puppies that resembled Chinook were kept and bred until Walden virtually established a line
of large, yellowish, lop-eared dogs that bred true to type. These dogs, which
he called "Chinooks," became something of a tourist attraction at Wonalancet Farm, and visitors would come for the opportunity of riding behind a real
dog team. Indeed, the team was so superbly trained, legend has it that one of
Walden's favorite tricks was to send Chinook, his teammates, and a driverless
sled out into an open field across from Wonalancet Farm, and put them
through their paces by issuing "Gee" and "Haw" commands by megaphone
from the porch of his home. This expertise with dogs undoubtedly was the
factor in his win of the first International Race, and was later (in 1928) to earn
Walden appointment as head driver on the first Byrd Antarctic Expedition.

Monadnock's first all Siberian team.

The New England Sled Dog Club

This first race sparked so much enthusiasm that, largely through the efforts of Walden himself, the New England Sled Dog Club was formed in 1924, and began sponsoring their own races in the winter of 1925. Its other organizers included: Fred Lovejoy, a Boston business man; Walter Channing, a well-known real estate man, also from Boston; Moseley Taylor, whose family owned (and still does) *The Boston Globe*; and Milton Seeley, about whom more will be said later. Walden was the first president. The vice-presidents were: Dr. Harry Souther of Boston, Charles DeForest of New Haven, Everett Rutter and Percival Estes of New Hampshire, Styles Oxford of Maine, and Dustin White of Vermont. Claude Calvert of Meredith, New Hampshire, became the club's first secretary-treasurer.

The early New England racing scene was quite different from that of today. In the first place, the races were generally longer. Also, since the roads were generally not plowed, many of the courses could be along the main streets of towns. The crowds were large and the newspaper coverage extensive. The towns where the races were held were eager to play host and even paid the Club a nominal amount for the honor of holding the race. The drivers themselves were paid three dollars a day expense money and were, by and large, a tighter-knit group than today. This was in part because they were fewer. normally less than 25, and because, due to more primitive modes of travel, they spent more time together. There were no super highways, and in winter even a journey of twenty miles was an undertaking. Consequently, most drivers arrived at the course on the day before the race and stayed in guest houses, tourist homes, or the local hotel; there were no motels. The dogs were often brought in on trucks—not pickups, but large, covered trucks—and bedded down in various barns, the use of which had been pre-arranged. Every Saturday night the host town would hold a "Mushers' Ball" and crown a "Mushers' Queen"—an honor usually accorded the girl who managed to sell the most buttons, one of the ways in which the towns raised the money to hold the event.

The races themselves were in some ways more exciting for the spectator than those of today. Because there were fewer teams, there was usually a handicap division, which of course gave the race a handicap winner as well as an elapsed time winner. Each team was given a handicap based upon its previous performance time, calculated so that each team should theoretically finish as the same time. As a result, there were often very exciting finishes and even the slower teams had a chance at a trophy. Emile St. Goddard, driving his Canadian hounds, was one of the few drivers ever to win both the elapsed time and the handicap races. Since he started last, he had to pass every other team on the course to accomplish this feat.

The early races sponsored by the New England Sled Dog Club were largely dominated by Arthur Walden and his Chinooks. In fact, so handily did he win

Leonhard Seppala with Bonzo at Lake Placid, 1932.

			Sepp
		Fritz	
			Dolly
	Harry		
			Ugruk
		Shika	
			Boorka
TOSKA			
BONZO (Whelped 7/15/25)			
ROSIE			
			Kyak
		Putza	
			Sigrid
	Kolyma		
			Naguruk
		Duska	
			Melba

these races, it was felt he just couldn't be beaten. In 1927, however, Leonhard Seppala came to race at Poland Spring, Maine.

After the famous Serum Drive, Seppala had been touring the United States with a team of Siberians, and when it was known that he would be in the area, he was challenged to race against Walden.

The impression that Seppala and his dogs made upon the New England sled dog enthusiasts was not particularly overwhelming. "Siberian rats" they had been originally dubbed in Alaska, and the New Englanders' viewpoint was not much different. In fact, the Siberians appeared so small next to the huge New England sled dogs that some people objected, on humanitarian grounds, to the Siberians being allowed to race at all.

The Siberians' first performance in New England has become something of a legend, no doubt richly embellished with time and telling. But since the legend is by now more accessible than any bare assemblage of facts, we tell it in its entirety.

In the first place the cards seemed stacked against the Siberian entry from the beginning. For one, while Walden's Chinooks were in excellent racing condition, the little Siberians had been on exhibition and marching in parades, and were soft. Consequently, when Seppala and Walden traveled the 90 miles from Wonalancet Farm to the race site at Poland Spring together, the Chinooks spent the three-day trip considerably outdistancing the Siberians, and word got around that the Siberians were small and slow.

Furthermore, on the day of the race, Seppala, who had brought some forty-odd dogs with him, was informed that he would be allowed to race only seven. He vigorously argued that since his dogs weighed only 50–55 pounds, as opposed to the 100 pound dogs that were being used by the majority of drivers, he should be allowed to use at least eleven dogs to equal their pulling power. The judges, however, ruled otherwise.

And things went from bad to worse. On the morning of the race, the noise of the crowd frightened the Siberians at the starting line; when the starter said "Go," they plunged over a stone fence and down a hill behind the line itself. With the clock already running, it was all Seppala could do to get the team back up the hill and over the fence.

Once back on the trail things went smoothly for about two miles until the team suddenly bolted into the front door of a house they were passing. As it turned out, it was the aroma of frying mutton chops that had overcome the dogs. As the woman who was frying the chops looked up and saw what she believed was a pack of wolves descending upon her, she let out a piercing scream and fainted. The chops fell to the floor, but were too hot for the dogs to handle and Seppala managed to untangle them and get underway again.

About ten miles out, Seppala overtook a team of Chinooks driven by the Poland Spring Hotel owner's wife, Mrs. Elizabeth Ricker. A few minutes after passing the team, Seppala felt something touching his leg. It proved to be Mrs. Ricker's team without Mrs. Ricker. This put Seppala in a dilemma. Should he stop and untangle her team, and wait for her to catch up and there-

White Water Lake Knight, owned by Roland Bowles' Calivali Kennels.

Sapsuk of Seppala.

Belford's Wolf, owned by Alec Belford.

by lose the race, or should he continue? As he later put it, he felt "they would likely kill each other and her too" if they were not untangled. The race was not worth such a risk, so Seppala stopped his dogs and left them standing on the trail — an extremely risky act since they might take off at any moment — and went back to straighten out the badly-tangled team. Mrs. Ricker came running up and thanked him but said the delay would surely lose him the race. Seppala concurred but was determined to give it his best and got underway again.

As if enough ill fate had not befallen the Siberians, a skunk crossed their trail shortly before the finish line, and the dogs, picking up the scent, began running for all they were worth. Fortunately for Seppala, the skunk hid in an old sled track by the side of the trail and the dogs did not see him as they passed.

The result turned out to be a shocker. For despite the many mishaps, the Siberian team came in first, seven minutes ahead of Walden. The crowd went wild and that night Seppala was interviewed and the dogs photographed.

It also rained that night, and cars cut deep ruts in the road. Then it froze and the trails became icy and rough. These conditions favored Seppala who knew that with his lighter dogs with their tough feet he would surely win the next day's conclusion of the race. Unfortunately, the other drivers and the judges decided to cancel the remainder of the race in order to save the dogs' feet for the big New England point-to-point race of 133 miles to be run the following month. As it turned out, Seppala won that race as well.

The Siberian Husky Club of America

As the Siberians continued to dominate the New England racing scene, more and more sled dog enthusiasts began switching from the local large freighting dogs to the Siberians. Not only were they faster, but they were far less inclined to fight, required less food, and were much more attractive.

This attractiveness, however, was relative, for it should not be assumed that these early Siberians possessed the uniformity of structure, coat, and markings they do today. It is true that the Chukchi had spent centuries perfecting these dogs as long distance, low energy consuming, sled dogs possessing incredible endurance and a degree of uniformity that was obvious to even the most untrained eye. The goal of the Chukchi breeders, however, had always been function; and where the rudiments of survival are hard come by, aesthetics seldom enter the picture. Even the dogs bred in different regions of the Chukchi domain, although similar, differed somewhat in structure and coat length.

Seppala, although obviously also concerned with function had already begun breeding with an eye toward greater uniformity. His color preference was light gray, while his wife's was white. Normally it was she who chose the puppies while he did the training; in the years to come, they would prove to be a formidable team, especially when working with Earle Snodie at his Bow Lake Kennels in Washington where some very fine white Siberians were produced.

But at the time the first Siberians were seen in New England, there was quite a variety in the specimens. Some were long and leggy, others shorter coupled and heavier boned; some were marked symmetrically, many were not. The job of modifying this existing breed of moderately attractive, moderately uniform sled dogs into a dual-purpose breed—one that could not only perform its original function in harness, but could also conform to a detailed standard of uniformity that would enable it to compete in the conformation ring on equal footing with breeds that had been specifically bred for the show ring for decades—was a monumental task. The fact that this feat was largely accomplished within a few short years speaks for the energy, know-how, and dedication of the pioneers of the breed.

Not the least of the problems facing these early breeders was the need to create a standard of conformation. After the breed was officially recognized by the American Kennel Club in 1930, the first standard was published in *The American Kennel Gazette* in April of 1932. It read as follows:

General Appearance—For hundreds of years the Siberian Husky has been used as a sled dog in northeastern Asia. He should be exceptionally active, quick and light on his feet, able to run in harness with a load, at a speed of twenty miles an hour for short distances. He should be strong, courageous and tireless on the trail. He should have a deep strong chest, heavy bone, strong legs and feet, straight powerful back and well muscled hindquarters. A grown dog should stand about 23 inches at the shoulders and weigh about 60 pounds. A bitch should be smaller and weigh about 10 or 12 pounds less.

Head—The size of the head should be in proportion to the body, but not clumsy or too large. It should be of medium width between the ears. The ears should be erect, set high on the head, medium in size, pointed at the tops and well covered with hair on the inside. It should be of medium length and slightly wedge shaped. The jaws and teeth are very strong, and should be neither overshot nor undershot. The eyes may be either blue or brown, with a keen, friendly, and intelligent expression. Eye rims dark. The nose may be either light brown or black. The muzzle should be strong, the lips dark and firmly fitting together.

Chest and Ribs—Chest should be deep and strong, but not too broad. The ribs should be well arched and deep.

Back, Quarters and Stifles—The loins should be slightly arched and especially well muscled. The stifles should be well let down and very muscular. The back should be straight, not too long, and strongly developed.

Legs—Straight of good length, well muscled and good bone.

Feet—Strong, not too compact, with exceptionally tough pads protected with hair.

Tail—Long, and usually carried over back but sometimes dropped down, especially when tired. Should be well protected with fur and hair, but bushy tails not desirable.

Size and Weight—Dogs, 22 to 23½ inches at shoulder, 54 to 64 pounds; bitches, 21 to 22½ inches, 44 to 54 pounds.

Color—All colors permissible from white to black including many variations of grays and mixed wolf colorings.

Coat—Should be thick with a very soft and warm under fur next to the skin. The guard hairs should not be too long, and should be straight, not too coarse, and fairly close to the body so that the graceful lines of the dogs are not obscured. A bushy or shaggy coat is not desirable.

Scale of Points—Size and general appearance, 25; head and neck, 10; coat and color, 10; chest and ribs, 10; quarters and stifles, 15; back, 10; legs, 10; feet, 5; tail, 5. **Total**—100.

It should be noted how closely this standard resembles the one used today. Except for phrasing, various clarifications, and changes in minor details, the only change has been to drop the point scale. The degree to which the basic tenets of this standard have survived indicates the kind of in-depth study that went into its composition. This standard and, perhaps even more so, the standard submitted after the formation of The Siberian Husky of America in 1938 were the results of years of intensive study of various breed characteristics found in several generations of Siberians. And, although there were some differences of opinion on some details, there was, by and large, a surprising degree of agreement among these early fanciers. When difficulties developed over these details, it was often Seppala, himself, who was called upon for advice. It was he, for instance, who described the majority of Siberian tails that he had seen as being like a "fox brush" rather than like a plume. Although a variety in coat length and coupling could be observed among the early imports, he stated that his preference, and those he felt to be most typical, were the relatively short-coupled, medium-coated dogs.

The first official meeting of The Siberian Husky Club of America was held at Milton and Eva Seeley's on June 10, 1938. Dean C. F. Jackson served as the club's first president, with Mrs. Samuel Post as vice-president and Mrs. Seeley as secretary-treasurer. On the board of standards were Dean and Mrs. Jackson, Mrs. Moseley Taylor, Mr. and Mrs. Seeley, Miss Margaret Dewey, Miss Millie Turner, and Charles Roberts. The advisory committee consisted of Mrs. Kaare Nansen (formerly Mrs. Elizabeth Ricker), Leonhard Seppala, judge Coke Hill, Clarence Grey and Mrs. Birdsall Darling. It was at this meeting that the 1938 standard was drawn up; it was adopted by the AKC two months later, in August.

FOUNDATION KENNELS OF THE BREED

Insofar as the formation of The Siberian Husky Club of America established a channel of communication among breeders, provided a more comprehensive standard of conformation, and fostered greater interest in the show ring — an interest not easily fostered among many of the early dyed-in-the wool dog drivers — 1938 represents a milestone in the history of the breed. However, much of the work toward greater standardization had already taken place in the decade prior to the founding of the club.

The absence of records, and the vagueness of memory, make it impossible to acknowledge everyone who, in one way or another, contributed to the development of the breed during these formative years. Immunization was not developed to the extent it is today, with result that many good dogs died young. This, and other quirks of fate caused some of the early lines to die out completely, and explains why some top quality dogs of the time have had little influence on the breed except as a treasured memory in the minds of some old-timers.

Northern Light

Such was the case, for instance, with the line of the predominantely white Siberians bred by Julian Hurley of Alaska. Hurley, a lawyer and judge, purchased his first dogs from Frank Dufresne, one time head of the Alaskan Game Commission, and an avid racing enthusiast. Many of these dogs were imported to Michigan and New England. Most of them were white, and one— Northern Light Kobuck, in September, 1932, became the first Siberian Husky AKC champion of record. Kobuck, whelped in 1928, was owned by Oliver R. Shattuck of Alton, N. H., who, along with Hurley, registered many of the first Siberians.

The first Siberian Husky to be registered by the American Kennel Club was listed in the December 1930 Stud Register as follows: Fairbanks Princess Chena, 758,529—By Bingo II ex Alaska Princess (by Jack Frost ex Snowflake). Jack Frost by Scotty ex Vasta. Bingo II by Bingo ex Topsy. Owner— Mrs. Elsie K. Reeser. Breeder, Julien A. Hurley, Fairbanks, Alaska. Whelped 9/16/27. White. Then in the January 1931 Stud Register, 21 Siberians bearing the Northern Light prefix were listed, all bred by Mr. Hurley. Unfortunately, the Northern Light strains have all but disappeared.

But some strains of this pioneer period have left their impact. In turning to them now, we first note that two of them take on such importance that we have chosen to tell the story of the Chinook Kennels of Milton and Short Seeley, and of the Monadnock Kennels of Lorna Demidoff, in a chapter to themselves. It follows this chapter.

Harry Wheeler's team at St. Jovite. Shown with loose leader and no neck lines except on wheel dogs.

Cold River team, owned by Mrs. M. Lee Frothingham and her daughter Millie Turner of Beverly Farm, Massachusetts. Leader, Sapsuk of Seppala.

Elizabeth Ricker and the Seppala Siberian Kennels

The meeting of Leonhard Seppala and Elizabeth Ricker, the Poland Spring Hotel owner's wife, on the trail of that first New England race which Seppala entered, was a fortuitous one in terms of the breed's subsequent history. So impressed was Mrs. Ricker with the performance of these little dogs that she immediately sold her entire stock of cross-bred sled dogs and bought all forty-odd Siberians that Seppala had brought with him. Although many of these dogs were neutered, as was the custom with the majority of sled dogs, her breeding program was extensive, and at times there were over 160 dogs, including puppies, at her kennel.

Although she remained an active breeder only a relatively short time, from 1926 to 1932, Elizabeth Ricker's contribution to the breed was an extremely significant one. Among the outstanding dogs bred or housed at this first New England kennel were the famous Togo (presented to Mrs. Ricker by Seppala as a token of his esteem); Kreevanka, Tserko, Volchok and Laika's Bilka, all selected and imported from Siberia by Olaf Swenson, the fur trader; and Bonzo and Tosca, littermates, whelped in July 1925, and imported from Alaska. Bonzo became an outstanding leader, first on Mrs. Ricker's team and later on Harry Wheeler's, and Tosca proved an outstanding brood bitch, producing some of the most outstanding of the early specimens, especially when bred to Kreevanka.

Kingeak, a Togo son, was also at this kennel. Another Togo son, Sepp III, was acquired from Mrs. Ricker by Dean Jackson and went on to produce the famous Ch. Shankhassock Lobo, second AKC registered Siberian Husky to attain championship and the dog that for many years was used to illustrate the breed in the AKC's publication, *The Complete Dog Book*.

In 1932, when Mrs. Ricker—divorced from Ted Ricker—was married to Kaare Nansen, son of the famous polar explorer, her dogs were acquired by Harry Wheeler of St. Jovite, Canada; and from there they influenced the breeding program of almost every New England kennel. Mrs. Ricker's, or Mrs. Nansen's, influence on the breed, however, was not limited to her role as a breeder and driver. She served for many years on the advisory committee of The Siberian Husky Club of America. She is also the author of *Seppala, Alaskan Dog Driver* and *Togo's Fireside Reflections*, both invaluable to the student of the early days of sled dog driving and racing. Currently she is working on a book depicting the early Siberian scene in New England.

Kreevanka.

Ch. Vanka of Seppala II.

Valuiki of Cold River.

Harry Wheeler

Harry Wheeler's kennels at the Grey Rocks Inn in St. Jovite was based upon the stock he obtained from Mrs. Ricker as well as upon numerous dogs that came directly from Alaska. Like many of the early breeders, Mr. Wheeler's primary concern was racing, but he did provide influential stock to many of the early New England kennels. To Mrs. Frothingham's Cold River Kennels went several dogs including Ch. Vanka of Seppala II, an offspring of Kreevanka and Tosca and an outstanding stud. William Shearer's Foxstand Kennels was also based upon Wheeler stock.

In the late 1940s, when the responsibilities of managing his Grey Rocks Inn became too time-consuming, Wheeler sold his dogs to Don McFaul of Maniwaki, Quebec, who thus established his Gatineau Kennels which continued to exert an influence on the breed until the early 1960s.

Wheeler, like Seppala and Ricker before him, often used the suffix "of Seppala" when naming his dogs. Renowned for their racing ability, Wheeler dogs were highly prized by many early fanciers of the breed, and today some people still speak of the "pure Seppala strain" that emanated from this kennel. In all fairness, however, it should be pointed out that, given the fact that almost all the early stock came directly from Seppala or related breeding, the dogs coming from this kennel were no more "pure Seppala" than those from most other foundation kennels, the only difference being that Wheeler perpetuated the name longer.

Mrs. Marie Lee Frothingham and The Cold River Kennels

Established in 1936 by Mrs. Marie Lee Frothingham and her daughter, Marie Turner (now Mrs. M. Turner Remick) in Beverly Farms, Massachusetts, the Cold River Kennel was named after the river that flowed behind their property in Sandwich, New Hampshire.

Although Mrs. Frothingham, known to her friends as "The Duchess," never drove a team, she oversaw the training and masterminded the racing strategy of some of the most successful teams of that era. For many years the Cold River Kennel team #1 was driven by Don Shaw, a professional driver, while Cold River Kennel team #2 was driven by Millie Turner. While Shaw won the majority of races entered in both the United States and Canada, Miss Turner's team placed consistently, very often being the highest placing team driven by a woman. For those who think the red, or copper, Siberian is a fairly recent development, it is interesting to note that one of Millie Turner's early dogs, which had been bred by Moseley Taylor, was a red (appropriately named "Red").

Millie Turner Remick with Cold River Kennels' team. L. to r: Juneau, Tongass, Ch. Vanka of Seppala II, Putsa, Sapsuk of Seppala and Surgut.

Two very influential Cold River bitches:

```
                                                          Unknown
                                        Unknown
                                                          Unknown
                        Kreevanka
                                                          Unknown
                                        Unknown
                                                          Unknown
        Ch. Vanka of Seppala II*
                                                          Fritz
                                        Harry
                                                          Shika
                        Tosca
                                                          Putza
                                        Shika
                                                          Duska

CH. HELEN OF COLD RIVER
DUCHESS OF COLD RIVER        (Whelped 11/6/42)

                                                          Togo
                                        Kingeak
                                                          Rosie
                        Smokey of Seppala
                                                          Nutok
                                        Pearl
                                                          Czarina
        Sky of Seppala
                                                          Unknown
                                        Wolf
                                                          Unknown
                        Nanna
                                                          Unknown
                                        Nan
                                                          Unknown
```

*Brother of Vanka of Seppala and Burka of Seppala.

71

Bill Belletete in Laconia race. Izok of Gap Mountain is dog at right point.

Izok of Gap Mountain, very influential stud.

After Miss Turner, who is also a well-known animal portraitist, married and moved to Alaska, Mrs. Frothingham hired a number of drivers, the last of which were Lyle and Marguerite Grant. The Grants trained and drove the Cold River teams from 1949 until 1956, when they acquired the last of Mrs. Frothingham's dogs as the foundation for their own Marlytuk Kennels in Carlisle, Massachusetts.

Although Cold River Kennels was primarily oriented to turning out top racing dogs, some of their dogs were shown by Miss Turner on a limited basis. In 1940, Ch. Vanka of Seppala II, known as "Cossack," completed his championship. He, his full brothers Vanka of Seppala and Burka of Seppala, as well as Sapsuk of Seppala, Ch. Helen of Cold River (an outstanding lead dog), Duchess of Cold River, Valuiki of Cold River, Rola, Bugs, Delzeue of Cold River, Enara of Cold River and a bitch named Sky of Seppala, all appear often in pedigrees.

Mrs. Frothingham's many contributions in behalf of the breed included service as president of the Siberian Husky Club of America. She died in September, 1969, at age of 82.

Other Foundation Kennels:

Margaret Dewey's Komitik Kennels bred many of the early outstanding dogs. Miss Dewey was a very conscientious student of the breed, and was an active member—and secretary for several years—of the Siberian Husky Club of America. But unfortunately, although it is possible to find the Komitik name far back in some of today's pedigrees, it is rare.

Other kennels that got their start during this period were Roland Bowles' Calivali Kennels, Dr. Roland Lombard's Igloo Pac Kennels and the kennels of Alec Belford in Laconia, New Hampshire. During these formative years, Belford—whose enthusiasm for sled dog racing has been carried on for many years by his son Dr. Charles Belford—owned one of the most influential dogs in the breed, Belford's Wolf, another dog from Mrs. Ricker's kennel.

Others, not kennel owners per se but who nevertheless owned dogs that made significant contributions to the breed, included Walter Channing, who owned a Togo daughter named Toto, and Leonard Chapman, who owned an outstanding gray male out of John "Iron Man" Johnson's kennels in Alaska named Duke.

Somewhat later, in the early 1940s, William Belletete and J. August Duval came upon the scene. Both had worked with sled dogs during the war and both were avid racing enthusiasts. Belletete acquired his dogs primarily from William Shearer who had acquired them from the Army after the war. The most significant of these was Duchess of Cold River out of Mrs. Frothingham's breeding, who, when bred to Ch. Wonalancet's Baldy of Alyeska, produced two outstanding specimens: Kiev of Gap Mountain and Izok of Gap

Tat Duval's matched team, Jaffrey, N.H.

Tat Duval's famous "Aleka" litter who, along with their parents, comprised one of the most famous matched teams in the history of the breed. Many of these dogs figure in contemporary pedigrees.

```
                                            Burka of Seppala
                            Valuiki of Cold River
                                            Delzeue of Cold River
                    Ch. Vanya of Monadnock III
                                            Belford's Wolf
                            Ch. Panda
                                            Tosca of Alyeska
            Chort of Monadnock
                                            Kreevanka
                            Vanka of Seppala I
                                            Tosca
                    Ch. Kira of Monadnock
                                            Duke
                            Tosca of Alyeska
                                            Tanta of Alyeska
```

CH. ALEKA'S CZARINA
ALEKA'S KHAN
ALEKA'S SONYA
ALEKA'S CZAR   (Whelped 3/15/48)
ALEKA'S OKA
ALEKA'S RUSKA

```
                                            Duke
                            Ch. Togo of Alyeska
                                            Tanta of Alyeska
                    Nicholas of Monadnock
                                            Vanka of Seppala I
                            Ch. Kira of Monadmock
                                            Tosca of Alyeska
            Ch. Aleka of Monadnock
                                            Burka of Seppala
                            Valuiki of Cold River
                                            Delzeue of Cold River
                    Ch. Belka of Monadnock II
                                            Belford's Wolf
                            Ch. Panda
                                            Tosca of Alyeska
```

Note - Vanka of Seppala I, Burka of Seppala, and Ch. Vanka of Seppala II were brothers.

74

Mountain. Kiev was used to illustrate the standard for many years and Izok went on to become one of the most influential studs in the breed.

Duval purchased two dogs from Monadnock Kennels, Chort of Monadnock and Aleka of Monadnock, and a mating of these produced one of the most impressive matched teams in the history of the breed, as well as some very important dogs in terms of genetic influence. All named for their dam, this litter consisted of Aleka's Czar, Czarina, Khan, Oka, Ruska and Sonya. Jean Lane (now Jean Bryan) later acquired this team and showed both Aleka of Monadnock and Aleka's Czarina to their championships. When the time came to breed Aleka's Czarina, Izok of Gap Mountain was chosen as a stud, and out of this mating came the famous and highly influential Mulpus Brook's The Roadmaster.

Ch. Aleka of Monadnock and Chort of Monadnock, owned by J. August Duval.

Short Seeley with Ch. Wonalancet's Baldy of Alyeska and Ch. Wonalancet's Disko of Alyeska.

4

Chinook And Monadnock

by Michael Jennings

ALTHOUGH all of the breeders mentioned in the preceeding chapter contributed greatly in furthering the cause of the Siberian Husky, two of the foundation kennels, whether because of circumstance, or greater dedication or perserverance managed to produce such consistently outstanding stock that their names have become synonymous with excellence in the breed. And, indeed, it is extremely difficult today to find a Siberian Husky whose background cannot be traced back to one or, in most cases, both of these kennels.

More than any other of the foundation kennels, Chinook and Monadnock remained dedicated to the concept of a dual-purpose Siberian, one who could win in the show ring as well as on the trail. Too often today one hears the argument of show dogs versus sled dogs and forgets that not only did Chinook and Monadnock produce the foundation stock for almost every show kennel in the country, but they also fielded some of the top racing teams of their day. Indeed, even today when the sport of sled dog racing has grown so popular, Mrs. Seeley and Mrs. Demidoff—the women behind these two kennels—are ranked among the top women drivers of all time. And the teams they drove contained many bench show champions, many of them outstanding leaders.

Chinook Kennels

When Eva, known to her friends as "Short", and Milton Seeley were married in May of 1924, they elected to spend their honeymoon mountain climbing in New England. There they witnessed their first sled dog team in action, a team of Arthur Walden's Chinooks, and were so impressed, particularly by Chinook himself, that they immediately ordered one of his puppies to become their housepet in their home on the Hudson River near Nyack, New York, where Milton owned a successful chemical business.

And this might have been the extent of the Seeleys' involvement with the world of sled dogs had not Milton, stricken with diabetes in the days before insulin, been advised by his doctors to give up the world of business and move to the mountains. The year of this prescribed early retirement was 1928, the same year Arthur Walden was preparing to accompany the first Byrd Antarctic expedition as head dog driver. Walden needed someone to manage Wonalancet Farms during his absence, and the Seeleys were available. Out of these circumstances developed one of the most impressive careers in the world of sled dogs.

In the winter of 1929, "Short" learned to drive a dog team composed of Chinooks. Having been a physical education teacher, she took to the rigors of the sport naturally, although for years she was the only woman to actively participate. And even though she was small, she was probably foremost among all women drivers in her ability to handle a sled.

It was also in the winter of 1929 that the Seeleys saw their first team of Siberians at a race in Poland Spring and decided to eventually own and breed some of their own. Subsequently they also became involved in Alaskan Malamutes. Today, these two breeds—although not invented by the Seeleys—are acknowledged to have become what they are largely because of the foundation breeding at this kennel.

When Walden returned from the Antarctic he sold his share of the kennel to the Seeleys, who moved it to its present site in Wonalancet and named it Chinook in honor of Walden's great leader, who died in the Antarctic. In the years that followed the Seeleys were an active force in getting both the Siberian and the Alaskan Malamute recognized by the AKC and in forming the Siberian Husky Club of America.

It was also at Chinook that the dogs were trained for the second and third Byrd expeditions, and that the training of many of the sled dogs used in the Second World War took place. Originally the Army planned to use sled dogs to assist the Ski Troops in the reinvasion of Norway. But when this plan was abandoned, the dogs were used in Greenland, Labrador, Alaska, Italy, and to rescue the wounded in the Battle of the Bulge.

The Arctic Search and Rescue Unit, found to be so much more effective than mechanized transport in saving the lives of pilots downed in frozen Arctic wastes, and the first Dog Ambulance Corps, assigned to rescue the wounded of the Third Army from the snow-buried fields of France in 1945, both contained dogs trained at Chinook.

But although Chinook Kennels has been active in every phase of the sled dog world, from training to racing to developing more nutritional food formulas, it was the Seeleys' painstaking care in determining what was ideal in

Milton Seeley with Toska of Wonalancet (at right) and her sister Cherie. Toska was dam of Ch. Wonalancet's Baldy of Alyeska.

Cheeak of Alyeska, foundation bitch of the Chinook Kennels.

both the Siberian Husky and the Alaskan Malamute, and breeding toward that ideal, that has made the kennel the shrine of these breeds it is today.

In creating their Siberian line, the Seeleys managed, through the help of Mrs. Ricker, to lease Toto, a Togo daughter, from Walter Channing. They then succeeded in getting her approved by the AKC as a trial bitch, this being in the days when the Siberian was first getting recognized. Toto was then bred to Moseley Taylor's Tuck and produced one lone female, Tanta of Alyeska. Tanta was first shown at Manchester, New Hampshire where, as the only bitch entry, she went Best of Breed over nine males. Tanta was then bred to Leonard Chapman's Duke and produced nine puppies. Two of these, Yukon and Sitka, eventually went to William Shearer's Foxstand Kennels. Seven of the puppies went to Moseley Taylor to form his wife's highly successful matched racing team. Although Mr. Taylor succeeded in talking the Seeleys into selling six outright, the seventh, Cheeak of Alyeska (the Seeleys choice of the litter) was only leased and had to be returned each year to Chinook for breeding.

In 1934 Cheeak was bred to Belford's Wolf, and out of this great combination came many of the first AKC registered Siberian Husky champions. Among these was Ch. Laddy of Wonalancet, who went on to sire some of the first dogs registered with the Igloo Pak kennel name, and Ch. Turu of Wonlancet. Out of the combination of Mrs. Frothingham's Sapsuk of Seppala and Tosca of Alyeska (a littermate of Cheeak of Alyeska) came Toska of Wonalancet who, when bred to Ch. Turu of Wonalancet produced perhaps the first really exceptional specimen of the breed, Ch. Wonalancet's Baldy of Alyeska. Baldy attained his championship in 1941 and shortly thereafter became the first Siberian Husky to win the Working Group, (at the North Shore Kennel Club). Baldy was also shown with his brother, Wonalancet's Disko of Alyeska, in brace competition. Together they won several Best Brace in Group awards, and at the Eastern Dog Club Show in Boston went all the way to Best Brace in Show.

Baldy turned out to be not only a great show dog but a great stud as well, siring many outstanding dogs including the famous Izok of Gap Mountain.

From the beginning, the Seeleys were staunch supporters of the standard and recognized the weaknesses as well as the strength of their dogs. Although Cheeak of Alyeska was an excellent example of the breed, and although she was the shortest coupled of the litter, the Seeleys realized that the tendency of her parents and the rest of her otherwise outstanding litter was toward ranginess. For this reason, after being bred to Belford's Wolf and producing Turu and Laddy, she was bred to Dean Jackson's Sepp III, a Togo son who, like his father, was quite close-coupled. This mating produced Ch. Cheenah of Alyeska who, in 1938, became the first Siberian Husky female to attain her championship. Cheenah was then bred to a male of Harry Wheeler's kennels, a grandson of both Kingeak and Tserko named Wolfe of Seppala. Out of this breeding came Bonzo of Taku who, when bred to Kituh of Taku, a grand-

Ch. Wonalancet's Baldy of Alyeska.

			Unknown
		Smoky	
	Belford's Wolf		Unknown
		Tosca	Harry
	Ch. Turu of Alyeska		Kolyma
			Ici
		Duke	
	Cheeak of Alyeska		Wanda
		Tanta of Alyeska	Tuck
			Toto

CH. WONALANCET'S BALDY OF ALYESKA   (Whelped 6/10/40)

			Unknown
		Tserko	
	Sapsuk of Seppala		Unknown
		Dushka	Bonzo
	Toska of Wonalancet		Nanuk
			Ici
		Duke	
	Tosca of Alyeska		Wanda
		Tanta of Alyeska	Tuck
			Toto

81

One of the first outstanding black and white Siberians and a high-ly influential stud:

```
                                        Kingeak
                              Smokey of Seppala
                                        Pearl
                 Wolfe of Seppala
                                        Tserko
                              Sigrid of Seppala
                                        Dushka
        Bonzo of Taku
                                        Togo
                              Sepp III
                                        Unknown
                 Ch. Cheenah of Alyeska
                                        Duke
                              Tosca of Alyeska
                                        Tanta of Alyeska
CH. ALYESKA'S SUGGEN OF CHINOOK    (Whelped 6/2/49)
                                        Ch. Turu of Alyeska
                              Ch. Wonalancet's Baldy of Alyeska
                                        Toska of Wonalancet
                 King Husky of Wonalancet
                                        Belford's Wolf
                              Tcheeakio of Alyeska
                                        Cheeak of Alyeska
        Kituh of Taku
                                        Ch. Laddy of Wonalancet
                              Igloo Pak Chuckchee
                                        Tchuchis of Wonalancet
                 Igloo Pak's Kresta
                                        Ch. Laddy of Wonalancet
                              Igloo Pak Vixen
                                        Tchuchis of Wonalancet
```

Short Seeley with leader Waska, followed by (r. to l.) Ch. Turu of Alyeska, Ch. Wonalancet's Disko of Alyeska, Tosca of Wonalancet and Ch. Laddy of Wonalancet.

daughter of Ch. Wonalancet's Baldy of Alyeska, produced one of the all-time greats of the breed—a black and white, blue-eyed male named Ch. Alyeska's Suggen of Chinook.

For many years Suggen was Mrs. Seeley's personal companion and official greeter of all visitors to Chinook Kennels. Until very recently, his portrait was the one used to head the Siberian column of the *AKC-Gazette*. Not only was Suggen a great show dog and stud, he was an extremely long lived one, siring litters well into his teens and being bred, at least on one occasion, to his great, great granddaughter, Ch. Yeso Pac's Aurora. And not to be outdone by his kennelmate, Ch. Wonalancet's Baldy of Alyeska — who could claim among his influential progeny his grandson Mulpus Brook's The Roadmaster, of later Monadnock fame — Suggen was grandsire of the other mainstay of that illustrious breeding program, Ch. Monadnock's Pando.

Milton Seeley died in 1944, but "Short" continues to remain a dominant force in both Malamutes and Siberians to this day. Not only is she an active breeder, judge, and Honorary Life President of the Siberian Husky Club of America, she remains an ardent and outspoken teacher of newcomers and a vigilant protector of these breeds she all but invented almost half a century ago. Honored at a banquet in 1971 on her eightieth birthday where she received greetings from such people as Richard Nixon and Sherman Adams, she received this salutation from the noted judge, Maxwell Riddle:

"For me you have long been America's First Lady of Dogdom. And surely you rank as the world's first lady of sled dogs."

Few would disagree.

Monadnock Kennels

I think it fair to say that no kennel has had as much impact upon the Siberian Husky breed as has Monadnock Kennels.

For old timers and newcomers alike, there is a certain excitement at ringside when the catalog reveals that a dog bearing Monadnock prefix is to be exhibited. And though such dogs are unfortunately rarer now than they have been over the past 45 years, the name still holds a mystique for Siberian Husky enthusiasts that is unequaled.

But ironically, the name has become such an institution as to occasionally dwarf the rather quiet, unassuming, albeit stately, woman behind it. This fact was brought home to me at a recent show. I had been admiring the dog of an intense young exhibitor, who was obviously new to the breed, and asked her regarding its background. She replied that although she was uncertain of its more immediate background, further back it was "mostly Monadnock." She then asked if I knew anything about the judge. I assured her, "No matter what happens, with Mrs. Demidoff judging, one knows that the dog who will eventually take the honors will be a good one." To which the young lady, rather

Lorna B. Taylor and Short Seeley in race at Manchester, Vermont 1936.

Lorna Taylor (Demidoff) with Ch. Togo of Alyeska (finished in 1939) and Short Seeley with Ch. Cheenah of Alyeska (finished in 1938), two of the earliest AKC champions of the breed.

challengingly, responded, "Well, I only hope she appreciates a Monadnock type of dog." In my shock, I could barely get out: "But Mrs. Demidoff IS Monadnock!"

Almost anyone who has ever owned a Siberian Husky knows the name Monadnock; and virtually everyone who has ever shown a Siberian knows that the Monadnock show record stands unchallenged. But I doubt that many are aware of the incredible dedication that has gone into the building of the Monadnock success.

There was, for example, the nightmarish summer that Mrs. Demidoff suffered when some thirty of her puppies died from distemper as she valiantly tried to save even one and failed.

Then there is the story of Ch. Otchki of Monadnock, four time National Specialty winner, and the only Siberian of his time to have the triple distinction of being a bench show champion, an Obedience title holder, and a racing leader. Otchki was unquestionably one of the best dogs produced at Monadnock Kennels, but today few know his name—for Otchki turned out to be sterile.

These and other setbacks would have made anyone with less fortitude and determination take up basket-weaving or some other less harrowing hobby. But Lorna Barnes had had a dream.

The story of Monadnock Kennels really had its start in Tenafly, New Jersey some sixty years ago, when a little girl of six got her first ride in a dog cart behind a small collie-shepherd type dog named "Beans". So thrilled was she by the experience that Lorna Barnes began reading everything she could find about sled dogs. And when she was lucky enough to get a glimpse of one in a movie, she nearly fell out of her seat with excitement. Finally, when she was sixteen and living with her family in Fitzwilliam, New Hampshire, her father arranged for her to ride behind a real dog team. This was a team of Eskimo dogs belonging to a man named Ed Clark who, for a publicity stunt of some kind, was driving them from Woodstock, N.H. to Boston and return. They were being kenneled for the night in a stable in Keene, and while they were there, Mr. Barnes drove his daughter over by horse and sleigh and she got to ride behind the dogs on a run of some five miles. From that day on, it was her dream to one day own a team of her very own.

In 1929 at Laconia, she got to see her first race. Although she was not overly impressed with the motley appearance of most of the dogs, she was very much impressed with their performance. She also learned a very valuable lesson in training and conditioning. It seems that one of the first teams to start that day took off at such incredible speed that she naturally assumed this to be one of the better teams, if not the very best. Shorty Russick's team, on the other hand, down from Flin Flon, Manitoba, starting later, actually started at a walk, and seemed "really rather pathetic." In those days, the Laconia race

The Monadnock matched team in action at Sandwich, New Hampshire, 1937.

Lorna Taylor with Ch. Togo of Alyeska, first Siberian Husky to place in the Group (at Newport, R.I. 1939).

consisted of 30 miles a day for three consecutive days, and Russick's team, trained for long distances and in excellent condition, won the race, while the team that had started so fast finished well back in the field. It was a lesson Lorna never forgot, and in the twenty years of active competition that followed, the teams fielded by Monadnock Kennels were always in excellent condition, regularly covering as much as 35 miles a day during mid-winter training.

In 1930, Leonhard Seppala drove a team of Siberians in the Laconia race, and Lorna saw for the first time what she had found lacking the year before; dogs of outstanding beauty and uniformity who were also excellent in harness. Seppala, of course, won the race with ease, and from that day on Lorna was a devotee of the Siberian.

In 1931 she married Moseley Taylor, son of the publisher of the *Boston Globe* and an avid sled dog enthusiast. Lorna learned to drive a team, and for a year or so drove the dogs considered not fast enough for Moseley's first string team. These dogs were mostly cross-breds, for Moseley was not particularly concerned with the looks of his dogs so long as they were fast. But Lorna did such a commendable job with this second string team and obviously enjoyed it so much that Moseley, knowing her weakness for the beautiful little Siberians, bought her the Seeleys' matched team. This team, consisting of Togo of Alyeska, Anvik of Alyeska, Cheeak of Alyeska, Tosca of Alyeska, Flash, Laska and Toto, were young but had been beautifully trained at the Seeleys by Nate Budgell. It was with this team that Lorna entered the ranks of sled dog racing's top drivers, becoming the first woman driver ever to win a race and placing consistently near the top in races she didn't win.

It was also in the 1930s that Mrs. Taylor began showing her dogs, simply to have something to do in the warmer months when she was not driving. Today, as a seasoned judge, she has considerable sympathy for the occasional moments of embarrassment experienced at one time or another by most novice handlers, for she vividly remembers her first show in which, having shown horses as a girl she followed the standard procedure for horse shows and entered every class for which her dogs were eligible. To make matters worse, hers were the only two Siberians entered. And so, for four straight classes, she and the friend who was handling her other dog trotted in and out of the ring, feeling very foolish but accumulating quite a number of ribbons. She has always remained grateful to judge Louis Murr, who, she says, never cracked a smile or became impatient, but approached each class with the same air of seriousness.

Togo of Alyeska completed his championship in 1939 but was never used extensively at stud, since, at the time, Mrs. Taylor did not fully realize what a remarkable dog he was. In retrospect, this is regrettable, for today she feels he may well have been the best all-round Siberian she ever owned. Exceptionally loyal for a Siberian, he was also what could only be described as a truly gifted leader. Once, on a bet, for instance, she was able to write her name in a field of new snow with a three dog team simply by issuing directional commands to Togo.

Lorna Taylor with Tuck, 1932. Tuck was bred by Mike Cooney, Fairbanks, Alaska.

An unregistered Togo daughter, bred to Tuck by the Seeleys to produce the influential Tanta of Alyeska.

```
                              Ugruk
                   Suggen
                              Liska
          Togo
                              Unknown
                   Dolly
                              Unknown
TOTO    (Whelped probably in the mid-1920s)
                              Nansen
                   Jafet
                              Tacoma
          Nome
                              Hans
                   Alma
                              Ada
```

An incident in Togo's life demonstrates not only the incredible instinctive drive of these dogs, but how the instinct for their particular kind of work, once properly nurtured, gains supremacy over all others. It has been mentioned that Togo was exceptionally loyal for a Siberian—loyal almost to a fault. Once, for instance, when Mrs. Taylor was forced to leave him at home with her parents, he refused to eat and going to her closet pulled down a pair of her ski pants, curled up on these and did not budge until she returned several days later. Knowing the degree of his devotion, which, of course, was reciprocated, Lorna seldom went anywhere without Togo. So when she went to visit friends, some 60 to 70 miles from where she was then living in Fitzwilliam, she naturally took him along. Most of her dogs were at this time on temporary loan to a young man named John Chase; but there were a few dogs left at home in Fitzwilliam, including a bitch in season. Being an unusual Siberian, Togo could be let out of the house wherever Lorna happened to be and could be counted upon to come immediately when called. So on the first morning of the visit, Togo was let out. This time, however, he did not come when called. The area was searched, the police were informed, but all to no avail. Finally, after several hours, a call came from John Chase saying that, by way of an extraordinary set of circumstances, he actually had Togo there. By good luck, he had happened to be driving on a highway about 20 miles from where Lorna was visiting and had seen the dog running for all he was worth, apparently trying to get back to the bitch in season. He called to the dog, but Togo never even broke stride. Finally after driving several miles alongside the dog, trying frantically to figure out how he might apprehend him, he remembered that they were approaching a turn off to the right that ended in a dead end at a high fence. Remembering also that Togo was a lead dog, Mr. Chase leaned out of the car window and gave the command, "Togo, Gee". Togo took the turn, found himself at the fence and gave up the chase.

Although seldom bred, as leader of the most impressive matched team of the era, a team that was not only a top contender on the course but the one that elicited the greatest response from the spectators off the course, Togo made many friends for the breed, and so was not without influence. His litter sister, Tosca of Alyeska, on the other hand, was bred, and it is from her that Monadnock Kennels descends.

The name Monadnock was not actually registered until 1940, the year before Lorna having divorced Mosley Taylor, married Prince Nikolai Alexandrovitch Lopouchine-Demidoff, a Russian prince who had emigrated to the States after the Revolution and a top sled dog driver in his own right until a back injury forced him to retire from competion. So not until 1940 do dogs bred by Lorna bear the Monadnock prefix.

In 1938, Tosca was bred to Belford's Wolf to produce Lorna's first home-bred champion and an excellent racing leader, Ch. Panda. In 1940 Tosca was bred to Millie Turner's Ch. Vanka of Seppala II and produced outstanding

The litter that started it all at Monadnock. L. to r. are: Anvik of Alyeska, Ch. Togo of Alyeska, Laska (spayed), Toto (spayed), Tosca of Alyeska (foundation bitch of Monadnock) and lying down, Cheeak of Alyeska. Pictured in 1935.

The most historically significant members of the first well-known matched team in the history of the breed:

			Thor	Unknown
				Unknown
		Ici		Unknown
			Unknown	Unknown
	Duke			Unknown
			Unknown	Unknown
		Wanda		Unknown
			Unknown	Unknown

CH. TOGO OF ALYESKA
CHEEAK OF ALYESKA   (Whelped 7/2/32)
TOSCA OF ALYESKA
also SITKA OF FOXSTAND

			Unknown	Unknown
		Tuck		Unknown
			Unknown	Unknown
	Tanta of Alyeska			Suggen
			Togo	Dolly
		Toto		Jafet
			Nome	Alma

90

dogs including Ch. Kira of Monadnock (not to be confused with Monadnock's Kira), and Ch. Kolya of Monadnock (not to be confused with Monadnock's Kolya), who became the foundation male at the Nagle's Kabkol Kennels.

Ch. Panda was then bred to Millie Turner's Valuiki of Cold River to produce two very outstanding specimens of the breed, Ch. Vanya of Monadnock III and Ch. Belka of Monadnock II (not to be confused with a later bitch belonging to Kathrine Hulen named Ch. Monadnock's Belka) Belka was also a racing leader and, although bred only once, produced Ch. Aleka of Monadnock who, along with Chort of Monadnock and their offspring, comprised the famous matched team of J. August Duval.

At this point Mrs. Demidoff felt that she had what she wanted in the way of outside influences and confined her breeding, for the most part, to within her own kennel. Ch. Vanya of Monadnock III was bred many times to Ch. Kira of Monadnock, producing such dogs as Pando of Monadnock, who, owned by the McInnes's Tyndrum Kennel in Alaska, greatly influenced the Siberian in that part of the country; Chort of Monadnock, sire and member of Duval's matched team; and Ch. Monadnock's Otchki C.D. who, although sterile, gave the Siberian world something to shoot for in terms of all around excellence.

What might be considered the final phase of the Monadnock breeding program, came some years later. In 1954 Jean Lane (now Jean Bryar), having acquired Duval's matched team, bred Ch. Aleka's Czarina to the famous Izok of Gap Mountain. From this litter she elected to keep a very striking black and white, blue-eyed male whom she named Mulpus Brook's The Roadmaster (after the latest top-of-the-line Buick). Although his dam, Czarina, continued her show career and went on to take Best-of-Opposite Sex at three consecutive National Specialities, The Roadmaster was to see the inside of the ring only once in his life. This was at the Manchester (N.H.) Kennel Club Show, where he went all the way to Best of Breed from the puppy class. Unfortunately, it was at this show that he contracted distemper, which left him totally blind in his right eye.

At the time, Mrs. Lane was in process of building a fast racing team and felt a dog with impaired vision might be a liability. Mrs. Demidoff, on the other hand, had just retired from racing after twenty years of competition, and thought the young dog might not only be able to function adequately on her pleasure team, but be an asset to her breeding program. Thus, The Roadmaster took up residence at Monadnock.

During this same period Ch. Alyeska's Suggen of Chinook had been bred to Monadnock's Kira, an Izok of Gap Mountain daughter. Out of this litter Lorna selected an attractive black and white, blue-eyed male whom she named Monadnock's Kolya. Unfortunately Kolya died very young of distemper, but not before siring two litters. Bred in 1954 to Ch. Monadnock's Nina, he sired Monadnock's Zora who, when later bred to Roadmaster, produced

Ch. Vanya of Monadnock III, winner of the SHCA National Specialty in 1946. His dam, Ch. Panda of Monadnock was BOS.

Ch. Belka of Monadnock II.
1950 National Specialty winner.

```
                                              Unknown
                              Kreevanka
                                              Unknown
               Burka of Seppala
                                              Harry
                              Tosca
                                              Kolyma
        Valuiki of Cold River
                                              Tserko
                              Sapsuk of Seppala
                                              Dushka
               Delzeue of Cold River
                                              Tserko
                              Chuchi of Seppala
                                              Bilka of Seppala
```

CH. VANYA OF MONADNOCK III (Whelped 12/15/44)

CH. BELKA OF MONADNOCK II

```
                                              Unknown
                              Smoky
                                              Unknown
               Belford's Wolf
                                              Harry
                              Tosca
                                              Kolyma
        Ch. Panda
                                              Ici
                              Duke
                                              Wanda
               Tosca of Alyeska
                                              Tuck
                              Tanta of Alyeska
                                              Toto
```

92

Ch. Belka of Monadnock, Ch. Kira, Zoya, Kimmy, Ch. Vanya, Ch. Otchki (front) and Mitya.

Nicholas Demidoff on the runners at Chester, Vermont race, 1941.

the very influential Ch. Monadnock's Konyak of Kazan. Nina was a double Izok granddaughter and an outstanding bitch. She was, in fact, the first Siberian bitch ever to place in Group, which she did three times. The breeding was repeated in 1955, shortly before Kolya's death, and produced what is usually somewhat disappointing to a breeder—a litter of one. But with that one puppy, in whom it seems all the right genes had congregated after years of selective breeding, the course of Siberian Husky history was drastically changed. For he was Ch. Monadnock's Pando.

The name "Pando" was the suggestion of a friend and Lorna has since somewhat regretted not thinking of something more original or dignified. But because of the dog who wore it, the name has come to have a majesty it might not otherwise have had; for what Togo had been to the trail, Pando was to the show ring. Although never extensively compaigned, he was, nevertheless, rarely defeated in breed competition and was winning and placing in the Working Group at a time when Siberians were rarely even looked at. From 1957 through 1961, he won four Specialty Shows and five consecutive Bests of Breed at Westminster.

But Pando's greatness lay not only in his outstanding record as a show dog, but in his ability to produce. An extremely prepotent sire, he was able to consistently produce offspring who were not only good specimens of the breed, but remarkably like himself in appearance. This was most strikingly the case with his son Ch. Monadnock's King, who was so similar to his father that even Mrs. Demidoff occasionally confused them. Shown as a brace only in large shows, they were Best-Brace-in-Show at every major show in which they were entered, including the International and Eastern dog shows twice. When teams of four were still being shown, Pando and three sons, usually Ch. Monadnock's King, Ch. Monadnock's Savda Bakko, and Monadnock's Czar, often stole the show. This was especially true when the competition consisted of four dogs handled by four different handlers. When it came time for the Monadnock team to move and Lorna single-handedly gaited all four dogs in perfect unison around the ring, there was never any doubt in the spectators' minds as to who should win.

In addition to Ch. Monadnock's King, a National Specialty Winner and the first Siberian Husky in the continental United States ever to win a Best in Show, Pando's outstanding offspring included: Ch. Monadnock's Dmitri, the first Siberian to win two Best-in-Show awards and the foundation stud of Koryak Kennels; Ch. Frosty-Aire's Alcan King, a Best in Show winner and foundation stud of Fra-Mar Kennels; and Specialty winners—Ch. Monadnock's Prince Igor CD, Ch. Foxhaunt's Tovarisch CD, Ch. Monadnock's Rurik of Nanook, and Ninaki of Monadnock. Among his grandsons to have won Specialty Shows are Ch. Savdajaure's Cognac, Ch. Kronprinz of Kazan, Ch. Dichoda's Yukon Red, and Ch. Fra-Mar's Soan Diavol, who is also a Best in Show winner.

So extensive has been Pando's influence, however, that it is impossible to

Ch. Monadnock's Pando.

Wolfe of Seppala
Bonzo of Taku
Ch. Cheenah of Alyeska
Ch. Alyeska's Suggen of Chinook
King Husky of Wonalancet
Kituh of Taku
Igloo Pak's Kresta
Monadnock's Kolya
Ch. Wonalancet's Baldy of Alyeska
Izok of Gap Mountain
Duchess of Cold River
Monadnock's Kira
Ch. Vanya of Monadnock III
Panda Girl
Nadejda

CH. MONADNOCK'S PANDO (Whelped 4/4/55)
and MONADNOCK'S ZORA (Whelped 10/26/54)

Ch. Wonalancet's Baldy of Alyeska
Izok of Gap Mountain
Duchess of Cold River
Monadnock's Petya
Ch. Vanya of Monadnock III
Tanya of Monadnock
Ch. Kira of Monadnock
Ch. Monadnock's Nina
Ch. Wonalancet's Baldy of Alyeska
Izok of Gap Mountain
Duchess of Cold River
Monadnock's Laska
Ch. Vanya of Monadnock III
Panda Girl
Nadejda

95

Four generations of champions. In top photo (r. to l.) are Champions Panda and Belka. Below (also r. to l.) are Champions Aleka and Aleka's Czarina.

enumerate all the dogs produced by him who have had in turn been an influence on the breed. Suffice it to say that at the 1966 Speciality Show held in Philadelphia, it was discovered that of the 103 dogs being exhibited, 100 were direct descendants of Pando. Pando, himself, made his final ring appearance at this show, winning the Veteran Dog class at eleven years of age and receiving a standing ovation from ringside.

The final phase of the Monadnock breeding program can then be seen as a process of amalgamating the assets of these two great studs, Pando and Roadmaster. From Pando came class, bearing and elegance, while Roadmaster provided his beautiful head and his somewhat more robust, deep-chested structure. And although Pando's influence may have been more far reaching, since he was in greater breeding demand outside of the kennel, Roadmaster produced around a dozen champions in his own right, including the last great Monadnock stud, Ch. Monadnock's Akela, who, along with Ch. Frosty-Aire's Banner Boy, Ch. Savdajure's Cognac, Ch. Baron of Karnovanda and Ch. Frosty-Aire's Beau-Tuk-Balto, ranks as one of the top producing studs of all time.

Ch. Monadnock's King and Ch. Monadnock's Pando, Best Brace in Show at Eastern Dog Club, 1961.

Best in Show team: Champions Monadnock's Savda Bakko, Serge, King, Pando.

In retrospect, Mrs. Demidoff consistently downplays her role of mastermind of probably the most consistently successful breeding program in the history of the breed. Her first love, she insists, was driving: not winning per se, but the sheer pleasure of working with a team of beautiful, excellently trained animals. If she managed to produce beautiful specimens, she says, it was because she enjoyed working with beautiful animals, not because she had her heart set on the accumulation of ribbons. And there has never been a dog at Monadnock who was only a show dog. Even Pando, for all his success in the ring, spent many more hours as leader of the Monadnock pleasure team than he did at shows. And, of course, enviable as the Monadnock show record is, Lorna's racing record still places her among the best woman drivers in the history of the sport, a career that hit its peak in 1945 with firsts at Fitzwilliam, Newport, and East Jaffrey, New Hampshire.

When asked about her mistakes, or what she might have done differently, Mrs. Demidoff says that she probably should not have let Pando be used on so

The bitch most frequently bred to Ch. Monadnock's Pando. Czarina was the dam of such champions as Monadnock's King, Serge, Prince Igor CD, Tasco del Norte, Red Tango of Murex and Rurik of Nanook.

```
                                              Wolfe of Seppala
                              Bonzo of Taku
                                              Ch. Cheenah of Alyeska
              Ch. Alyeska's Suggen of Chinook
                                              King Husky of Wonalancet
                              Kituh of Taku
                                              Igloo Pak's Kresta
        Monadnock's Nikko
                                              Ch. Wonalancet's Baldy of Alyeska
                              Izok of Gap Mountain
                                              Duchess of Cold River
              Monadnock's Kira
                                              Ch. Vanya of Monadnock III
                              Panda Girl
                                              Nadejda

MONADNOCK'S CZARINA   (Whelped 10/14/54)

                                              Ch. Togo of Alyeska
                              Nicholas of Monadnock
                                              Ch. Kira of Monadnock
              Sasha of Monadnock
                                              Belford's Wolf
                              Ch. Panda
                                              Tosca of Alyeska
        Monadnock's Nadya
                                              Czar of Alyeska
                              Chinook's Alladin of Alyeska
                                              Tcheeakio of Alyeska
              Akiak of Anadyr
                                              Chinook's Alladin of Alyeska
                              Dirka of Anadyr
                                              Candia
```

**Mulpus Brooks the Roadmaster
at 12 years of age.**

```
                                    Belford's Wolf
                        Ch. Turu of Alyeska
                                    Cheeak of Alyeska
            Ch. Wonalancet's Baldy of Alyeska
                                    Sapsuk of Seppala
                        Toska of Wonalancet
                                    Tosca of Alyeska
Izok of Gap Mountain
                                    Kreevanka
                        Ch. Vanka of Seppala II
                                    Tosca
            Duchess of Cold River
                                    Smokey of Seppala
                        Sky of Seppala
                                    Nanna
```

MULPUS BROOK'S THE ROADMASTER   (Whelped 5/31/54)

```
                                    Valuiki of Cold River
                        Ch. Vanya of Monadnock III
                                    Ch. Panda
            Chort of Monadnock
                                    Vanka of Seppala I
                        Ch. Kira of Monadnock
                                    Tosca of Alyeska
Ch. Aleka's Czarina
                                    Ch. Togo of Alyeska
                        Nicholas of Monadnock
                                    Ch. Kira of Monadnock
            Ch. Aleka of Monadnock
                                    Valuiki of Cold River
                        Ch. Belka of Monadnock II
                                    Ch. Panda
```

Ch. Monadnock's King, Best in Show at Mohawk Valley Kennel Club, Schenectady, N.Y. 1961.

At left, Ch. Monadnock's Akela, distinguished son of Roadmaster. Right, Ch. Monadnock's Zita, a Pando daughter and an outstanding producer in her own right.

many outside bitches. In explanation she says, temperament was a far greater problem then than today, as many of the early Siberians were shy. So when a bitch was brought to be bred to Pando, she often accepted it if it exhibited a friendly, outgoing nature, even though it might have been less than perfect structurally. In this respect, it was Marie Turner Remick who once made the statement that future breeders could thank Lorna Demidoff for the beautiful temperament of the contemporary Siberian. When one considers that she is also credited with bringing the Siberian to its highest level of physical perfection, it is no wonder that the name Monadnock carries the prestige it does today.

The only other regret that Mrs. Demidoff occasionally voices is that Pando started such craze for black and white, blue-eyed Siberians that many new people think that is the only criteria for excellence. Fortunately the presence of the beautiful copper and white, bi-color-eyed male, Ch. Monadnock's Akela at Monadnock did much to dispel the myth that the only good Siberian was a black and white, blue eyed one. And for the record, Pando's show record would probably have been exactly the same had he been gray and white and brown eyed.

Nor was Pando simply a show and working dog. For many years he was the house pet and official greeter at Monadnock. He was also the mascot of the Monadnock Regional High School, whose Senior Yearbook is still called the Pandorian. In his advanced years he suffered from nephritis, and Lorna was afraid that his activities as mascot might be more than he was up to. But not wanting to disappoint the kids, she simply sent King along as his stand-in, and the student body never knew the difference.

Unfortunately, even the last of the Monadnock studs, Akela, a son of Roadmaster and Ch. Monadnock's Norina, (a double Pando granddaughter) is now gone, having died unexpectedly in December 1976. But with his champion get numbering some 31 at last count, it is unlikely he will be forgotten any sooner than any of his remarkable forebears.

Once, several years ago, I visited Monadnock Kennels for the first time. After standing and marveling at Akela and the handful of beautiful Monadnock bitches, all well past ten and beautifully cared for, I was invited inside by Lorna, who by now has grown fairly accustomed to having her afternoons interupted by intense young fanciers of the breed eager to have some particle of knowledge bestowed on them. Once inside and past the almost overwhelming array of trophies, I sat under the beautiful wall-size photograph of Pando, King and Roadmaster lying in the snow in harness and listened as she talked dogs and showed old photographs in her quiet, moving way. When I finally managed to tear myself away, knowing I had taken up her entire afternoon, but knowing it was not one I'd soon forget, I happened to notice the license plate on the station wagon outside. It read, "PANDO," above which was written the motto of the state of New Hampshire, "Live Free or Die." And I thought how for a little girl in Tenafly, New Jersey, a dream had surely been realized.

Two distinguished Alakazan producers. At left, Alakazan's Kristi, a top dam. Right, Ch. Alakazan's Nikolai, noted stud.

Kameo of Kazan, at age 11.

Ch. Monadnock's Serge and Ch. Monadnock's Konyak of Kazan, influential studs of the Alakazan Kennels.

5

Outstanding Kennels

O F THE 122 BREEDS recognized by the American Kennel
Club, the Siberian Husky now ranks 14th in popularity. Despite this popularity, the fact that the majority of dogs exhibited today still evidence the qualities of type, temperament and soundness found in previous generations speaks
well for the dedication of the fanciers who nurtured this once obscure breed
into its present position of popularity.

What follows is a description of what might be called the "second generation" of Siberian kennels which fostered the breed during its slow growth during the 1940s and '50s and even into the '60s and '70s. While all of these kennels were established prior to 1960, many are still active today. But even
those now defunct have left an indelible mark on the breed.

In all fairness, however, it should be emphasized that today, throughout
America (and even abroad) there are more kennels than ever dedicated to producing top quality Siberians, kennels that are alert to the dangers engendered
by the breed's fantastic popularity and that are zealously guarding the qualities that make the breed the unique one it is today. May their success continue.

Alakazan

The real beginning of Alakazan Kennels was a vacation trip to the Adiron-
dacks in 1954. There Paul and Margaret Koehler saw their first Siberians and
brought back to their home in Pittsford, New York, near Rochester, a black
and white puppy bitch whom they named Laska of Kazan. Kazan was chosen

Two contemporary Alakazan bitches who exhibit the kind of balanced pedigrees sought at Alakazan:

                                    Ch. Frosty Aire's Beauchien, CD
                          Ch. Frosty Aire's Beau-Tuk Balto
                                    Ch. Klutuk's Carrie
                  Ch. Frosty Aire's Banner Boy, CD
                                    Ch. Monadnock's Red Tango of Murex
                          Frosty Aire's Suntrana
                                    Ch. Kenai Kittee of Beauchien, CDX
        Alakazan's Gunnar

                                    Ch. Monadnock's Savda Bakko
                          Ch. Savdajaure's Cognac
                                    Monadnock's Savda Pandi
                  Alakazan's Kristi
                                    Ch. Alyeska's Suggen of Chinook
                          Ch. Yeso Pac's Tamara
                                    Ch. Yeso Pac's Aurora

CH. ALAKAZAN'S KIRA   (Whelped 9/12/70)

                                    Izok of Gap Mountain
                          Mulpus Brook's The Roadmaster
                                    Ch. Aleka's Czarina
                  Ch. Monadnock's Konyak of Kazan
                                    Monadnock's Kolya
                          Monadnock's Zora
                                    Ch. Monadnock's Nina
        Kameo of Kazan
                                    Ch. Monadnock's Pando
                          Frosty Aire's Chenik
                                    Kura
                  Czarina Alexandria
                                    Ch. Monadnock's Pando
                          Monadnock's Natasha
                                    Monadnock's Czarina

                                    Ch. Frosty Aire's Beauchien, CD
                          Ch. Frosty Aire's Beau-Tuk Balto
                                    Ch. Klutuk's Carrie
                  Ch. Frosty Aire's Banner Boy, CD
                                    Ch. Monadnock's Red Tango of Murex
                          Frosty Aire's Suntrana
                                    Ch. Kenai Kittee of Beauchien, CDX
        Ch. Alakazan's Banner Blue
                                    Mulpus Brook's The Roadmaster
                          Ch. Monadnock's Konyak of Kazan
                                    Monadnock's Zora
                  Kameo of Kazan
                                    Frosty Aire's Chenik
                          Czarina Alexandria
                                    Monadnock's Natasha

ALAKAZAN'S BANNER BLUE LADY (Whelped 1974)
                                    Izok of Gap Mountain
                          Mulpus Brook's The Roadmaster
                                    Ch. Aleka's Czarina
                  Ch. Monadnock's Akela
                                    Frosty Aire's Chenik
                          Ch. Monadnock's Norina
                                    Monadnock's Natasha
        Ch. Monadnock's Volcana
                                    Ch. Monadnock's Pando
                          Ch. Monadnock's Tasco del Norte
                                    Monadnock's Czarina
                  Monadnock's Tia Valeska
                                    Mulpus Brook's The Roadmaster
                          Ch. Monadnock's Lisa
                                    Ninaki of Monadnock

as a kennel name because of its Siberian associations. Years later, however, when the Koehlers decided to register the name with the AKC, they were informed that proper nouns were no longer allowed. To circumvent the problem, they simply appended the expression "a la" to the name and Alakazan became a registered kennel name.

At the time they bought Laska, the Koehlers knew nothing about Siberian bloodlines. Fortunately for them, Laska was from the very best. Her sire was Aleka's Ruska (Chort of Monadnock out of Aleka of Monadnock) a member of Tat Duval's famous matched team, and her dam was Monadnock's Laska (Izok of Gap Mountain out of Panda Girl).

The Koehlers' next acquisition was a large wolf-gray male named Nordholm's Jonas. Jonas was purchased from Joel Nordholm, some of whose dogs came from William Shearer's Foxstand lines. Jonas was shown to his championship, bred to Laska to produce Agfa of Kazan and then bred to Agfa to produce the Koehlers' first homebred champion—the bitch Peggy considers the real foundation bitch of Alakazan—Ch. Kira of Kazan. Kira's show record was outstanding. Finishing her championship by taking the points in four out of the six shows in which she was entered, she went on to take Best-of-Opposite Sex to Ch. Monadnock's King at the 1962 National Speciality.

Kira was then bred to Ch. Monadnock's Serge, a Pando son whom the Koehlers acquired from Frosty Aire Kennels, to produce Ch. Kronpinz of Kazan, a great team dog, the 1965 National Specialty Winner, Best of Breed winner at Westminster in 1966, and a Working Group winner.

In 1960 the Koehlers acquired another young male from Monadnock Kennels, a son of Roadmaster and Pando's sister, Monadnock's Zora, who went on to become Ch. Monadnock's Konyak of Kazan, probably the most influential of all Alakazan studs and the one who is largely responsible for the kind of exciting physical presence associated with Alakazan dogs. Among his more famous offspring are Ch. Alakazan's Satan Sitka, Ch. Yankee Czar's Yogi, Ch. Alakazan's Nikki, Ch. Snoridge's Lorelei, and the very influential Kameo of Kazan, through whom Konyak maintained his influence in the Alakazan breeding program.

Kameo's dam was Czarina Alexandria, a double Pando granddaughter and litter sister of Ch. Monadnock's Norina. Although never shown, Kameo was an outstanding bitch. Bred four times to Ch. Frosty-Aire's Banner Boy, she produced such dogs as Ch. Alakazan's Kossak, Ch. Alakazan's Kio Kam of Snoana, Ch. Alakazan's Saanki, Ch. Alakazan's Banner Blue, and Ch. Alakazan's Nikolai. And today, Nikolai himself can claim around a dozen champion offspring so far to his credit, including the multi-Best in Show winner Ch. Dudley's Tavar of Innisfree.

The bitch that has served largely to complement the strengths of Kameo in the Koehlers' breeding program is Alakazan's Kristi, a daughter of Ch. Savdajaure's Cognac and Ch. Yeso Pac's Tamara, purchased from the Poseys' Yeso Pac Kennels. Like Kameo, Kristi was never shown, but like Kameo she

Ch. Monadnock's Volcana, a top copper bitch of the Alakazan Kennels.

Ch. Alakazan's Banner Blue.

has made her presence felt. More delicate than her kennel mate, she is responsible for much of the "classiness" of Alakazan dogs. Bred to Banner Boy she produced Alakazan's Gunnar who, when bred to Kameo, produced Ch. Alakazan's Kira. Kristi also produced several champion offspring in her own right.

But the dog which Peggy feels most closely resembles her ideal of all the dogs she has bred is the strikingly beautiful copper and white daughter of Ch. Monadnock's Akela and Alakazan's Tia Valeska named Ch. Monadnock's Volcana. Among her impressive wins, Volcana took Best-of-Opposite Sex to her half-brother Ch. Marlytuk's Red Sun of Kiska at the 1971 National Specialty.

Impressive as the Alakazan show record is, however, it is only part of the story. Seven years as one of the top drivers in the Arctic Sled Dog Club, Paul's racing career peaked in 1964 when he won the coveted Siberian Husky Club of America's racing trophy with an extremely impressive team composed of five bench show champions and two pointed dogs. He also served as president of the Siberian Husky Club of America from 1962 to 1964. Jointly the Koehlers have been putting out the Siberian Husky Club of America's *Newsletter* for many years and are largely responsible for its current award-winning format. They have also provided the foundation stock to kennels all over the United States and sent dogs to such places as Finland, Germany, France and Italy.

Although it was Paul who first got the Koehlers into Siberians and whose enthusiasm and eye for dogs put them on the road to being one of the top kennels in the country, his business responsibilities have required more and more of his time in recent years, and it is now Peggy who is most closely associated with the activities of the kennel. She too has held various offices in the Siberian Husky Club, including first Vice President, member of the Board of Directors, Editor of the *Newsletter*, and head of the Standards Committee set up to revise the standard in 1971.

Impressive as her official activities have been, however, her greatest influence has probably been in a subtler capacity. Trained as an English teacher and librarian, it has been many years since Peggy has been in a classroom. However, over the past twenty-odd years she has devoted her particular talents to the meticulous study and teaching of her favorite subject, the Siberian Husky. And whether from her chair at ringside, in her capacity of writer of various columns and articles, or over coffee in her kitchen, she has probably disseminated as much down-to-earth, common-sense information about the breeding, raising and appreciation of the Siberian Husky as anyone alive.

Asked about the theories behind her own breeding program, she considers her own "recipe for stew" to be an attempt to synthesize the strengths of three of the great dogs of the breed: Pando, Roadmaster, and Banner Boy. Over the years her particular concerns, beyond maintaining the basic requisites of type, have been movement, strong, well-angulated fronts and rears, sufficient length of neck, a silhouette that is somewhat longer than tall, small high-set ears, a muzzle that is somewhat longer than that sought by some breeders (and thus more compatible with the standard), and, above all, that a Siberian should be a delight to be with.

Alaskan Kennels

Earl and Natalie Norris' Alaskan Kennel is probably better known to Siberian fanciers by the Anadyr prefix which they use in naming their Siberians. Nevertheless, the kennel name is *Alaskan*.

To the Norrises, raising and driving sled dogs had been a way of life long before they met each other in Alaska. Natalie started driving dogs at the age of ten in Lake Placid, New York, where she made sufficient money to support her dogs by giving rides to wealthy tourists. Her reputation as a dog driver became such that in 1940, at the age of sixteen, she exhibited her dog team at a sport show in Madison Square Garden. During the war she sold her dogs to the Seeleys to be used by the Army Search and Rescue Units. After the war, when she had finished college, she went to work as a kennel helper at the Seeleys' Chinook Kennels. This was in 1945.

In 1946, she decided to go to Alaska and, after consulting with Short Seeley, took along two dogs to act as foundation studs of the kennel she proposed to set up there. These were Chinook's Alladin of Alyeska (Czar of Alyeska out of Tcheeakio of Alyeska) and a dog named Terry who was subsequently discarded. Arriving in Alaska with eleven dogs, she met Earl Norris whose kennel at that time contained 15 dogs, and the rest is history.

Earl himself, began driving dogs at the age of ten in his hometown, Orofino, Idaho, and by the age of 12 owned his first Siberian. Determined to be where the action was in the world of sled dogs, Earl moved to Alaska in 1945 and started a small but high calibre racing kennel. The primary interest of both Earl and Natalie was to develop a kennel of high quality purebred dogs, both Siberians and Malamutes. In 1946, however, when Natalie arrived in Anchorage, no one in Alaska seemed to be breeding registered Siberians, so the Norrises virtually had to start from scratch. Basically, three dogs are responsible for what became their Anadyr line: Chinook's Alladin of Alyeska, and two bitches, Bayou of Foxstand and Candia.

Bayou of Foxstand was bred by Joe Booth of Massachusetts and registered by William Shearer. Bred to Alladin she produced Ch. U-chee of Anadyr who, along with Pando of Monadnock (not to be confused with Ch. Monadnock's Pando) became the foundation of Charles and Kit McInnes' Tyndrum Kennels in Anchorage. A breeding of these two subsequently produced Ch. Tyndrum's Oslo, CDX from whom came the foundation stock of Bob and Lou Richardson's S-K-Mo Kennels, Frosty-Aire Kennels, and in turn Innisfree, Snoana, Chotovotka and many others.

Candia, sired by Bugs of Cold River out of Foxstand's Sukey, was obtained directly from Foxstand Kennels. Bred to Alladin in 1947, she produced the first homebred Anadyr bitch, Dirka of Anadyr, who in turn produced Ch. Noho of Anadyr, who was undefeated in the conformation ring during his five-year career.

Ch. Bonzo of Anadyr CD, however, is probably the most famous dog produced by the Norrises. A grandson of Alladin, he was an outstanding lead dog, the fourth champion Siberian in the United States to earn an Obedience degree, and, in 1955, became the first Siberian in the world to win a Best in Show.

Unique among Siberian kennels who can boast a Best-in-Show winner, Alaskan Kennels is and always has been first and foremost a racing kennel. Indeed it is Earl's boast that while others race their show dogs, the Norrises show their racing dogs. While this may be something of an over-simplification, it does serve to underline the Norrises primary orientation. And, indeed, their racing record and record as producers of top lead and team dogs that have been exported all over the world is probably incomparable.

Alladin was the foundation stud of Alaskan Kennels, and Nanuk the foundation bitch of Kabkol Kennels.

```
                                              Kingeak
                                  Smokey of Seppala
                                              Pearl
                    Wolfe of Seppala
                                              Tserko
                                  Sigrid of Seppala
                                              Dushka
        Czar of Alyeska
                                              Togo
                          Sepp III
                                              Unknown
                    Ch. Cheenah of Alyeska
                                              Duke
                          Tosca of Alyeska
                                              Tanta of Alyeska

CHINOOK'S ALLADIN OF ALYESKA
NANUK OF ALYESKA   (Whelped 5/9/44)

                                              Unknown
                          Smoky
                                              Unknown
                    Belford's Wolf
                                              Harry
                          Tosca
                                              Kolyma
        Tscheeakio of Alyeska
                                              Ici
                          Duke
                                              Wanda
                    Cheeak of Alyeska
                                              Tuck
                          Tanta of Alyeska
                                              Toto
```

Ch. Noho of Anadyr, c. 1956.

Imported from the Norris' Alaskan Kennels, Noho became very influential in the Dichoda and S-K-Mo breeding programs.

```
                                              Smokey of Seppala
                              Bonanza of Seppala
                                              Sigrid of Seppala
                  Charney of Seppala
                                              Kreevanka
                              Dushka of Seppala II
                                              Tosca
        Yaddam of Huskie Haven
                                              Ch. Vanka of Seppala II
                              Mitya of Monadnock
                                              Ch. Panda
                  Nony of White Water
                                              Sedanka of Gatineau
                              Queen of Gatineau II
                                              Queen of Gatineau

CH. NOHO OF ANADYR    (Whelped 5/23/50)

                                              Wolfe of Seppala
                              Czar of Alyeska
                                              Ch. Cheenah of Alyeska
                  Chinook's Alladin of Alyeska
                                              Belford's Wolf
                              Tcheeakio of Alyeska
                                              Cheeak of Alyeska
        Dirka of Anadyr
                                              Burka of Seppala
                              Bugs
                                              Delzeue of Cold River
                  Candia
                                              Ch. Vanka of Seppala II
                              Foxstand's Sukey
                                              Sigrid III of Foxstand
```

Dichoda

It was at their first dog show in 1945, while living in Alexandria, Virginia, that Frank and Phyllis Brayton saw their first Siberian Huskies. Earl Nagle told them what kind of dogs they were, and when the Braytons returned home to California in 1946 they took with them a male from the Nagles' Kabkol Kennels named Dingo Dmitri of Kabkol. Unfortunately Dingo was struck by a car at eight months of age and died in Frank's arms, but he nevertheless played a significant role in the kennel. From him comes the *Di* in Dichoda, and from his unfortunate death comes the rule that no Dichoda dog is sold to anyone without an adequately fenced yard, no matter what.

The rest of the Dichoda name came from the next two Siberians acquired by the Braytons, Echo of Kabkol and Gouda of Kabkol. Echo, a bitch out of Ch. Kolya of Monadnock and Nanuk of Alyeska, provided the *cho* while Gouda, a male out Ch. Kolya of Monadnock and Kabloona, provided the *da*. A litter out of these two in 1948 provided the Braytons with their first homebred champion, Ch. Dichoda's Aurelia, CD, who, in 1952, became the third Siberian in the United States to earn both her bench show championship and an Obedience title.

In 1953, Noho of Anadyr was purchased from Earl and Natalie Norris' Alaskan Kennels. Noho, a son of Yaddam of Huskie Haven and Dirka of Anadyr, completed his championship in 1958 and was undefeated in breed competition during the five years he was shown. Bred to Aurelia he produced the first of the Dichoda reds, and in 1960, Dichoda's Gjoa, the bitch the Braytons kept from this litter, became the second red Siberian Husky to attain championship status, and the first female.

In 1960 Noho sired a litter out of Lou Richardson's Ch. Atu of Glacier Valley, and Frank chose a beautiful bitch out of this litter who was named Dichoda's Beauty of S-K-Mo. Shown on a very limited basis, she nevertheless acquired seven points and went on to produce some of the best known Dichoda dogs.

In 1961 the Braytons acquired Ch. Monadnock's Rurik of Nanook from Virginia Emrich. Rurik was a son of Ch. Monadnock's Pando and Monadnock's Czarina, and, like Noho before him, he was never defeated in Best-of-Breed competition in all the years he was shown. He also produced twelve champions. Bred to Beauty, he sired a litter that contained five champions, the best known of which is the superlative red and white male, Ch. Dichoda's Yukon Red.

All the dogs at Dichoda prior to Yukon were owner-handled by Frank, and Yukon, himself, attained the majority of his points from the Bred-by-Exhibitor Class with Frank. Frank, however, was a victim of multiple sclerosis, and when his condition became more pronounced, the Braytons elected to have their good friend and former Obedience trainer, Tom Witcher, handle Yukon. It was with Tom that Yukon won his first Working Group at the Golden Gate

Three Dichoda Siberian Huskies, c. 1950. Left to right, Adak of Little Tanana, Echo of Kabkol, and Ch. Dichoda's Aurelia, CD.

An early Dichoda breeding:

```
                                          Kreevanka
                            Vanka of Seppala I
                                          Tosca
                Ch. Kolya of Monadnock
                                          Duke
                            Tosca of Alyeska
                                          Tanta of Alyeska
        Gouda of Kabkol
                                          Unknown
                            Ivan
                                          Unknown
                Kabloona
                                          Unknown
                            Duchess
                                          Unknown
```

CH. DICHODA'S AURELIA, CD   (Whelped 10/4/48)
DICHODA'S AKIA
DICHODA'S AKIMO KIO

```
                                          Kreevanka
                            Vanka of Seppala I
                                          Tosca
                Ch. Kolya of Monadnock
                                          Duke
                            Tosca of Alyeska
                                          Tanta of Alyeska
        Echo of Kabkol
                                          Wolfe of Seppala
                            Czar of Alyeska
                                          Ch. Cheenah of Alyeska
                Nanuk of Alyeska
                                          Belford's Wolf
                            Tcheeakio of Alyeska
                                          Cheeak of Alyeska
```

112

Kennel Club show under the noted judge Maxwell Riddle. Yukon subsequently placed in Group twelve times.

In 1967, Yukon was ranked the number one Siberian Husky in the United States, and for the next five years he remained in the top five. Normally such a ranking implies not only a very good specimen but one that is campaigned extensively. In 1967, however, the year he was ranked number one, Yukon was shown only 14 times.

In fact, the Braytons have never campaigned their dogs extensively. Nor have they bred that frequently or kept a large number of dogs. Rather they have bred slowly and carefully, never housing more than a dozen dogs at a time, but nevertheless making an enormous contribution to the breed.

They were the first Siberian kennel in California and one of the first in the West. They were also among the very first breeders in the country to X-ray their stock for hip dysplasia. And throughout the years they have not only contributed greatly to raising the calibre of the Siberian in the West but have held various offices in the national club as well.

In 1975 Frank died of multiple sclerosis, but Phyllis continues the Dichoda breeding program, a breeding program that in recent years has essentially been an attempt to maintain the overall typiness and beautiful movement of one of the truly great dogs in the breed, Ch. Dichoda's Yukon Red. To date, he has sired seven champions and many more with points. More importantly, he has contributed influential stock to some of the best known and most important kennels in the country.

After many years as its recording secretary, Phyllis was recently elected president of the SHCA.

Ch. Monadnock's Rurik of Nanook and Beauty of S-K-Mo going Best of Breed and Best of Opposite Sex, respectively, at Sacramento Kennel Club, 1963. Rurik was winner of the 1964 SHCA Specialty. Owned by Dichoda Kennels.

Ch. Dichoda's Yukon Red, one of the most outstanding copper Siberians in the history of the breed. Owned by Dichoda Kennels.

```
                              Ch. Alyeska's Suggen of Chinook
                    Monadnock's Kolya
                              Monadnock's Kira
          Ch. Monadnock's Pando
                              Monadnock's Petya
                    Ch. Monadnock's Nina
                              Monadnock Laska
     Ch. Monadnock's Rurik of Nanook
                              Ch. Alyeska's Suggen of Chinook
                    Monadnock's Nikko
                              Monadnock's Kira
          Monadnock's Czarina
                              Sasha of Monadnock
                    Monadnock's Nadya
                              Akiak of Anadyr

CH. DICHODA'S YUKON RED    (Whelped 1/18/65)

                              Charney of Seppala
                    Yaddam of Huskie Haven
                              Nony of White Water
          Ch. Noho of Anadyr
                              Chinook's Alladin of Alyeska
                    Dirka of Anadyr
                              Candia
     Dichoda's Beauty of S-K-Mo
                              Pando of Monadnock
                    Ch. Tyndrum's Oslo, CDX
                              Ch. U-Chee of Anadyr
          Ch. Atu of Glacier Valley
                              Yaddam of Huskie Haven
                    Cawkick of Lakota*
                              Nabesna of Polaris
```

*Poko Bueno of Lakota's sister.

114

Ch. Frosty Aire's Alcan King,
Best in Show winner.

Fra-Mar

Frank and Marie Wamser's Fra-Mar Kennels in Olmsted Falls, Ohio, began in the late '50s. Marie became interested in purebred dogs in 1954 when she acquired a Pug whom she worked to his CDX degree in Obedience. It was while showing him in Obedience that she became interested in Siberian Huskies. One Siberian, in particular, caught her eye at several shows and this was Ch. Kenai Kittee of Beauchien, CD. Finally, in 1959 she contacted the Fosters and obtained from them a young Pando son out of a bitch named Kura.

Marie's intention had been to work the puppy in Obedience. Instead, although he did get the first two legs toward his CD degree, he became Ch. Frosty-Aire's Alcan King, the second Pando son to win a Best-in-Show. He also became the first American Best-in-Show winning Siberian to sire an American Best-in-Show winner.

The next important dog the Wamsers acquired was a bitch from the Fosters, sired by Ch. Frosty-Aire's Beau-Tuk-Balto out of Laika of Monadnock, who became Ch. Fra-Mar's Misarah. Missy, in turn, was bred to Ch. Frosty-Aire's Eric to produce their first homebred champion bitch. Ch. Fra-Mar's Karo Mia Diavol. It is upon these three dogs that the Fra-Mar breeding program was based. Essentially it entailed line breeding on Ch. Monadnock's Pando, with Karo Mia being used as a partial outcross.

The most famous dog to come out of Fra-Mar Kennels was a product of Alcan King and Misarah—American, Bermudian and Canadian Ch. Fra-Mar's Soan Diavol. Not only was he, like his father, a Best-in-Show winner, but he was ranked as the top winning Siberian in the country in 1966, '68 and '69 and the top Siberian in Canada in 1970.

Like many of the better kennels in the country, Fra-Mar is a relatively small kennel whose breeding program is conducted slowly and carefully. Among the impressive dogs to come out of this kennel are Ch. Fra-Mar's Czarina Diavol, Ch. Fra-Mar's Troisk Diavol, Ch. Fra-Mar's Challa Diavol, Ch. Fra-Mar's Shiva Diavol, Ch. Fra-Mar's Aja-Tu Diavol, Ch. Fra-Mar's Cherry Puff Diavol, and Ch. Fra-Mar's Nicholai Diavol. Diavol means devil and has always been used in naming dogs of Marie's own breeding. As she says, "All the little devils are mine."

Ch. Fra-Mar's Misarah.

Ch. Fra-Mar's Karo Mia Diavol.

116

Ch. Fra-Mar's Soan Diavol, Best in Show winning son of a Best in Show winner.

<pre>
                                          Ch. Alyeska's Suggen of Chinook
                            Monadnock's Kolya
                                          Monadnock's Kira
                  Ch. Monadnock's Pando
                                          Monadnock's Petya
                            Ch. Monadnock's Nina
                                          Monadnock's Laska
      Ch. Frosty Aire's Alcan King
                                          Czar of Anadyr
                            Ch. Stony River 's Ootah
                                          Ch. Stony River's Karluk
            Kura
                                          Aleka's Khan
                            Stony River's Kayenta
                                          Tanya of Monadnock

American, Bermudian & Canadian CH. FRA-MAR'S SOAN DIAVOL   (Whelped 1/17/65)

                                          Frosty Aire's Tobuk
                            Ch. Frosty Aire's Beauchien, CD
                                          Snow Bird
                  Ch. Frosty Aire's Beau-Tuk Balto
                                          Snow Sepp of Bow Lake
                            Ch. Klutuk's Carrie
                                          Klutuk of Long's Peak
      Ch. Fra-Mar's Misarah
                                          Monadnock's Kolya
                            Ch. Monadnock's Pando
                                          Ch. Monandnock's Nina
            Laika of Monadnock
                                          Monadnock's Nikko
                  Music
                                          Spider
</pre>

Ch. Kenai Kittee of Beauchien, CDX, foundation bitch of Frosty Aire Kennels, pictured at 10 months.

```
                                                    Valuiki of Cold River
                                       Ch. Vanya of Monadnock III
                                                    Ch. Panda
                          Pando of Monadnock
                                                    Belford's Wolf
                                       Ch. Panda
                                                    Tosca of Alyeska
              Ch. Tyndrum's Oslo, CDX
                                                    Czar of Alyeska
                                       Chinook's Alladin of Alyeska
                                                    Tcheeakio of Alyeska
                          Ch. U-Chee of Anadyr
                                                    Surgut of Seppala
                                       Bayou of Foxstand
                                                    Duchess of Huskyland

CH. KENAI KITTEE OF BEAUCHIEN, CDX   (Whelped 5/27/56)

                                                    Ch. Igloo Pak's Anvik
                                       Snow Storm
                                                    Nadejda
                          Misha of Breezymere
                                                    Dichoda's Akimo Kio
                                       Sikha
                                                    Doonah of Monadnock
              Tyndrum's Shiva
                                                    Ch. Vanya of Monadnock III
                                       Pando of Monadnock
                                                    Ch. Panda
                          Tyndrum's Comanchee
                                                    Keetna of Monadnock
                                       Gretel of Tyndrum
                                                    Ch. U-Chee of Anadyr
```

118

Frosty Aire

Jack and Donna Foster's interest in Siberians began in 1955 in Alaska where Jack was stationed in the army. Upon returning to Indiana, they brought with them a male, later Ch. Kenai Krystee of Lakota, CD, and immediately sent back to Alaska for a bitch who was to become Ch. Kenai Kittee of Beauchien, CDX, Frosty Aire's foundation bitch and a very important bitch to the history of the breed.

A daughter of Ch. Tyndrum's Oslo and Tyndrum's Shiva, Kittee had an outstanding show career (going either Best-of Breed or Best-of-Opposite Sex over 80 percent of the times she was shown) and an equally outstanding career in Obedience (winning the *Dog World* Award of Distinction for three consecutive scores of 195 or better.) Bred three times, to Sonya's Torger, to Ch. Stoney River's Ootah and to Ch. Red Tango of Murex, she produced such offspring as Ch. Frosty Aire's Tofty, Ch. Frosty Aire's Susitna and Frosty Aire's Suntrana, all of whom figure in contemporary pedigrees. Among her most outstanding grandsons were Ch. Frosty Aire's Beauchien, CD, and Ch. Frosty Aire's Banner Boy, CD.

Much of the breeding at Frosty Aire was aimed at producing dogs of the type and calibre of famous Izok of Gap Mountain, whom the Fosters saw on a trip to the East. Sonya's Torger was chosen as a stud for Kittee because he was an Izok son. Marina of Mulpus Brook Farm was then purchased because she was a daughter of Baldy of Gap Mountain, an Izok brother. Laika of Monadnock was also purchased because she was linebred to Izok. Another of the Frosty Aire foundation bitches was Kura, who, when bred to Pando, produced Marie Wamser's Best-in-Show winner Ch. Frosty Aire's Alcan King.

One breeding, that of Kittee to Ch. Monadnock's Red Tango of Murex was done specifically to obtain red puppies. There were, however, no red puppies in the litter; but a great grandson, Ch. Frosty Aire's Eric, did become the foundation sire for reds, producing such dogs as Ch. Frosty Aire's Red Devil Beau and Ch. Frosty Aire's Jolly Red Giant as well as a number of black and white and gray titled dogs. And subsequently Red Beau, himself, became a top producing sire.

Perhaps the real peak in the Frosty Aire breeding program began in 1960 when Ch. Frosty Aire's Beauchien, a Kittee grandson, was bred to Ch. Klutuk's Carrie, owned by Dr. Mary Helen Cameron, to produce the famous "Beau-Tuk" litter, the only litter in the history of the breed in which all became champions. They were Ch. Frosty Aire's Beau-Tuk Balto, Ch. Frosty Aire's Beau-Tuk Belka, Ch. Frosty Aire's Beau-Tuk Katrina, CD, Ch. Beau-Tuk Beauvallon and Ch. Frosty Aire's Beau-Tuk Evil One, CD. And this was

The historic Beau Tuk litter—only Siberian litter of size in which all members became champions. L. to r., back row: sire, Ch. Frosty Aire's Beauchien, CD; Ch. Frosty Aire's Beau-Tuk Balto (dog); Ch. Frosty Aire's Beau-Tuk Belka (bitch) and dam, Ch. Klutuk's Carrie. Front, lying down, Ch. Beau-Tuk Evil One, CD (bitch); Ch. Beau-Tuk Katrina, CD (bitch) and Ch. Beau-Tuk Beauvallan.

Ch. Frosty Aire's Beauchien, CD.

120

only the beginning. Balto finished at eight months 23 days and then proved to be what all breeders hope for—that truly prepotent sire capable of producing get that are consistently as good or better than himself. Balto produced 24 champions, which ranks him among the five or ten top producing studs in the history of the breed. But his most outstanding offspring was Ch. Frosty Aire's Banner Boy, CD, owned by the Piuntis, who was not only a truly great specimen of the breed but the sire of some 35 champions to date, making him the breed's number one champion-producing sire of all time.

Balto was not the only member of his litter to exert a strong influence on today's Siberians. Belka was the granddam of Ch. Frosty Aire's Bittersweet, Ch. Frosty Aire's So Cold and Ch. Frosty Aire's Persimmon, all by Ch. Frosty Aire's Red Devil Beau. And Persimmon is still the youngest Siberian to attain her championship, doing so at seven months, 21 days, and with three strikes against her: she was a red in a day when reds were still rare in the show

The famous "Beau-Tuk" litter, the only sizable litter in the history of the breed in which all finished to their championships:

```
                                                    Izok of Gap Mountain
                                    Sonya's Torger
                                                    Aleka's Sonya
                    Frosty Aire's Tobuk
                                                    Ch. Tyndrum's Oslo, CDX
                                    Ch. Kenai Kittee of Beauchien, CDX
                                                    Tyndrum's Shiva
    Ch. Frosty Aire's Beauchien, CD
                                                    Ch. Igloo Pak's Anvik
                                    Snow Storm
                                                    Nadejda
                    Snow Bird
                                                    Dichoda's Akimo Kio
                                    Sihka
                                                    Doonah of Monadnock

CH. FROSTY AIRE'S BEAU-TUK BALTO
CH. FROSTY AIRE'S BEAU-TUK BELKA
CH. FROSTY AIRE'S BEAU-TUK KATRINA, CD
CH. FROSTY AIRE'S BEAU-TUK BEAUVALLON
CH. FROSTY AIRE'S BEAU-TUK EVIL ONE, CD
    (Whelped 12/9/60)
                                                    Torr of Seppala
                                    Little Sepp of Bow Lake
                                                    Leda of Bow Lake
                    Snow Sepp of Bow Lake
                                                    Igloo Pak's Chukchee
                                    Mitzy of Bow Lake
                                                    Malinka of Bow Lake
    Ch. Klutuk's Carrie
                                                    Valuiki of Cold River
                                    Ch. Vanya of Monadnock III
                                                    Ch. Panda
                    Klutuk of Long's Peak
                                                    Izok of Gap Mountain
                                    Alaskan Twilight of Long's Peak
                                                    Tanya of Monadnock
```

ring, a bitch, and a puppy. Shown out of the puppy class only, she amassed three Best of Breed, three Best of Opposite Sex, three Best-of-Winners, two Winner's Bitch and one class first awards in 12 shows, and went third in Working Group the day she finished.

Over the years Frosty Aire has remained a dominant force in the Midwest, from where their meticulous breeding program has influenced kennels all over the country, including Sihu, Susitna, Snoana, Alakazan, Innisfree, Chotovotka, Weldon, So-Huck, Wintersett, Klutuk, Sno-Mound and others.

Igloo Pak

Dr. Roland Lombard's career as a sled dog driver has been so remarkable that his career as a breeder of registered Siberians is occasionally overlooked. Nevertheless, the Igloo Pak prefix is frequently found in the pedigrees of some of the most outstanding show dogs in the breed today, and their names are pointed to with great pride.

Igloo Pak was registered by Roland and his wife Louise about 1940 and was one of the first Siberian kennels to become registered. It means, simply, "the house of the white man." But the story of Igloo Pak really goes back to the 1920s when Roland, then a high school student, first saw and fell in love with Siberian Huskies. His first Siberians were given to him by Seppala and Mrs. Ricker and were named Arctic, Paddy and Frosty.

After he completed his education, and after the war, he was able to acquire Helen of Cold River from William Shearer. Helen was a daughter of Ch. Vanka of Seppala II and Sky of Seppala and was a sister of Duchess of Cold River. She had been in the Army's Search and Rescue unit and proved to be an outstanding lead dog. The Lombards also showed her to her championship.

Another of the outstanding dogs to have come to Igloo Pak was Monadnock's Vickie of Igloo Pak, a trained tracker and racing leader. Before the age of super highways when the drivers gathered together the night before the races, it was often Vickie who kept them entertained by putting on demonstrations of scent discrimination that included picking up dimes placed on the floor among various other objects. Unfortunately she died very young.

Ch. Sitka's Wona of Alyeska was also an Igloo Pak dog and winner of a Group Fourth in an age when Siberians were rarely even looked at in Group. A Wona son, Igloo Pak's Anvic (pedigree herewith), was Best of Breed at the 1947 SHCA Specialty under Mrs. Seeley.

For the most part Igloo Pak stock was based upon Chinook, along with some Monadnock, Foxstand, Belford and Cold River dogs. But undoubtedly the most influential dog to have come out of Igloo Pak in terms of contemporary pedigrees was Igloo Pak's Tok, a son of Alyeska's Sugrut of Chinook and Igloo Pak's Misty, and the sire of many outstanding dogs. Tok has proved influential in many lines, especially in the Yeso Pac breeding program.

Ch. Frosty Aire's Beau-Tuk Balto. Finishing at 8 months and 23 days, Balto went on to produce 24 champions to become one of the breed's top producers.

Ch. Frosty Aire's Banner Boy, top stud at Art and Mary Ann Piunti's Snoanna Kennels. At last count, Banner had sired some 35 champions.

Ch. Frosty Aire's Eric, at 10 months, foundation sire at Frosty Aire for reds.

123

While "Doc" has been in the spotlight of the racing world for some fifty years now, Louise has also contributed a great deal to the world of sled dogs. Her first love was Alaskan Malamutes, and she showed a pure white one and then proceeded to make him the first individual of a northern breed to hold a CD. For many years she also raced Malamutes, but later changed to Siberians. Among her achievements was a second in the Women's Championship race in Alaska in 1969, coming in just fifteen seconds behind the winner.

But the real contribution of Igloo Pak goes far beyond the various outstanding specimens that have been produced there. Rather, in their life-long commitment to the breed, the Lombards have kept the Siberian "on the map" as a running dog for, although they run quite a few cross-breds, there are always a number of purebred Siberians on their teams, and in 1957 "Doc" won the North American Championship race with a team composed entirely of registered Siberians. It is this sort of example that has served as an inspiration to fanciers of the breed for so many years.

An early Igloo Pak dog who was influential on the East Coast, especially through his daughter, Igloo Pak's Kresta, and later on the West Coast at Earl Snodie's Bow Lake Kennels:

```
                                                    Unknown
                                    Smoky
                                                    Unknown
                    Belford's Wolf
                                                    Harry
                                    Tosca
                                                    Kolyma
        Laddy of Wonalancet
                                                    Ici
                                    Duke
                                                    Wanda
                    Cheeak of Alyeska
                                                    Tuck
                    Tanta of Alyeska
                                                    Toto
IGLOO PAK CHUCKCHEE   (Whelped 7/1/45)
                                                    Tserko
                                    Sapsuk of Seppala
                                                    Dushka
                    Suggen of Wonalancet
                                                    Duke
                                    Tosca of Alyeska
                                                    Tanta of Alyeska
        Tchuchis of Wonalancet
                                                    Togo
                                    Sepp III
                                                    Unknown
                    Lassie of Wonalancet
                                                    Duke
                    Cheeak of Alyeska
                                                    Tanta of Alyeska
```

Another early Igloo Pak dog whose influence is still in evidence on contemporary pedigrees. Note the influence of litter sisters, Cheeak of Alyeska, Tosca of Alyeska and Sitka of Foxstand.

```
                                        Belford's Wolf
                            Ch. Turu of Alyeska
                                        Cheeak of Alyeska
                Ch. Wonalancet's Baldy of Alyeska
                                        Sapsuk of Seppala
                            Toska of Wonalancet
                                        Tosca of Alyeska
        Bluie of Chinook
                                        Smooky
                            Belford's Wolf
                                        Tosca
                Tcheeakio of Alyeska
                                        Duke
                            Cheeak of Alyeska
                                        Tanta of Alyeska

CH. IGLOO PAK'S ANVIC     (Whelped 10/3/45)

                                        Unknown
                            Smoky
                                        Unknown
                Belford's Wolf
                                        Harry
                            Tosca
                                        Kolyma
        Sitka's Wona of Alyeska
                                        Ici
                            Duke
                                        Wanda
                Sitka of Foxstand
                                        Tuck
                            Tanta of Alyeska
                                        Toto
```

A later Igloo Pak stud who has been extremely influential:

```
                                        Ch. Turu of Alyeska
                            Ch. Wonalancet's Baldy of Alyeska
                                        Toska of Wonalancet
                Alyeska's Kobuk of Chinook
                                        Belford's Wolf
                            Tcheeakio of Alyeska
                                        Cheeak of Alyeska
        Alyeska's Sugrut of Chinook
                                        Ch. Wonalancet's Baldy of Alyeska
                            Ipuk of Alyeska
                                        Cheeak of Alyeska
                Keo of Alyeska
                                        Belford's Wolf
                            Tcheeakio of Alyeska
                                        Cheeak of Alyeska

IGLOO PAK'S TOK   (Whelped 11/17/57)

                                        Polaris of Sapawe
                            Foxstand's Lippy
                                        Foxstand's Sukey
                Foxstand's Pontiac
                                        Foxstand's Suggen
                            Foxstand's Cleo
                                        Foxstand's Colleen
        Igloo Pak's Misty
                                        Kobe of Gatineau
                            White Water Lake Knight
                                        Nanuk of White Water
                Chogoandoe's Vanya
                                        Ipuk of Alyeska
                            Nikki's Ningo of Alyeska
                                        Tcheeakio of Alyeska
```

125

Kathleen and Norbert Kanzler and friends: wheel dogs, l. to r., Ch. Innisfree's El Ferro, Am. & Can. Ch. Frosty Aire's Starfire; point, left - Innisfree's Rashiri of A-Baska, right - Ch. Innisfree's Krimbo. Lead, Ch. Innisfree's Lobo.

One of two foundation bitches of Innisfree Kennels imported from Alaska:

<pre>
                                        Ch. Vanya of Monadnock III
                        Pando of Monadnock
                                        Ch. Panda
            Ch. Tyndrum's Oslo, CDX
                                        Chinook's Alladin of Alyeska
                        Ch. U-Chee of Anadyr
                                        Bayou of Foxstand
    Siya of A'Baska
                                        Carka of Anadyr
                        Tofta of Nobilis
                                        Cheechee of Anadyr
            Cheena of Nobilis
                                        Chinook's Alladin of Alyeska
                        Cheechee of Anadyr
                                        Ch. U-Chee of Anadyr

INNISFREE'S RASHIRI OF A'BASKA

                                        Skipper of Bow Lake
                        Sash of Bow Lake
                                        Shuska of Bow Lake
            Loki
                                        Igloo Pak Chuckchee
                        Ingrid of Bow Lake
                                        Leda of Bow Lake
    Takla Ananen
                                        Chinook's Alladin of Alyeska
                        T-Serko of Anadyr
                                        Candia
            Tyone of Anadyr
                                        Foxstand's Saint
                        Starina of Gatineau
                                        Ilona of Seppala
</pre>

126

Innisfree

Lieutenant-Colonel Norbert Kanzler and his wife Kathleen's involvement with purebred dogs goes well back into the 1950s when they bred Miniature Schnauzers which they showed both in conformation and Obedience. And although they only obtained their first Siberian in 1960, as originators of one of the most broadly based and influential breeding programs in the country, it is impossible to give an accurate picture of the development of the Siberian without including the Kanzlers.

Having been located in Michigan, Kansas, California and Maryland, Innisfree has been among the most mobile of Siberian kennels, and its record in the show ring has been one of the most impressive. However, when asked to write something about the history and specific character of her kennel, Kathleen tends to minimize the individual accomplishments of her dogs in favor of discussing some of the more crucial issues in establishing a breeding program. As she once said, she can often recall the precise set of a given dog's shoulders without recalling whether or not he completed his championship. What she has written provides such an incisive picture of the concerns that a breeder has, a picture that in so many ways is more important than a given breeder's show record, we feel it should be included in its entirety. What follows, then, are her words:

> Innisfree Siberians are based on two foundation brood bitches purchased in Alaska. Innisfree's Rashiri of A-Baska and Tanio were whelped in 1960–61 in Alaska. Both these bitches were bred by people that were racing purebred Siberians in the heyday of registered Siberians in Alaska.
>
> Innisfree's Rashiri of A-Baska was bred to Frosty Aire stud dogs. Rashiri's

At left, Ch. Innisfree's Beau-Tuk. Right, Ch. Weldon's Beau-Buk, bred by Nancy Perkins' Weldon Kennels in Michigan, and owned by Innisfree Kennels.

127

Ch. Innisfree's Oomachuk and Ch. Innisfree's Barbarossa.

A truly outstanding bitch in her own right, Oomachuk figures significantly in contemporary pedigrees.

<pre>
                                              Izok of Gap Mountain
                               Sonya's Torger
                                              Aleka's Sonya
                  Ch. Frosty Aire's Tofty
                                              Ch. Tyndrum's Oslo, CDX
                               Ch. Kenai Kittee of Beauchien, CDX
                                              Tyndrum's Shiva
     Ch. Innisfree's El Ferro
                                              Poko Bueno of Lakota
                               Ch. Kenai Kristyee of Lakota
                                              Tyee
                  Ch. Frosty Aire's Chena
                                              Ch. Stoney River's Ootah
                               Kura
                                              Stony River's Kayenta

CH. INNISFREE'S OOMACHUK   (Whelped 8/31/65)

                                              Ch. Frosty Aire's Beauchien, CD
                               Ch. Frosty Aire's Beau-Tuk Balto
                                              Ch. Klutuk's Carrie
                  Ch. Innisfree's Beau-Tuk
                                              Ch. Frosty Aire's Beau-Tuk Balto
                               Am. & Can. Ch. Frosty Aire's Starfire
                                              Frosty Aire's Starina
     Innisfree's Banshee
                                              Ch. Tyndrum's Oslo, CDX
                               Siya of A'Baska
                                              Cheena of Nobilis
                  Innisfree's Bashire of A'Baska
                                              Loki
                               Takla of Ananen
                                              Tyone of Anadyr
</pre>

first litter with Ch. Frosty Aire's Beauchien, CD, produced two females that became the foundation bitches of two Michigan kennels. Rashiri's second breeding was with Ch. Frosty Aire's Beau-Tuk Balto and produced Ch. Frosty Aire's Masked Bandit, the foundation of Chotovotka Kennels, Bob and Dorothy Page; and Ch. Innisfrees' Lobo, our Siberian companion on our travels around the world.

Innisfree's initial breedings were aimed toward preserving the soundness and type of our two original bitches, and toward introducing the showiness and eye appeal of the Frosty Aire studs. At this point in the breed it seemed important to linebreed to stabilize the traits we felt were important. American and Canadian Ch. Frosty Aire's Starfire, a Balto daughter, Group placer, top producing brood bitch of the year, and undefeated by any other Siberian in Canada, was bred to her sire, Ch. Frosty Aire's Beau-Tuk Balto. This mating produced three champions. One of these, Ch. Innisfree's Beau-Tuk, was the foundation of Weldon Kennels, Nancy T. Perkins. This linebred Balto son in turn was a keystone of Innisfree. Ch. Weldon's Beau-Buck, a son of Ch. Innisfree's Beau-Tuk, and Ch. Weldon's Beau-Tukker, a grandson of Beau-Tuk, are current studs at Innisfree.

Ch. Innisfree's Beau-Tuk was bred to Innisfree's Rashiri of A-Baska and produced Ch. Innisfree's Chilka, producer of many champions for her owner, Nancy Perkins. Most notable of these was Ch. Weldon's Enuk Balto, producer of two Best-in-Show winners, Ch. Weldon's Beau-Phunsi and Ch. Innisfree's O'Murtagh. Innisfree's Banshee, a sister of Chilka's, also produced many champions, among them Ch. Innisfree's Banshee Tu, American and Canadian Ch. Kler's Rosie and most notably, Ch. Innisfree's Oomachuk.

Tanio, bred to Ch. Innisfree's Beau-Tuk produced Ch. Innisfree's Kitka, Winners' Bitch and Best of Winners at the Siberian Husky Club of America Specialty, and the foundation bitch for another Michigan kennel. Another Tanio daughter, Arctic's Angel of Innisfree (Tanner) produced Ch. Innisfree's Sierra Beau-Jack (Burnside) and Ch. Innisfree's Beau-Kara and Innisfree's Beau-Biddy. Angel was sired by Ch. Innisfree's Krimbo. Krimbo was a Balto son bred to a Balto daughter out of Rashiri.

Our consistent use of Balto, inbred to one of his daughters out of Rashiri or his linebred son, Ch. Innisfree's Beau-Tuk, produced one major line that exists at Innisfree today. However, an enduring kennel must have several options. All breeding cannot go in one direction. A breeder must have other ways to go if his original plans do not materialize. Even if the original linebreeding is going successfully, outcrosses must be introduced regularly. Many great lines in a breed are apt to fade away when one great producing dog ages. A viable kennel must consistently produce good dogs year after year, with the offspring produced being as good or, hopefully better, than the foundation stock. These offspring, besides being good or great specimens of the breed, must be capable of producing quality if one's kennel is to remain significant on the breed scene. Adhering to this theory of developing compatible lines that could be introduced to each other as outcrosses, Innisfree worked on two more strains.

The most important of these was the offspring of Ch. Innisfree's El Ferro. El Ferro was a small in stature, black and white brown-eyed male. He was a beautiful-headed dog with lovely movement. El Ferro bred to Innisfree's Banshee produced the great producing bitch Ch. Innisfree's Oomachuk who, when bred to Ch. Alakazan's Nikolai, produced American and Canadian Ch. Dudley's Tavar of Innisfree's two time Best-in Show Winner, Ch. Innisfree's Pegasus, current important stud at Innisfree, and Ch. Alakazan's Dak Rambo. El Ferro, bred to Zucane's Puna of Bluebell, produced American, Canadian and Bermudian Ch. Innisfree's King Karl (Weir). King Karl was the first Bermudian champion Siberian and the first Siberian to earn three championships.

The crossing of offspring of Ch. Innisfree's Beau-Tuk with Ch. Innisfree's El Ferro continues to be an important part of Innisfree's breeding programs.

The third option we used was the introduction of reds into the breeding program. Breeding for one trait should always be approached with caution. In the early 1960s red Siberians were a phenomenon. It was a challenge to develop dogs that would produce quality red Siberians. Zucane's Puna of Bluebelle was bred to Ch. Frosty Aire's Eric (red) and produced Ch. Innisfree's Barbarossa, a red. Barbarossa was used as an outcross for more leg and his offspring brought this back, successfully, into the lines of Beau-Tuk and the original bitches. Ch. Innisfree's Royal Purple, a Barbarossa son, is currently used for this purpose. Royal's dam, Innisfree's Fireweed was a surprise indeed. A mating with Innisfree's Rashiri of A-Baska and her grandson, Innisfree's Tonto, out of Ch. Innisfree's Lobo and Tanio, produced Fireweed. A light red, she was not recognized as a red until she was five weeks old. She opened up many directions for the reds to go. Through Fireweed we discovered that Rashiri was a red carrier and of course many of her offspring carried the red gene. This was good news for the red Siberians of the time. The few available reds were closely related and the introduction of a strong outcross red line was of value.

The current top studs at Innisfree are Ch. Innisfree's Pegasus and Ch. Weldon's Beau-Tukker, with Ch. Innisfree's Sierra Cinnar, becoming, we hope, the ideal coming-on young stud, along with Innisfree's Import and Innisfree's Targhee.

The outstanding bitches are Ch. Innisfree's Meghan, Ch. Innisfree's Beau-Kara and Innisfree's Beau-Biddy. These are third generation bitches bred here who, together with outcross bitches, Innisfree's Kathleen and Innisfree's Kismet (a product of Ch. Monadnock's Akela, Ch. Koonah's Red Kiska), Ch. Marytuk's Red Sun of Kiska and Ch. Dichoda's Yukon Red, will enable Innisfree to continue building on the near forty Innisfree Champions produced so far.

Our breeding philosophy and concerns are to utilize the best dogs available at any given time. No kennel stays in the running by using their own dogs exclusively. Pride in your dogs is misplaced if you build a line on anything less than the best available.

Many dogs that are fine animals in themselves are not capable of reproducing themselves, because their four grandparents were not exceptional animals. The longer one looks at dogs the more one sees that a grandmother with no outstand-

Ch. Innisfree's Chilka, owned by Nancy Perkins' Weldon Kennels.

Ch. Weldon's Beau Tukker, bred by Nancy Perkins, owned by Innisfree Kennels.

Ch. Innisfree's Pegasus, bred by Margaret Koehler (Alakazan Kennels) and Kathleen Kanzler. Owned by Innisfree Kennels.

ing virtues that was used out of misplaced emotion by a fond owner has undue influence on her grandchildren. How much further ahead a breeding program would be if that fond owner had looked with less love and more awareness at the bitch. Perhaps then the mature decision would have been to love her as a pet and buy the best bred female available to build upon.

The other basic breeding principle is to never compromise on temperament. The unique, friendly personality of the Siberian cannot take second place to quality. Aggressive or shy traits are inherited and cause nothing but heartache for the sincere breeder. You have to live with a dog first, then show him. A dog's temperament is basically aggressive or soft. A decided tendency to too aggressive (vicious) or to too soft (shy) are judgements a breeder must consider in breeding animals. Personality is an offshoot of temperament. Personality traits are the traits that make a dog an individual. A happy, outgoing, willing-to-please Siberian that takes correction with no resentment is our picture of breed temperament.

The original Innisfree bitches were very sound and typy. Both were greys and not flashy—plain jane types, perhaps. When they were bred it was the soundest that were kept. Often these were not the flashiest. When building for future generations, it is imperative that soundness and breed type be the first considerations in selecting puppies for breeding stock.

Pitfalls are falling for that dramatic black and white, blue-eyed pup, the darkest red one and perhaps overlooking the superior soundness that may be present in the grey or dilute black pup with bi-colored eyes or a white break in his coat.

The breed is not yet at a stage where one can breed all top quality, dark black or red dogs with blue eyes. Serious breeders must still pursue perfection through the soundest animals of proper type regardless of color.

Another pitfall that entraps breeders is searching for more size, more specifically a bit longer leg. This is a nagging problem. Many of our greatest producing dogs would have been closer to the ideal if they were a bit higher on leg. The way to ruin your breeding program is to breed the small, typy, refined bitch to the big, long stationed, long backed male. Genes do not mix. Some pups will be small, some large and long. Two different types of dogs are not going to produce the ideal. If you are going to genetically outcross for size, breed phenotypes (dogs that look alike). Then breed back toward the family lines that work for you. Outcrosses, for whatever reason, are usually most useful in a breeding program when bred back into the original family. Your results are in the second generation, not the outcross itself.

Although Innisfree doesn't have a name in racing, all of the original dogs through 1968 were raced in Michigan. The team was composed of six champions on the seven dog team. The will to work is an important facet of Siberians that should be preserved. The dogs are harness trained and run for fun by Norb, Trish, John and Sheila. The terrain and climate of southern Maryland are not conducive to serious running.

Innisfree is a family affair. Trish, John and Sheila are most often seen in the ring handling the dogs while Norb gets the kennel moved, built and set up at whatever spot the Army sends us. So far Innisfree has been in Michigan, Maryland, New York State, Kansas, California and returned to Maryland.

132

Ch. Baron of Karnovanda, CD, sire of 25 champions.

Ch. Karnovanda's Zenda, CD, dam of 10 champions—to date the record for the breed.

Foundation bitch of Karnovanda Kennels:

                                              Aleka's Khan
                               Baloo of Komatik
                                              Waska of Komatik
                  Misha of Monadnock
                                              Izok of Gap Mountain
                               Tamara
                                              Aleka's Sonya
    Baron von Richthoven
                                              Czar of Alyeska
                  Chinook's Alladin of Alyeska
                                              Tcheeakio of Alyeska
                  Alaskan Cheeakio of Anadyr
                                              Chinook's Alladin of Alyeska
                               Dirka of Anadyr
                                              Candia

CH. ESKA'S NONIE, UD   (Whelped 11/18/58)

                                              Ch. Wonalancet's Baldy of Alyeska
                               Izok of Gap Mountain
                                              Duchess of Cold River
                  Sonya's Torger
                                              Chort of Monadnock
                               Aleka's Sonya
                                              Ch. Aleka of Monadnock
    Eska of Timberland
                                              Ch. Igloo Pak's Anvik
                               Snow Storm
                                              Nadejda
                  Akia's Kenai of Timberland
                                              Gouda of Kabkol
                               Dichoda's Akia
                                              Echo of Kabkol

**Ch. Karnovanda's Ivan Groznyi.
A champion at 8 months, winner
of 15 Group placements, and
sire of 20 champions.**

134

Karnovanda

Judy Russell has probably never done anything half-way in her life when it comes to animals. An animal "nut" as a child, she had dogs, cats, hamsters, mice, rabbits, birds, fish or whatever happened along. She began riding at seven, competing in saddle horse events at nine, owned her first horse at ten, and by the time she retired from competition in the late '50s, she had won just about every Saddle Horse or Horsemanship championship open to a juvenile, a woman or an amateur, including the "good hands" championship at the Kentucky State Fair in 1954, '55 and '56. And much of her success in Siberians she feels is probably directly attributable to her background in horses.

It was actually her long time trainer, Chris Reardon, who gave her her first Siberian for her 19th birthday. He had first seen some at the American Royal Horse Show in Kansas City, Missouri, and had ordered a pair. He offered Judy her choice of puppies and she chose the bitch who became Ch. Eska's Nonie, UD. Nonie became Judy's constant companion through college and presented her with a litter of eight puppies in her senior year. Judy kept a bitch, which she named Karen. Karen completed her championship and attained a UD degree in Obedience. She later produced Ch. Karen's Token of Karnovanda, CD who produced some nice puppies. Nothing at Karnovanda today, however, descends from her.

Nonie, on the other hand, was bred again and from her Karnovanda Kennels descends. It was after Judy had married Joel Russell and while they were both doing graduate work at Berkeley that Nonie was bred a second time. This time she was shipped all the way across the country for a mating with Pando, and out of this breeding came the last two syllables of the name Karnovanda, Ivan and Zenda. "Kar" for Karen, "no" for Nonie, "van" for Ivan and "da" for Zenda. The two important puppies from this litter were Ch. Baron of Karnovanda, CD and Ch. Karnovanda's Zenda, CD. Baron amassed some 16 Group placings during his career and sired 25 champions, while Zenda became a top ranking brood bitch, producing ten champions in her own right, the record in the breed to date.

The next step in the Karnovanda breeding program came after the Russells had moved to Michigan. Once there, they purchased an inbred son of Ch. Frosty Aire's Eric and his daughter, Frosty Aire's Miss Erica, who became Ch. Frosty Aire's Jolly Red Giant. He was acquired specifically to be bred to Zenda, a breeding which produced Ch. Karnovanda's Zenzarya, who, when bred back to her uncle, Ch. Baron of Karnovanda, produced a total of six champions. The most important of these was Ch. Karnovanda's Lara Baronovna, dam of six champions herself, the most famous of which is Ch. Karnovanda's Wolfgang, whelped March 11, 1970 and winner of six Group firsts and a Best in Show.

Meanwhile, back in 1966, Zenda had been bred to Ch. Foxhaunt's Glacier Blu and had produced a bitch who became Ch. Karnovanda's Koyukuk. This litter also contained the second of the Russells' Ivans, Ch. Karnovanda's Ivan Groznyi. Finishing his championship at eight months, which is a breed record for males, Ivan won some 90 Best of Breed awards and placed 15 times in Group. Extremely useful when bred to daughters and granddaughters of Baron, he produced twenty champions, and five of his get reside at Karnovanda today.

Karnovanda is a relatively large kennel, housing usually between twenty and thirty dogs at a time. Since her divorce in 1971, Judy teaches full time, raises her three children, takes care of several horses and ponies, and, with the help of friend and fellow Siberian enthusiast, Nancy Hanes, operates the kennel. As if these activities weren't enough, Judy, Nancy and the three children all race with the Great Lakes' Sled Dog Association, so that the fall and winter months are taken up entirely with training and racing. The rest of the year is devoted to showing which Judy approaches with the same energy and singleness of purpose, as attested by the fact the number of champions owned or bred by Karnovanda now stands at over fifty.

Koryak

The story of Dr. James Brillhart's Koryak Kennels is a story of determination. Losing the first three purebred dogs he purchased to hereditary and congenital defects, Jim became interested in Siberians, whose looks, temperament and intelligence appealed to him and who seemed free of many of the hereditary defects he had found in other breeds.

His run of bad luck however, was not over, and he lost the first three Siberians he purchased as well. Through a freakish set of circumstances, two were shot, and the third, well on his way to his championship, contracted distemper and died.

At this point he was ready to give up dogs altogether, but hearing that Monadnock Kennels had a promising puppy for sale, he decided to take one last chance. Driving all the way to New Hampshire from Indiana, he returned with a black and white, blue-eyed puppy who, indeed, was to bring a change of luck. For he grew up to be Ch. Monadnock's Dmitri, the first Siberian to win two Best in Show awards and the top ranked Siberian in the country in 1964 and '65. In his best year, he was also ranked among the Top Ten Working Dogs. He then went on to become what too few top winners manage to become, a top producer. In 1967 and '68 he was ranked the number one producing Siberian sire in the country and in 1968 tied for eleventh place among the 25 top producing Working Group sires.

Ch. Karnovanda's Wolfgang, Best in Show winner. A current stud at Karnovanda.

<pre>
                                                Ch. Frosty Aire's Beau-Tuk Balto
                                  Ch. Frosty Aire's Banner Boy, CD
                                                Frosty Aire's Suntrana
                      Ch. Foxhaunt's Glacier Blue
                                                Igloo Pak's Tok
                                  Foxhaunt's Kaytee
                                                Yeso Pac's Sandy
           Ch. Karnovanda's Ivan Groznyi
                                                Monadnock's Kolya
                                  Ch. Monadnock's Pando
                                                Ch. Monadnock's Nina
                      Ch. Karnovanda's Zenda, CD
                                                Baron von Richthoven
                                  Ch. Eska's Nonie, UD
                                                Eska of Timberland

CH. KARNOVANDA'S WOLFGANG   (Whelped 3/11/70)

                                                Monadnock's Kolya
                                  Ch. Monadnock's Pando
                                                Ch. Monadnock's Nina
                      Ch. Baron of Karnovanda, CD
                                                Baron von Richthoven
                                  Ch. Eska's Nonie, UD
                                                Eska of Timberland
           Ch. Karnovanda's Lara Baronovna
                                                Ch. Frosty Aire's Eric
                                  Ch. Frosty Aire's Jolly Red Giant
                                                Frosty Aire's Miss Erica
                      Ch. Karnovanda's Zenzarya
                                                Ch. Monadnock's Pando
                                  Ch. Karnovanda's Zenda, CD
                                                Ch. Eska's Nonie, UD
</pre>

Ch. Mikhail of Koryak and his father, Ch. Monadnock's Dmitri, owned by Dr. James Brillhart. Dmitri was the first Siberian to win two Bests in Show, and was top winning Siberian of the mid-60's.

Koryak champions. L. to r.: Ch. Tova II of Koryak, Ch. Koryak's Pandy, Ch. Monadnock's Dmitri and Ch. Mikhail of Koryak.

Two influential Koryak dogs:

```
                                    Ch. Alyeska's Suggen of Chinook
                        Monadnock Kolya
                                    Monadnock's Kira
            Ch. Monadnock's Pando
                                    Monadnock's Petya
                        Ch. Monadnock's Nina
                                    Monadnock's Laska
Ch. Monadnock's Dmitri
                                    Izok of Gap Mountain
                        Mulpus Brook's The Roadmaster
                                    Ch. Aleka's Czarina
            Mondadnock's Ekatrina
                                    Izok of Gap Mountain
                        Monadnock's Aleka
                                    Monadnock's Czarina
```

CH. MIKHAIL OF KORYAK (Whelped 3/10/63)
CH. GALYA OF KORYAK

```
                                    Ch. Wonalancet's Baldy of Alyeska
                        Izok of Gap Mountain
                                    Duchess of Cold River
            Mulpus Brook's The Roadmaster
                                    Chort of Monadnock
                        Ch. Aleka's Czarina
                                    Ch. Aleka of Monadnock
Monadnock's Kira of Koryak
                                    Monadnock's Kolya
                        Ch. Monadnock's Pando
                                    Ch. Monadnock's Nina
            Monadnock's Volna
                                    Monadnock's Nikko
                        Monadnock's Czarina
                                    Monadnock's Nadya
```

139

Bred to Monadnock's Kira of Koryak, a Roadmaster daughter acquired from Monadnock Kennels, Dmitri produced the first homebred Koryak champions, Ch. Mikhail of Koryak and Ch. Galya of Koryak. Shown as a brace, Dmitri and Mikhail won five Best Brace in Show awards, including the International Kennel Club show in Chicago in 1968. And Galya, bred back to her grandfather, Pando, provided the first red in the Koryak line, Ch. Tova II of Koryak.

Although Koryak's breeding and showing activities are less extensive today than in the past, it remains one of the foremost Midwestern kennels and has provided influential stock to kennels all over the country. Among Dimitri's more famous progeny are Mikhail, Galya, Ch. Romka Koryak of Bolshoi, Ch. Kincki of Koryak, and his granddaughter, Ch. Koryak's Scarlet Scandal, who, in 1968, tied for first place with Ch. Karnovanda's Zenda, as the top producing dam in the country.

Marlytuk

Lyle and Marguerite Grant began their career in Siberians in 1950 as trainers of Mrs. Frothingham's Cold River Kennel racing team. While Lyle did the actual competing, Peggy did much of the training during the week. This arrangement continued through the winter of 1956 when Mrs. Frothingham found she could no longer keep her kennel and offered the Grants any of her dogs and equipment they wanted. Thus began Marlytuk Kennels: *Mar* for Marguerite, *ly* for Lyle and *tuk* for Ahkeetuk, the first Siberian pup owned by the Grants.

From Mrs. Frothingham's dogs the Grants selected one male, Ninga of Cold River, and four females, Lena of Cold River, Enara of Cold River, Tongass of Cold River and Rola. Of these Rola proved the most significant. A daughter of Igloo Pak's Blui and Ch. Helen of Cold River, Dr Lombard's famous lead dog, she was bred to Izok of Gap Mountain to produce two very influential dogs in the Marlytuk breeding program, a bitch named Wanee of Marly and a dog named Ch. Noonok of Marly.

While Wanee, bred to a Roadmaster son, Monadnock's White Xmas, produced Marlytuk's Ahrigah Nakoo, dam of both Ch. Koonah's Red Kiska and Ch. Koonah's Red Gold, Noonok produced such offspring as Ch. Marlytuk's Ahkee, Marlytuk's Tukki and Ch. Marlytuk's Nonah who, in turn, were influential in the Savdajaure and Doonauk lines as well as in the Marlytuk breeding program.

Ch. Koonah's Red Kiska, one of the most outstanding copper bitches in the history of the breed. Dam of Ch. Marlytuk's Red Sun of Kiska.

<table>
<tr><td></td><td></td><td></td><td>Ch. Wonalancet's Baldy of Alyeska</td></tr>
<tr><td></td><td></td><td>Alyeska's Kobuk of Chinook</td><td></td></tr>
<tr><td></td><td></td><td></td><td>Tcheeakio of Alyeska</td></tr>
<tr><td></td><td>Alyeska's Sugrut of Chinook</td><td></td><td></td></tr>
<tr><td></td><td></td><td></td><td>Ipuk of Alyeska</td></tr>
<tr><td></td><td></td><td>Keo of Alyeska</td><td></td></tr>
<tr><td></td><td></td><td></td><td>Tcheeakio of Alyeska</td></tr>
<tr><td>Columbia's Admiral</td><td></td><td></td><td></td></tr>
<tr><td></td><td></td><td></td><td>Monadnock's Kolya</td></tr>
<tr><td></td><td></td><td>Ch. Monadnock's Pando</td><td></td></tr>
<tr><td></td><td></td><td></td><td>Ch. Monadnock's Nina</td></tr>
<tr><td></td><td>Monadnock's Flash</td><td></td><td></td></tr>
<tr><td></td><td></td><td></td><td>Monadnock's Nikko</td></tr>
<tr><td></td><td></td><td>Monadnock's Czarina</td><td></td></tr>
<tr><td></td><td></td><td></td><td>Monadnock's Nadya</td></tr>
</table>

CH. KOONAH'S RED KISKA   (Whelped 10/19/63)

<table>
<tr><td></td><td></td><td></td><td>Izok of Gap Mountain</td></tr>
<tr><td></td><td></td><td>Mulpus Brook's The Roadmaster</td><td></td></tr>
<tr><td></td><td></td><td></td><td>Ch. Aleka's Czarina</td></tr>
<tr><td></td><td>Monadnock's White Xmas</td><td></td><td></td></tr>
<tr><td></td><td></td><td></td><td>Kita Kituh of Chebacco</td></tr>
<tr><td></td><td></td><td>Dama of Monadnock</td><td></td></tr>
<tr><td></td><td></td><td></td><td>Star of Chebacco</td></tr>
<tr><td>Marlytuk's Ahrigah Nakoo</td><td></td><td></td><td></td></tr>
<tr><td></td><td></td><td></td><td>Ch. Wonalancet's Baldy of Alyeska</td></tr>
<tr><td></td><td></td><td>Izok of Gap Mountain</td><td></td></tr>
<tr><td></td><td></td><td></td><td>Duchess of Cold River</td></tr>
<tr><td></td><td>Wanee of Marly</td><td></td><td></td></tr>
<tr><td></td><td></td><td></td><td>Igloo Pak's Blui</td></tr>
<tr><td></td><td></td><td>Rola</td><td></td></tr>
<tr><td></td><td></td><td></td><td>Ch. Helen of Cold River</td></tr>
</table>

141

Acquired from the Dennisons, Koonah's Red Kiska became one of the truly outstanding copper bitches in the breed. Completing her championship at the age of nine months, she enjoyed a highly successful and extremely long show career, going Best of Opposite Sex, for instance, at Westminster Kennel Club in 1973 at the age of nine years.

Over the years, largely because of Kiska and her sister Ch. Koonah's Red Gold, Marlytuk has become particularly well known for red Siberians, although all colors are produced there. When the time came to breed Kiska, Ch. Monadnock's Akela was chosen as the stud and this breeding was done five times. Among the many truly outstanding offspring produced by this combination, the most famous has undoubtedly been Ch. Marlytuk's Red Sun of Kiska, known in the Siberian world as "Sunny." Completing his championship in 1968 by winning four out of five shows, all of them four point majors, Sunny went on to win two National Specialty Shows and to accumulate well over fifty Best of Breed ribbons, feats which kept him near the top in both Phillips System and *Kennel Review* rankings for a number of years. Not only was Sunny a great show dog, however, but a highly prepotent stud who has left an indelible mark on the breed, especially at Marlytuk where a great deal of work has been done to insure that his soundness, type, and above all, his beautiful movement are maintained.

It is not surprising, however, that both Sunny and Kiska are renowned for their movement, since Marlytuk has always been a top working dog kennel as well as a show kennel, and most of their top show dogs have spent a number of years in harness. In fact, Marlytuk is the only kennel to win the Siberian Husky Club of America's racing trophy four times.

It is probably due in part to the fact that Marlytuk dogs are worked in harness that Peggy has always taken a great interest in brace and team competition; Marlytuk brace teams have won eight Best Brace in Show awards to date, five of which were won by Sunny and Kiska. In fact, in 1975, they took Best Brace in Show at all three specialty shows, Sunny at the age of nine and a half and Kiska at the age of 12, a feat for which they are now known at Marlytuk as "the Geritol twins." So not only has Marlytuk's racing and show records been remarkable but their record for endurance has been equally enviable.

Among the many outstanding dogs produced or housed at Marlytuk have been Ch. Marlytuk's Ahkee, Ch. Marlytuk's Nonah, Ch. Marlytuk's Dom, Ch. Marlytuk's Chena, Ch. Marlytuk's Tongass, Ch. Marlytuk's Jeuahnee, and Ch. Marlytuk's Red Kira of Yukon, daughter of Ch. Koonah's Red Gold and Ch. Dichoda's Yukon Red. Today, with Sunny and Kiska past their prime in terms of ring performance, the current top show dogs are Ch. Kiska Too of Chaku, a daughter of Sunny and one of the few bitches in the breed to have won a Group first, and Ch. Marlytuk's Kiska Trey, a full sister of Sunny from the last breeding of Akela and Kiska.

The Geritol Twins. Ch. Marlytuk's Red Sun of Kiska (at 9 1/2 years) and Ch. Koonah's Red Kiska (at 12 years) winning Best Brace at the 1975 National Specialty at Keene, N.H.

Ch. Marlytuk's Red Sun of Kiska stepping out at the 1975 Specialty.

Ch. Marlytuk's Kiska-Too of Chaku.

143

Savdajaure

Situated in Ashland, Massachusetts, Savdajaure Kennels is the result of the combined efforts of three people, Ragnar and Ingrid Forsberg, and their daughter Anna Mae. In the mid 1950s the Forsbergs began raising Norwegian Elkhounds, and their dogs carried the kennel name Lapp. When the family moved to Ashland where their kennel could be larger, they decided to add another breed. And it was at a dog show shortly thereafter that they saw the Monadnock brace of King and Pando and decided then and there that this was the breed.

From Monadnock they acquired two dogs, a bitch who became Monadnock's Savda Pandi and, shortly thereafter, a male named Monadnock's Savda Bakko. Pandi had been bred by Muriel Stumpfer and was out of Ch. Monadnock's Red Tango of Murex, a copper and white son of Pando, and Monadnock's Eb'ny Lass of Murex. This being in the days when bitches were frequently left home to produce puppies while the males were shown, Pandi did not complete her championship. Bred only to Bakko, however, she did produce six champions and has certainly left her stamp on the breed.

Bakko, on the other hand, was shown. Bred by Ella H. Shovah out of a mating of Pando and Ch. Sintulata, he, like Pandi, was born in September of 1958. He won his first five points at the National Specialty in Washington in 1959 at the age of six months and went Best of Winners at the Specialty Show in Philadelphia nine months later. In all he completed his championship in only ten shows, never placing lower than Reserve Winners' Dog. He was also a member of the famous team of Pando, King, Bakko and Monadnock's Czar and was a Group winner in 1964. During his career he sired nine champions and was twice winner of the Stud Dog Class at National Specialties.

As impressive an animal as Bakko was, however, he had the capacity to produce better than himself. And, indeed, in July of 1960, there was a puppy born at the Forsbergs who, like Togo and Pando before him, was the only live puppy in the litter. In 1958 the name Savdajuare, meaning "mountain lake" in the Swedish Lapp language had been registered by the AKC, and this puppy became Ch. Savdajaure's Cognac, Best of Breed at two National Specialties, three Area Supported Shows, and three-time winner of the Working Group. He also lived to produce 24 champions to make him one of the top producing Siberian sires of all time.

Among Cognac's most influential offspring has been Ch. Savdajaure's Miuk, CD, a copper and white male by Cognac out of Ch. Snoridge's Lorelei, bred by Anna C. Schmale and sent to the Forsbergs as a stud fee puppy. Winner of the Stud Dog Class at the National Specialty in Philadelphia in 1970, Miuk, himself, has sired 12 champions to date.

Other influential dogs to have resided at Savdajaure have been Ch. Savdajaure's Keema Tova, Ch. Savdajaure's Mekki, Ch. Savdajaure's Vackra

Ch. Savdajaure's Cognac, two time National Specialty winner, and a very influential stud with 24 champions to his credit.

```
                                             Ch. Alyeska's Suggen of Chinook
                                   Monadnick's Kolya
                                             Monadnock's Kira
                      Ch. Monadnock's Pando
                                             Monadnock's Petya
                                   Monadnock's Nina
                                             Monadnock's Laska
            Ch. Monadnock's Savda Bakko
                                             Ch. Vanya of Monadnock III
                                   Nikki of Monadnock
                                             Monadnock's Blitzen
                      Ch. Sintaluta
                                             White Water Lake Knight
                                   Dushka of Monadnock
                                             Tanya of Monadnock
CH. SAVDAJAURE'S COGNAC    (Whelped 7/3/60)
                                             Monadnock's Kolya
                                   Ch. Monadnock's Pando
                                             Ch. Monadnock's Nina
                      Ch. Monadnock's Red Tango of Murex
                                             Monadnock's Nikko
                                   Monadnock's Czarina
                                             Monadnock's Nadya
            Monadnock's Savda Pandi
                                             Foxstand's Pontiac
                                   Vanya's Frosty of Chogoandoe
                                             Chogoandoe's Vanya
                      Monadnock's Eb 'Ny Lass of Murex
                                             Izok of Gap Mountain
                                   Monadnock's Aleka
                                             Monadnock's Czarina
```

Monadnock's Savda Pandi, dam of Cognac.

Ch. Monadnock's Savda Bakko, sire of Ch. Savdajaure's Cognac.

Dockra, Ch. Savdajaure's Bushka, Ch. Savdajaure's Tanni and Miuk's son Ch. Savdajaure's Kalle Brun (Swedish for Charlie Brown.)

As large a contribution to the breed as Savdajaure has made, however, it is interesting to note that it is quite a small kennel where breeding is done very rarely. Each dog is, in effect a family pet — and a testimonial to the research, dedication and teamwork that has made Savdajaure what it is today.

While being a full-time nurse and now an AKC licensed judge, Anna Mae has also managed to serve in almost every capacity in the Siberian Club of America including being the official historian.

Ch. Savdajaure's Miuk CD, an outstanding Cognac son and himself a sire of many champions.

Bred at the MacInnes' Tyndrum Kennels in Alaska, Oslo figures significantly in the pedigrees of Dichoda, S-K-Mo, Frosty Aire and Innisfree.

```
                                              Burka of Seppala
                                Valuiki of Cold River
                                              Delzeue of Cold River
                   Ch. Vanya of Monadnock III
                                              Belford's Wolf
                                Ch. Panda
                                              Tosca of Alyeska
        Pando of Monadnock
                                              Smoky
                                Belford's Wolf
                                              Tosca
                   Ch. Panda
                                              Duke
                                Tosca of Alyeska
                                              Tanta of Alyeska

CH. TYNDRUM'S OSLO, CDX   (Whelped 10/23/52)

                                              Wolfe of Seppala
                                Czar of Alyeska
                                              Ch. Cheenah of Alyeska
                   Chinook's Alladin of Alyeska
                                              Belford's Wolf
                                Tcheeakio of Alyeska
                                              Cheeak of Alyeska
        Ch. U-Chee of Anadyr
                                              Kreevanka
                                Surgut of Seppala
                                              Duska of Seppala II
                   Bayou of Foxstand
                                              Sapsuk of Seppala
                                Duchess of Huskyland
                                              Rollongsford Nina
```

A highly influential dog in the S-K-Mo breeding program:

```
                                              Bonanza of Seppala
                                Charney of Seppala
                                              Duska of Seppala II*
                   Yaddam of Huskie Haven
                                              Mitya of Mondnock
                                Nony of White Water
                                              Queen of Gatineau II
        Carka of Anadyr
                                              Ch. Vanka of Seppala II
                                Mitya of Monadnock
                                              Ch. Panda
                   Nony of White Water
                                              Sedanka of Gatineau
                                Queen of Gatineau II
                                              Queen of Gatineau

CH. KOLA OF ANADYR   (Whelped 12/11/51)

                                              Burka of Seppala
                                Valuiki of Cold River
                                              Delzeue of Cold River
                   Ch. Vanya of Monadnock III
                                              Belford's Wolf
                                Ch. Panda
                                              Tosca of Alyeska
        Zoya of Monadnock
                                              Smoky
                                Belford's Wolf
                                              Tosca
                   Ch. Panda
                                              Duke
                                Tosca of Alyeska
                                              Tanta of Alyeska
```

148

*Duska of Seppala II appears on many pedigrees as Dushka of Seppala II.

Ch. S-K-Mo's Charney Korsar.

S-K-Mo

Robert and Lou Richardson's interest in Siberians began in the mid-50s while Bob was serving in the Air Force in Alaska. Returning to southern California in 1957, they brought with them down the Alcan Highway a small ball of grey fur who subsequently became Ch. Sassara's Ozera, their first champion and long-time racing leader.

Finding the sport of sled dog racing already established in southern California, the Richardsons began acquiring and breeding dogs for their team. And, like other Siberian enthusiasts in the area, they also began showing their dogs. From 1959 to 1966, they finished 15 champions, ten of which were bred by themselves, and acquired the enviable racing record of never having been beaten by any team of any breed trained in southern California.

Out of Ch. Sassara's Ozera, their first champion, came what was perhaps the most well-known of S-K-Mo dogs, Ch. S-K-Mo's Charney Sambo and his sister Ch. S-K-Mo's Charney Sooka. Not only did this team win five Best Brace in Show awards, but they won four of them consecutively the first four times they were shown together.

Basically, however, the S-K-Mo breeding program can be seen to be based primarily upon two dogs: Ch. Tyndrum's Oslo, CDX, and Ch. Kola of Anadyr. The influence of Oslo comes from two dogs brought down from Alaska,

149

Five time Best Brace in Show winners, Ch. S-K-Mo's Charney Sooka and her brother, Ch. S-K-Mo's Charney Sambo.

Ch. S-K-Mo's Charney Sobaka.

A current S-K-Mo champion showing the kind of careful line-breeding typical of the line:

```
                                                 Ch. Kola of Anadyr
                                  Ch. S-K-Mo's Charney Korsar
                                                 Ch. Atu of Glacier Valley
                    Ch. S-K-Mo's Charney Sobaka
                                                 Ch. Kola of Anadyr
                                  S-K-Mo's Malinkaya Lisa
                                                 Ch. S-K-Mo'- Charney Koshka
      Chandalar Pondo I
                                                 Ch. Tyndrum's Oslo, CDX
                                  Ch. Bennett's Digger
                                                 Tyone of Anadyr
                    S-K-Mo's Kenoos Nikki
                                                 Ch. Kola of Anadyr
                                  S-K-Mo's Kimo Charney
                                                 Ch. Atu of Glacier Valley

CH. S-K-MO'S J. P. McMORGAN  (Whelped 12/1/69)

                                                 Pando of Monadnock
                                  Ch. Tyndrum's Oslo, CDX
                                                 Ch. U-Chee of Anadyr
                    Ch. Bennett's Digger
                                                 T-Serko of Anadyr
                                  Tyone of Anadyr
                                                 Starina of Gatineau
      Ch. S-K-Mo's Jezebel Tu
                                                 Carka of Anadyr
                                  Ch. Kola of Anadyr
                                                 Zoya of Mondanock
                    Ch. S-K-Mo's Matushka Katrina
                                                 Ch. Tyndrum's Oslo, CDX
                                  Ch. Atu of Glacier Valley
                                                 Cawhick of Lakota
```

Ch. S-K-Mo's J.P. McMorgan. Owners: John and Laurel Tanner.

Ch. Bennett's Digger and an outstanding bitch named Ch. Atu of Glacier Valley; the influence of Kola, also brought down from Alaska and a brother of the very influential Ch. Noho of Anadyr owned by Dichoda Kennels, comes down through a number of progeny including Ch. Dichoda's Udacha of S-K-Mo, Ch. S-K-Mo's Kolyema Snova, Ch. S-K-Mo's Matushka Katrina and Ch. S-K-Mo's Charney Korsar.

Having tried unsuccessfully to introduce Eastern stock into their lines, the Richardsons finally leased Dr. Brillhart's Ch. Mikhail of Koryak in 1968 and were successful in introducing him into the S-K-Mo breeding program. Today, this line plus some stock introduced from Martha Lake Kennels serves to complement the carefully linebred stock that descends from the Richardsons' original Alaskan imports.

For many years Lou has been very influential in the Siberian Husky Club of America and in 1966 became an AKC licensed judge. Since that time there has been very little breeding done at S-K-Mo Kennels. Nevertheless, the influence that this kennel has exerted on the Siberians of the Far West is probably rivaled only by that of Dichoda.

A contemporary dog out of S-K-Mo breeding that shows the influence of Mikhail of Koryak, as well as the Anadyr influence:

```
                                        Carka of Anadyr
                              Ch. Kola of Anadyr
                                        Zoya of Monadnock
                    Ch. S-K-Mo's Kolyema Snova
                                        Ch. Tyndrum's Oslo, CDX
                              Ch. Atu of Glacier Valley
                                        Cawhick of Lakota
          S-K-Mo's Timuk of the Tundra
                                        Ch. Monadnock's Dmitri
                              Ch. Mikhail of Koryak
                                        Monadnock's Kira of Koryak
                    Natasha XVIII
                                        S-K-Mo's Volk of Table Mountain
                              S-K-Mo's Sheeka-Luk
                                        Ch. S-K-Mo's Charney Sooka
HUSHKYVARNA'S ON ANY SUNDAY   (Whelped 4/26/75)
                                        Ch. Monadnock's Pando
                              Ch. Monadnock's Dmitri
                                        Monadnock's Ekatrina
                    Ch. Mikhail of Koryak
                                        Mulpus Brook's The Roadmaster
                              Monadnock's Kira of Koryak
                                        Monadnock's Volna
          S-K-Mo's Oodachiney Bastion
                                        Carka of Anadyr
                              Ch. Kola of Anadyr
                                        Zoya of Monadnock
                    Ch. Dichoda's Udacha of S-K-Mo
                                        Ch. Noho of Anadyr
                              Dichoda's Beauty of S-K-Mo
                                        Ch. Atu of Glacier Valley
```

Ch. Monadnock's Prince Igor
CD, winner of the 1961 National
Specialty. Owned by Yeso Pac
Kennels.

Yeso Pac

In 1954 Charlie and Carolyn Posey established their Yeso Pac (C. A. Posey spelled backwards) Kennels with the intention of raising Boxers. No sooner had they moved into their new kennel property, however, than a friend offered them a Siberian bitch whose cat-chasing and fence-jumping he had found too much to cope with. Carolyn was against acquiring this scrawny, out-of-coat trouble maker who had already had five different owners at the age of four. Charlie, on the other hand, either out of curiosity, or a sense of challenge, or because even then he had a keen eye for dogs, wanted to take her. And so Kara came to live with the Poseys and the Boxers somehow got lost in the shuffle.

Kara, who came from Kabkol stock behind which was both Chinook and Monadnock breeding, turned out to be considerably more than the scrawny trouble maker she at first appeared. Not only did she rapidly win the affection and respect of both the Poseys, but, once back in coat and in good weight, she completed her championship with dispatch and then presented the Poseys with their first litter, one that contained three champions: Ch. Kara's Idyl, Ch. Kara's Aral, and Ch. Kara's Umlak.

153

Indeed, Kara, who Charlie says greatly resembled the Seeleys' Ch. Wonalancet's Baldy of Alyeska, became the foundation of Yeso Pac and produced a number of litters. Among them, the result of a mating with Pando, was one that contained another very significant bitch, Ch. Checkers of Yeso Pac.

The next important step in the Poseys' breeding program was the acquisition of a young male from Monadnock Kennels who became Ch. Monadnock's Prince Igor, CD. A Pando son and the Posey's only Obedience title holder, Igor went Best of Breed at Westminster in 1958 and was the 1961 National Specialty winner. Bred to Ch. Kara's Idyl, he produced Yeso Pac's Sandy who, when bred to the famous Igloo Pac's Tok, produced a number of exceptional dogs including Ch. Yeso Pac's Reynard who finished his championship at eleven months.

Bred to Checkers, Igor produced Ch. Yeso Pac's Aurora, a double Pando granddaughter who, when bred back to her great, great grandfather, Ch. Alyeska's Suggen of Chinook, produced a truly outstanding bitch Ch. Yeso Pac's Tamara. Tamara in turn was bred three times to Ch. Savdajaure's Cognac to produce such dogs as Alakazan's Kristi, extremely influential in the Alakazan line, Yeso Pac's Reddy Kilowatt and Ch. Yeso Pac's Minx, both

The foundation bitch of Yeso Pac Kennels:

```
                                                          Valuiki of Cold River
                                      Ch. Vanya of Monadnock III
                                                          Ch. Panda
                        Ataman of Monadnock
                                                          Vanka of Seppala I
                                      Ch. Kira of Monadnock
                                                          Tosca of Alyeska
          Cheracha's Chelo
                                                          Vanka of Seppala I
                                      Ch. Kolya of Monadnock
                                                          Tosca of Alyeska
                        Goody Girl of Kabkol
                                                          Ivan
                                      Kabloona
                                                          Duchess

CH. KARA   (Whelped 7/30/50)

                                                          Vanka of Seppala I
                                      Ch. Kolya of Monadnock
                                                          Tosca of Alyeska
                        Don Dee of Kabkol
                                                          Ivan
                                      Kabloona
                                                          Duchess
          Astra
                                                          Vanka of Seppala I
                                      Ch. Kolya of Monadnock
                                                          Tosca of Alyeska
                        Ekatrina of Kabkol
                                                          Czar of Alyeska
                                      Nanuk of Alyeska
                                                          Tcheeakio of Alyeska
```

Ch. Yeso Pac's Reynard (lying down) and Ch. Yeso Pac's Tamara

reds, and, perhaps most significantly, Ch. Yeso Pac's Vodka, an extremely important stud at Yeso Pac. During his lifetime Igor sired 12 champions while Vodka, now 11, has sired ten.

To complement this line of dogs, the Poseys introduced Igloo Pac stock, primarily through Igloo Pac's Tok, along with an intermingling of Calivali and Foxstand lines. Among their most outstanding show dogs was a bitch named Ch. Chebeo's Tashinka. Acquired from Walter Shanks, this exceptionally beautiful copper and white daughter of Ch. Monadnock's Akela and Ch. Chebeo's Copper Prestige was shown only seven times and finished with four majors.

But showing has only been part of Yeso Pac's commitment to the world of Siberians, and over the years their record on the trail has been as remarkable as their record in the ring. For over a dozen years Charlie has been one of the top contenders in the New England Sled Dog Club, and in 1974 the Yeso Pac racing team, led by Yeso Pac's Satan, winner of the Sled Dog Class at the Canadian Specialty in 1974, was ranked number two in the club, attesting to the fact that the Poseys' breeding program is still based on producing the same dual-purpose Siberian they first came to know and believe in.

One of Yeso Pac's most successful and influential breedings:

Monadnock's Kolya
Ch. Monadnock's Pando
Ch. Monadnock's Nina
Ch. Monadnock's Savda Bakko
Nikki of Monadnock
Ch. Sintaluta
Dushka of Monadnock
Ch. Savdajaure's Cognac
Ch. Monadnock's Pando
Ch. Monadnock's Red Tango of Murex
Monadnock's Czarina
Monadnock's Savda Pandi
Vanya's Frosty of Chogoandoe
Monadnock's Eb 'Ny Lass of Murex
Monadnock's Aleka

CH. YESO PAC'S VODKA
CH. YESO PAC'S MINX (Whelped 11/7/64)
YESO PAC'S REDDY KILOWATT
ALAKAZAN'S KRISTI

Wolfe of Seppala
Bonzo of Taku
Ch. Cheenah of Alyeska
Ch. Alyeska's Suggen of Chinook
King Husky of Wonalancet
Kituh of Taku
Igloo Pak's Kresta
Ch. Yeso Pac's Tamara
Ch. Monadnock's Pando
Ch. Monadnock's Prince Igor, CD
Monadnock's Czarina
Ch. Yeso Pac's Aurora
Ch. Monadnock's Pando
Ch. Checkers of Yeso Pac
Ch. Kara

Left, Ch. Chebco's Tashinka, bred by Walter Shanks and owned by Yeso Pac Kennels. Right, Ch. Yeso Pac's Vodka.

Ch. Baltic Pacesetter and Baltic Tor-Na-Do's Inuijak, bred by John and Ruth Cline and owned by Mr. and Mrs. R.B. Conyers' Taiga Kennels, California. Pacesetter continues as one of the leading winners and producers of today.

Four other kennels operating during the middle generation period of the breed, although no longer active today, contributed greatly to the progression of the breed. They were Baltic, Foxhaunt, Stoney River and Kabkol.

BALTIC KENNELS was established in the early 1950s in Commerce City, Colorado by John and Ruth Cline. Their first bitch, Baltic Chilla Chima, was acquired from Jerry Nemecek in 1955. Sired by Cheechako of Timberland out of Stoney River's Chima, she proved to be a foundation bitch in the truest sense of the word.

Bred to Ch. Stoney River's Jet Siobhan, Chilly provided the Clines with their first homebred champion, a bitch named Ch. Baltic Chilla's Gay Charmer, as well as another champion, Ch. Stoney River's Shutka. Charmer was then bred to Ch. Stoney River's Ootah to produce Teko Zema, an outstanding stud. Bred to Panda of Clear Creek, a Chilly daughter, he produced perhaps the most famous of Baltic dogs, Ch. Ty Cheeko of Baltic CD, the number one Siberian in the country in 1963 and sire of such dogs as Ch. Loki Easter of Baltic and Ch. Stashi's Ganya of Baltic. In a mating with another Chilly daughter, Baltic Chilla's Hao-Chi-La, Teko then produced the outstanding and influential bitch, Ch. Alapah Oonik of Baltic. And finally, bred directly back to Chilly for her last litter, he produced Ch. Reginald of Baltic who, in turn, sired Ed Samberson's Best in Show winner Ch. Darbo Domeyko of Long's Peak.

The Clines are both dead now, but the distinctive silver and gray dogs that descend from their line can be found in kennels all across the country, especially in the Rocky Mountain area where Baltic dogs and their descendants continue to be a dominant force to this day.

157

Ch. Kolya of Monadnock and Kabloona, owned by Earl and Margaret Nagle.

Dick Williams driving Foxhaunt's all Siberian racing team, 1968-69. Double lead: Foxhaunt's Suggen and Trina. Point: Ch. Foxhaunt's Zorina and Foxhaunt's Glacier Blu.

Foundation bitch of Baltic Kennels:

```
                                        Ch. Wonalancet's Baldy of Alyeska
                              Izok of Gap Mountain
                                        Duchess of Cold River
                    Sonya's Torger
                                        Chort of Monadnock
                              Aleka's Sonya
                                        Ch. Aleka of Monadnock
          Cheechako of Timberland
                                        Ch. Igloo Pak's Anvik
                              Snow Storm
                                        Nadejda
                    Akia's Kenai of Timberland
                                        Gouda of Kabkol
                              Dichoda's Akia
                                        Echo of Kabkol

BALTIC CHILLA CHIMA    (Whelped 1955)

                                        Burka of Seppala
                              Valuiki of Cold River
                                        Delzeue of Cold River
                    Ch. Vanya of Monadnock III
                                        Belford's Wolf
                              Ch. Panda
                                        Tosca of Alyeska
          Stony River's Chima
                                        Valuiki of Cold River
                              Ch. Vanya of Monadnock III
                                        Ch. Panda
                    Tanya of Monadnock
                                        Vanka of Seppala I
                              Ch. Kira of Monadnock
                                        Tosca of Alyeska
```

FOXHAUNT KENNELS was founded in the mid 1950s by Mr. and Mrs. Richard Williams. During its formative years the kennel was located in New Jersey before being moved to Algonquin, Illinois.

The Williams foundation stock came from Monadnock Kennels and consisted of a daughter of Pando and Czarina named Ninaki of Monadnock, who was later a National Specialty winner, and Monadnock's Kootenai, a son of Roadmaster and Monadnock's Zora and a full brother of Ch. Monadnock's Konyak of Kazan. A mating of these two produced Foxhaunt's first champion, Ch. Foxhaunt's Ziok. This breeding also produced a bitch named Foxhaunt's Sinopah who, when bred back to Pando, produced Ch. Foxhaunt's Tovarisch, the 1961 National Specialty winner.

Before leaving the East, the Williams acquired two more bitches, Foxhaunt's Ondine and Foxhaunt's Kaytee. Ondine came from Monadnock Kennels, was a double Pando granddaughter from a breeding of Frosty Aire's Chenik and Monadnock's Natasha, and was a full sister of Ch. Monadnock's Norina and Czarina Alexandria. After moving to the Midwest, she was bred

Left, Ch. Stony River's Frosty Boy. Right, Ch. Stony River's Miss Aurora, owned by Janie R. Church's Midnight Sun Kennels, Colorado.

Two significant Stony River dogs:

```
                                        Wolfe of Seppala
                            Czar of Alyeska
                                        Ch. Cheenah of Alyeska
                Chinook's Alladin of Alyeska
                                        Belford's Wolf
                            Tcheeakio of Alyeska
                                        Cheeak of Alyeska
        Czar of Anadyr
                                        Czar of Alyeska
                            Chinook's Alladin of Alyeska
                                        Tcheeakio of Alyeska
                Ch. U-Chee of Anadyr
                                        Surgut of Seppala
                            Bayou of Foxstand
                                        Duchess of Huskyland
CH. STONY RIVER'S OOTAH   (Whelped 8/10/55)
CH. STONY RIVER'S RINDA
                                        Ch. Vanya of Monadnock III
                            Chort of Monadnock
                                        Ch. Kira of Monadnock
                Aleka's Khan
                                        Nicholas of Monadnock
                            Ch. Aleka of Monadnock
                                        Ch. Belka of Monadnock II
        Ch. Stony River's Karluk
                                        Valuiki of Cold River
                            Ch. Vanya of Monadnock III
                                        Ch. Panda
                Stony River's Nanook
                                        Ch. Vanya of Monadnock III
                            Tanya of Monadnock
                                        Ch. Kira of Monadnock
```

160

to Ch. Frosty Aire's Banner Boy to produce Ch. Foxhaunt's Czarina. Kaytee, bred by Yeso Pac Kennels out of Igloo Pac's Tok and Sandy, was also bred to Banner Boy, a breeding which resulted in the last major step in the Foxhaunt breeding program. Out of it came both Ch. Foxhaunt's Glacier Blu and Foxhaunt's Suggen. Glacier Blu went Best of Breed at the International Dog Show in Chicago, while Suggen, although never campaigned to his championship, was a National Specialty winner.

Throughout their career, the Williams' primary concern was in breeding a standard Siberian who could also run on a team, and their racing record both in the East and the Midwest has been outstanding. Although other responsibilities have curtailed their activity in Siberians, the Williams still own a last son of Suggen.

KABKOL KENNELS, although active only a short time during the late 1940s and early 1950s, has had an influence on today's Siberians. Owned by Earl and Margaret Nagle, the foundation stock consisted of three dogs, a stud named Ch. Kolya of Monadnock, out of Ch. Vanya of Monadnock III and Ch. Kira of Monadnock, and two bitches, Nanuck of Alyeska and Kabloona. Nanuck was a product of Chinook Kennels sired by Czar of Alyeska out of Tcheeakio of Alyeska and Kabloona was unregistered. Out of these three dogs and their offspring came all the Siberians carrying the Kabkol name, some of whom appear in the pedigrees of some of the most influential kennels in the country, particularly in those of Dichoda and Yeso Pac.

STONY RIVER KENNELS belonged to James and Lucille Hudson and was in existence from 1952 to 1961, during which time they finished seven champions. Their foundation bitch was a daughter of Ch. Vanya of Monadnock III and Ch. Kira of Monadnock named Tanya of Monadnock. Their foundation stud was Aleka's Khan, a son of Chort of Monadnock and Ch. Aleka of Monadnock. A breeding of these two produced Ch. Stony River's Frosty Boy. A breeding of Tanya back to her father produced, among others, Ch. Stony River's Gay Panda, Stony River's Chima and Stony River's Nanuk. When Stony River's Chima was bred to Cheechako of Timberland, she produced Baltic Chilla Chima, the foundation bitch of Baltic Kennels. The breeding of Khan to Nanuk produced Ch. Stony River's Karluk, the first Siberian to place in the Group in Colorado. Tanya bred to Frosty Aire's Tobuk produced Ch. Stony River's Tikki-tue and Ch. Stony River's Taiki-O. Bred to Czar of Anadyr she produced the influential Ch. Stony River's Ootah and the equally outstanding Ch. Stony River's Rinda. Shown for the first time at age of six months and three days, Rinda took a five point major and proceeded to complete her championship in the next three shows, finishing at age of nine months, six days—for many years the youngest bitch in the breed to have finished her championship. For a time, the Hudsons also owned and showed Ch. Monadnock's Nina, the dam of Pando and a three-time Group placer.

TOP WINNING SIBERIANS OF THE 1970s

If the 1940s and '50s can be considered the formative years of the breed, and the '60s a decade of surging popularity among pet owners and exhibitors, then the 1970s should be considered the decade in which the Siberian Husky came into his own as a major inter-breed contender in the show ring.

From January 1970 through May 1977, 167 Siberians accounted for 700 Working Group wins or placements and 24 Best in Show awards.

What follows is an alphabetical listing of Siberians who placed two or more times in Working Groups during this period. Each listing includes their sex (m. for males, b. for bitches), the year that they finished championship, their parentage, breeders, owners, Group placement wins (GRI, GR2, GR3 and GR4), Best in Show wins, Specialty wins and the number of champion progeny (if any) they have produced. It should be noted that some of the older dogs had done most of their winning before January 1970, and these wins are not credited here. Also, no attempt has been made to account for Canadian show records; many of these dogs have compiled impressive records on that side of the border as well, both as competitors and producers.

It should be remembered that a list like this, while being indicative of an overall trend in a breed, is an arbitrary and somewhat vague indicator of an individual dog's worth, either as a show competitor or as a producer. Many of them are only approaching the zenith of their careers, while others (as we have noted) did much of their winning prior to this record. It also goes without saying that some dogs are campaigned more heavily than others.

CH. AJA-TU SHIVA SUNOMA, b. - WD-110804; Ch. 1977
(Ch. Fra-Mar's Nikolai Diavol ex Karnovanda's Kheta)
Breeders: Leslie and Daniel Haggard
Owners: Patricia and Michael Schloffeldt
1 GR3; 1 GR4

CH. ALAKAZAN'S KIEV, m. - WC-157788; Ch. 1974
(Ch. Alakazan's Nikolai ex Alakazan's Kundry)
Breeders: Richard Beams and Margaret Koehler
Owner: Barbara Young
1 GR1; 1 GR3; 1 GR4
1 champion offspring

CH. ALAKAZAN'S KIO KAM OF SNOANA, m. - WA-750606; Ch. 1968
(Ch. Frosty Aire's Banner Boy CD ex Kameo of Kazan)
Breeder: Alakazan Kennels
Owner: Mary Ann Piunti
3 GR3; 1 GR4
1 champion offspring

162

Ch. Monadnock's King, first Siberian Husky to win Best in Show in the continental USA, at Mohawk Valley KC 1961 under Mrs. Renner.

Ch. Monadnock's Dmitri, first Siberian to win two Bests in Show in the USA. Owned by Dr. James Brillhart. Pictured with handler Joe Gregory. (Mr. Gregory is now a widely respected judge.)

CH. ALMARING'S ALAI, m. - WB-279398; Ch. 1970
(Can. Ch. Petya of Monadnock ex Monadnock's Marina)
Breeder: Ingrid Brucato
Owners: D. Dugeon and C. Baumeister; then Sallye Davis and Ingrid Brucato.
2 GR2; 1 GR3; 4 GR4
1 champion offspring

CH. AMCHITKA'S AMIE VALENTINA, b. - WC-182203; Ch. 1974
(Ch. Knega's Total Eclipse ex Ch. Sobaka of Kistefjall)
Breeder-Owner: L. Stewart Cochrane
1 GR2; 2 GR3

CH. AMUR'S NATASHA OF NEWBURY, b. -WA-816003; Ch. 1968
(Kanangnark's Kiowa ex Amur's Tura Talsi)
Breeders: Kathleen and George Ruch
Owners: Lawrence and Suzanne Willson
1 GR2; 1 GR4
3 champion offspring

CH. ANIKO OF SO HUCK, m. - WB-409385; Ch. 1970
(Vicki and Cindy's Corporal ex Cheechako Black Party Punch)
Breeder: F. F. May
Owner: W. E. Kirkman
2 GR3; 1 GR4

CH. ARAHAZ TENGRI KHAN CD, m. - WB-19581; Ch. 1971
(Ch. Toki of Rockrimmon ex Ch. Arahaz Ebony Beauty)
Breeders: Edward and Rosemary Fischer
Owner: C. M. Windsor
2 GR4

CH. CHERSKI'S SANDOR CD, m. - WB803676; Ch. 1974
(Brendeara's Juneau Blanoir ex Cinnamon of Lustigleben)
Breeders: Brenda and Donald Randall
Owners: Hal and Mary Dufford
2 GR3; 1 GR4

CH. CHILKA'S ASTRA OF WELDON, b. - WB-496953; Ch. 1973
(Ch. Marlytuk's Red Sun of Kiska ex Ch. Innisfree's Chilka)
Breeder: Nancy Tucker Perkins
Owner: Roberta Denifrio
1 GR3; 1 GR4

CH. CHOTOVOTKA'S MS KITTY RUSSELL, b. - WC-787920; Ch. 1975
(Ch. Innisfree's Pegasus ex Ch. Chotovotka's Napachee)
Breeder-Owners: Bob and Dorothy Page
2 Bests in Show; 6 GR1; 3 GR2; 2 GR3; 3 GR4
2 Specialty BOBs and 1 Specialty BOS

CH. CHOTOVOTKA'S NOTA YANKIDRINK, m. - WB-819933; Ch. 1973
(Ch. Wintersett Bo Gentry ex Ch. Chotovotka's Kaytee)
Breeders: Bob and Dorothy Page
Owner: Kenneth Gentry, Jr.
2 GR2
1 champion offspring

CH. CINNAMINSON'S SOAYA FOURNIER, m. - WB-615666; Ch. 1970
(Ch. Tookany's Mitka ex Ch. Chachka of Cinnaminson)
Breeders: Sy and Ann Goldberg
Owners: Sy and Ann Goldberg and Jean Fournier
1 GR1; 1 GR3

Ch. Frosty Aire's Alcan King, Best in Show winner, owned by Fra-Mar Kennels. Pictured in his last showing, at just one month short of his twelfth birthday.

Am Can. & Bermudian Ch. Fra-Mar's Soan Diavol, son of Alcan King ex Ch. Fra-Mar's Misarah, the first Best in Show winning progeny of a Best in Show winner in the breed. Bred and owned by the Wamsers' Fra-Mar Kennels.

CH. DEERLAKE'S FROSTY KAZAN, m. - WB-928155; Ch. 1973
(Sandyhill's Black Bandit ex Hilltop's Czarina Tasha)
Breeder: Susanne Griffin
Owner: Randy Smeltzer
1 GR1; 5 GR2; 10 GR3; 2 GR4

CH. DESHA'S PRINCE JASCHA, m. - WC-748325; Ch. 1975
(Pinehill's Dakota CD ex Pinehill's Chena)
Breeder: Sandra K. Wacenske
Owners: Desmond T. and Sharon Cole
2 GR1, 2 GR3, 1 GR4

CH. DICHODA'S YUKON RED, m. - WA-440517; Ch. 1965
(Ch. Monadnock's Rurik of Nanook ex Dichoda's Beauty of S-K-Mo)
Breeder-owner: Dichoda Kennels
1 GR2; 2 GR4 (Most of his wins were scored in the 1960s.)
7 champion offspring

CH. DOMEYKO'S ZADAR, m. - WB-333090; Ch. 1971
(Ch. Darbo Domeyko of Long's Peak ex Ch. Takoka of Wabash Valley)
Breeders: Dale and Rachel Milam
Owners: Ed and Peg Samberson
2 GR1; 1 GR2; 2 GR3; 3 Gr4
1 champion offspring

CH. DOONAUK KEEMAH'S CHUCHI, b. - WA-462053; Ch. 1967
(Ch. Monadnock's Savda Bakko ex Ch. Doonauk's Keema)
Breeder-Owners: Amel R. and Viola B. Akers
2 GR3
3 champion offspring

CH. DUDLEY'S TAVAR OF INNISFREE, m. - WB-582471; Ch. 1971
(Ch. Alakazan's Nikolai ex Ch. Innisfree's Oomachuk)
Breeders: Kathleen Kanzler and Margaret Koehler
Owners: Clarence and Gladys Dudley
2 Bests in Show; 3 GR1; 7 GR2; 6 GR3; 5 GR4
6 champion offpsring

CH. DUDLEY'S VARSKA, m. - WC-330374; Ch. 1975
(Ch. Dudley's Tavar of Innisfree ex Ch. Dudley's Tava of Innisfree)
Breeders: Clarence and Gladys Dudley
Owners: Clarence and Gladys Dudley and Ginger Scott
3 Bests in Show; 12 GR1; 12 GR2; 10 GR3; 7 GR4
3 Specialty BOBs

CH. FRA-MAR'S NIKOLAI DIAVOL, m. - WC-25120; Ch. 1972
(Ch. Eu-Mor's Zhulek of Siber ex Ch. Fra-Mar's Aja-Tu Diavol)
Breeder: Marie Wamser
Owners: Leslie and Daniel Haggard
10 GR1; 10 GR2; 12 GR3; 13 GR4
8 champion offspring

CH. FRA-MAR'S SOAN DIAVOL, m. - WA-549611; Ch. 1966
(Ch. Frosty Aire's Alcan King ex Ch. Fra-Mar's Misarah)
Breeder; Nina Fischer
Owner: Marie Wamser
1 GR2; 1 GR4 (Most of his winning was prior to 1970)
10 champion offspring

Ch. Dudley's Tavar of Innisfree, two-time Best in Show winner. Wh. 1969, by Ch. Alakazan's Nikolai ex Ch. Innisfree's Oomachuk. Owned by Clarence and Gladys Dudley.

Ch. Dudley's Varska (by Ch. Dudley's Tavar of Innisfree ex Ch. Dudley's Tava of Innisfree). Varska has won 3 American all-breed Bests in Show, and 5 Canadian. He is co-owned by his breeders, Clarence and Gladys Dudley, and by Ginger Scott.

CH. FROSTLINE'S LORD BARNABY, m. - WC-143357; Ch. 1974
(Ch. Pixie Wim's Kawillaganuk ex Khan's Chikeeka of Green Tree)
Breeders: Jane and Thomas Hacker
Owner: G. Burzalski
2 GR4

CH. FROSTY AIRE'S AUSTRAL KNIGHT, m. - WC-793471; Ch. 1976
(Ch. Frosty Aire's Yukon Knight ex Ch. Klutuk's Funny Girl)
Breeder: Frosty Aire Kennels
Owners: Charles and Linda Clement
3 GR1; 1 GR2; 2 GR3; 1 GR4

CH. FROSTY AIRE'S RED BARON, m. - WB-91363; Ch. 1969
(Ch. Frosty Aire's Red Devil Beau ex Frosty Aire's Cinnamon Girl)
Breeder: Marilyn E. Stumpf
Owner: Dr. J. D. Guin
3 GR4
1 champion offspring

CH. GRE-TO-DA'S IESCHA MOON GLOW, b. - WB-810758; Ch. 1974
(Ch. Fra-Mar's Rising Sun Dancer ex Fra-Mar's Mide Noel)
Breeder: Julio A. Vale
Owners: Marie Wamser and Pat Corbin
1 GR1; 1 GR2; 2 GR3; 2 GR4
1 Specialty BOB

CH. HARM'S CHANUK PANDY, m. - WB-850; Ch. 1969
(Ch. Koryak's Pandy ex Stewart's Tawn-Ya)
Owners: L. W. and P. A. Harms
1GR2; 1 GR3
2 champion offspring

CH. INNISFREE'S O'MURTAGH, m. - WB-612050; Ch. 1972
(Ch. Baron of Karnovanda CD ex Ch. Weldon's Enuk Balto)
Breeder: Nancy Tucker Perkins
Owners: Major and Mrs. Milton Dohn
1 Best in Show; 3 GR1; 3 GR2
5 champion offspring

CH. INNISFREE'S SIERRA CINNAR, m. - WC-976104; Ch. 1975
(Ch. Innisfree's Sierra Beau-Jack ex Innisfree's Royal Kate)
Breeders: Michael Burnside and Sarah Higginbotham
Owner: Kathleen Kanzler
2 Bests in Show; 9 GR2; 9 GR3; 3 GR4
(Also the top rated breed dog for 1976 and 1977)

CH. INNISFREE'S TARCHEE, m. - WD-054798; Ch. 1976
(Ch. Weldon's Beau Tukker ex Ch. Innisfree's Bona Dea of Viking)
Breeder: Lois Proctor
Owners: Michael Burnside and Kathleen Kanzler
2 GR3

CH. INNISFREE'S TROIKA OF BAYKAL, m. - WC-833709; Ch. 1975
(Ch. Innisfree's Pegasus ex Vodka's Katrynka)
Breeders: Sheila and Kathleen Kanzler
Owner: John D. Zahrt
2 GR1; 1 GR2; 1 GR4
2 champion offspring

168

Ch. Darbo Domeyko of Long's Peak, Best in Show winner. Owner, Ed Somberson.

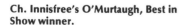

Ch. Innisfree's Sierra Cinnar, a Best in Show winner and one of the outstanding young males in the breed today. Owned by Kathleen Kanzler.

Ch. Innisfree's O'Murtaugh, Best in Show winner.

CH. JLAHKA'S CHOTOVOTKA BLACK JAC, m. - WC-740677; Ch. 1976
(Ch. Innisfree's Pegasus ex Ch. Chotovotka's Napachee)
Breeders: Bob and Dorothy Page
Owner: Larry Gehman
1 GR1; 1 GR2; 1 GR4

CH. JUNEAU OF TANDA, m. - WA-873739; Ch. 1969
(Ike of Bow Lake ex Ch. Kayak of Martha Lake CDX)
Breeder-Owner: Lynne Patterson
1 GR3; 1 GR4
2 champion offspring

CH. KARNOVANDA'S AKU AKU, m. - WC-152806;
(Ch. Karnovanda's Wolfgang ex Kler's Cindy)
Breeder-Owner: Judith M. Russell
1 GR2; 1 GR4
2 champion offspring

CH. KARNOVANDA'S EL BANDITO, m. - WB-461345; Ch. 1972
(Ch. Baron of Karnovanda CD ex Ch. Schneider's Angel)
Breeder: Judith M. Russell
Owners: M. and M. Miller
1 GR2; 1 GR3

CH. KARNOVANDA'S IVAN GROZNYI, m. - WA-801110; Ch. 1967
(Foxhaunt's Glacier Blu ex Ch. Karnovanda's Zenda CD)
Breeder-Owners: J. and R. W. Russell
1 GR1; 2 GR2; 3 GR3; 4 GR4
11 champion offspring

CH. KARNOVANDA'S KHAN OF KIEV, m. - WB-375788; Ch.
(Ch. Baron of Karnovanda CD ex Ch. Karnovanda's Zenzarya)
Breeder: Judith M. Russell
Owners: J. E. and M. V. Korn
1 GR2; 6 GR3; 4 GR4

CH. KARNOVANDA'S WOLFGANG, m. - WB-634168; Ch. 1971
(Ch. Karnovanda's Ivan Groznyi ex Ch. Karnovanda's Lara Baronovna)
Breeder-Owner: Judith M. Russell
1 Best in Show; 6 GR1; 5 GR2; 10 GR3; 9 GR4
6 champion offspring

CH. KOYUKUK'S MAKUKEK, m. - WC-207384; Ch. 1974
(Ch. Koyukuk's Nakomek CD ex Kaska Kimina)
Breeders: Neal and Kathi Farmer
Owners: George and Norma Marsh
2 GR3; 2 GR4

CH. LOBO REY, m. - WB-524509; Ch. 1972
(Ch. Baron Sasha ex Bro-Par's Babbs Ushka Onok)
Breeder: Gerald P. Pituch
Owner: Sylvia Gambosh
4 Bests in Show
9 GR1; 6 GR2; 3 Gr3; 8 GR4 (including Westminster)
2 Specialty BOBs

Ch. Weldon's Beau Phunsi, winner of 7 all-breed Bests in Show. Bred by Nancy T. Perkins, Beau Phunsi is by Ch. Weldon's Beau Buck ex Ch. Weldon's Enuk Balto, and was whelped 11-13-71. Owned by Anne P. Bruder, Sunset Hills Kennels, California.

Ch. Lobo Rey, winner of the 1973 National Specialty, and a 3- time Best in Show winner. Owned by Sylvia Gambosh.

171

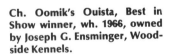

Best in Show winning Marlytuk team. L. to r., Ch. Marlytuk's Red Sun of Kiska, his mother—Ch. Koonah's Red Kiska, his sister—Marlytuk's Kiska Trey, and his daughter—Ch. Marlytuk's Kiska Too of Chaku.

Ch. Oomik's Ouista, Best in Show winner, wh. 1966, owned by Joseph G. Ensminger, Woodside Kennels.

172

CH. MARLYTUK'S KAJA, b. - WB-191335; Ch. 1973
(Ch. Monadnock's Akela ex Ch. Koonah's Red Kiska)
Breeder: Marguerite Grant
Owners: Duncan and Jorunn Wilson; then Dr. Cynthia Nist
1 GR2; 1 GR3; 1 GR4
1 champion offspring

CH. MARLYTUK'S KISKA TOO OF CHAKU, b. - WC-228556; Ch. 1974
(Ch. Marlytuk's Red Sun of Kiska ex Ch. Lamark's Chaku)
Breeder: Elsa Marchesano
Owner: Marguerite Grant
1 GR1; 1 GR2; 1 GR3; 1 GR4

CH. MARLYTUK'S RED SUN OF KISKA, m. - WA-782967; Ch. 1968
(Ch. Monadnock's Akela ex Ch. Koonah's Red Kiska)
Breeder-Owner: Marguerite Grant
1 GR2; 8 GR3;
2 Specialty BOBs
18 champion offspring

CH. MIDNIGHT SUN'S MONSTER, m. - WC-491590; Ch. 1975
(Midnight Sun III ex Midnight Sun's Jessica Marmik)
Breeder: Mary Best Morrisey
Owners: Peter and Carol Dane
1 GR3; 1 GR4

CH. MOKELUMNE'S THOR OF ZA-BA-VA, m. - WB-912801; Ch. 1973
(Mokelumne's Majestic Mouse ex Dean's Silver Mist Queen)
Breeder: Michaline Dean
Owners: E. and H. Dayton
3 GR3; 1 GR4

CH. NORSKA'S MISHKA, m. - WC-637381; Ch. 1975
(Ch. Karnovanda's Aku Aku ex Karnovanda's Adycha)
Breeder: Kenneth Wodtke
Owners: J. J. and K. M. Webb
2 GR2; 1 GR3; 1 GR4

CH. OOMIK'S OUISTA, m. - WA-790886; Ch. 1969
(Ch. Artic Flame of Long's Peak ex Oomik's Tasha)
Breeder: Marion A. Roof
Owner: Joseph G. Ensminger
1 Best in Show; 3 GR1; 2 GR2; 5 GR3
1 Specialty BOB

CH. POKEY ITASKA, m. - WB-736549; Ch. 1974
(Ch. Savdajaure's Miuk ex Chebco's Copper Prestige II)
Breeder-Owner: Paul and Carol Willhauk
3 GR4

CH. POW-UK'S NOLARINA, b. - WC-151554; Ch. 1974
(Ch. Itaska's Ah-New ex Pow-Uk's Rina of Tawny Hill)
Breeder: Judith Powers
Owner: Margaret Webber
1 GR1; 1 GR4
1 champion offspring

CH. ROB-IDA'S VOLCAN, m. - WA-954431; Ch. 1969
(Ch. Rob-Ida's Timiska Del Cerro ex Ch. Rob-Ida's Princess Natasha)
Breeder-Owners; Robert W. and Ida Mae Giddens
2 GR2; 3 GR3; 9 GR4
1 champion offspring

CH. SATEN'S SIN-SATION OF NIKINA, m. - WC-506962; Ch. 1976
(Ch. Nicholai of Sunnymead ex Moscow's Kneiona Toschia)
Breeder: Dick Moore
Owner: James Moore
2 GR2; 1 GR4

CH. SNOWMASS' COPPER KAYLEE, m.-WB-700217; Ch. 1972
(Ch. Chateauguay's Charlie ex Ch. Yankee Czar's Anya)
Breeders: Dr. Barry and Arthur Eton
Owners: Dr. Barry Eton; then Thomas F. and Christine LaDuke
1 GR2; 1 GR3; 2 GR4

CH. SNO WULF'S KOPPER CZARINA, b. - WD-40510; Ch. 1977
(Ch. Monadnock's Muktuk of Kaluna ex Ch. Abbik Khan of Snolance)
Breeder: Russ Blank
Owners: L. P. and B. A. White
2 GR3

CH. STEVENS' MIGHTY NOR-ELL KODIAK, m. - WB-272736; Ch. 1970
(Ch. Innisfree's Beau-Tuk ex Innisfree's Natasha II)
Breeders: James R. and Judith C. Walter
Owner: Joyce A. Stevens
1 GR2; 2 GR3; 2 GR4

CH. ST. NICHOLAS OF BLACKWATCH, m. - WC-36608; Ch. 1973
(Ch. Winsom's Salacious Sergei ex Sabrina of Blackwatch)
Breeders: MacKnight and Arlene Black
Owners: Robert and Katherine Bair
1 Best in Show; 6 GR1; 6 GR2; 2 GR3; 1 GR4
1 champion offspring

CH. SUNTAR'S ROUSTABOUT, m. - WC-337073; Ch. 1974
(Ch. Wind Country's Eskimo Boy ex Fireside's Konya of Kiev)
Breeder-Owners: Dave and Rachell Bell
1 GR1; 1 GR4
1 champion offspring

CH. TANDARA'S CHE KODIAK, m. - WC-925928; Ch. 1977
(The Bastion's Palachevyo ex Lubka of Tandara)
Breeders: Russell and Robin Wilson
Owner: Lynne Patterson
2 GR2

CH. TANYA OF SNOW VALLEY, b. - WB-345526; Ch. 1970
(Ch. Frosty Aire's Banner Boy CD ex Ch. Fort Salonga's Nada of Yeso Pac)
Breeder: Vincent Bouniello, Jr.
Owner: David A. Shank
1 GR1; 2 GR3

Ch. St. Nicholas of Blackwatch, Specialty winner and multiple Best in Show and Group winner. Bred by MacKnight and Arlene F. Black, and owned and shown by Robert Bair, Tighe-Mor Kennels, Maryland.

Ch. Karnovanda's Wolfgang, wh. 1970, Best in Show and multi-Group winner. Bred and owned by Karnovanda Kennels.

CH. TATARIAN'S SIERRA SMOKE CD, m. - WB-263609; Ch. 1970
(Smokey Tatarian ex Countess Tanya von Baronoff)
Breeders: Ronald and Jean Langford
Owners: Michael and Deena Burnside
1 GR3; 1 GR4
6 champion offspring

CH. TOTEM OF RABBIT VALLEY, m. - WC-56952; Ch. 1976
(Youkon of Rabbit Valley ex Tokeen of Rabbit Valley)
Breeders: Charles and Ruth M. Cannon
Owner: Betsy Randall
1 GR2; 1 GR4

CH. TRIK-TRAK'S ASSAGAI, m. - WC-180257; Ch. 1973
(Dichoda's Noho Karnovanda ex Ch. Karnovanda's Banner Bright)
Breeder-owner: Dr. Katherine J. Harmony (later Gardner).
1 GR1; 1 GR3

CH. WELDON'S BEAU PHUNSI, m. - WC-43966; Ch. 1974
(Ch. Weldon's Beau Buck ex Ch. Weldon's Enuk Balto)
Breeder: Nancy Tucker Perkins
Owners: Earl and Charlotte Reynolds; then Rev. and Mrs. J. R. Jones; then Anne Bruder
7 Bests in Show
32 GR1; 24 GR2; 12 GR3; 13 GR4

CH. WELDON'S BEAU-TUKKER, m. - WB-928752; Ch. 1973
(Ch. Weldon's Beau-Buck ex Ch. Weldon's Enuk Balto)
Breeder: Nancy Tucker Perkins
Owner: Kathleen Kanzler
1 GR1; 3 GR2; 3 GR3; 2 GR4
3 champion offspring

CH. WIND COUNTRY'S ESKIMO BOY, m. - WB-486540; Ch. 1971
(Ch. Riga of the Midnight Sun ex Wind Country's Chitina)
Breeders: O. S. and Ruth A. Junggren
Owner: Carol Deeks
1 GR3; 2 GR4
6 champion offspring

CH. WINTERSETT BO GENTRY, m. - Ch. 1969
(Ch. Frosty Aire's Banner Boy ex Ch. Klutuk's Kno-Kno of Sno-Ana)
Breeder-Owner: Joan Derek
1 GR1; 1 GR2
7 champion offspring

CH. WINTERSETT INSTANT REPLAY, m. - WB-464069; Ch. 1972
(Ch. Frosty Aire's Banner Boy ex Ch. Klutuk's Kno-Kno of Sno-Ana)
Breeder: Joan Derek
Owner: Judy Salaba
1 Best in show
9 GR1; 10 GR2; 9 GR3; 4 GR4
1 Specialty BOB
2 champion offspring

CH. WOLFDEN'S COPPER BULLET, m. - WB-359824; Ch. 1971
(Ch. Chebco's Copper Noya ex Alyeska Taku of Chinook)
Breeder-Owner: Beryl Allen
1 Gr1; 3 GR2; 1 GR3; 3 GR 4
1 Specialty BOB (at 1st independent SHCA Specialty, 1972)
5 Champion offspring

176

Ch. Chotovotka's Ms Kitty Russell, two time Best in Show winner. Kitty, winner of the 1976 National Specialty, is the first bitch in the breed to win Best in Show. Whelped 2-3-74, by Ch. Innisfree's Pegasus ex Ch. Chotovotka's Napachee, she was bred and is owned by Bob and Dorothy Page.

Ch. Wintersett Instant Replay, Best in Show and Specialty winner and sire of two champions. Owned by Judy Salaba of Doylestown, Pa.

CH. WOLFDEN'S FIONN MACCOOL, m. - WC-309230; Ch. 1976
(Ch. Wolfden's Copper Bullet ex Alakazan's Aneokle)
Breeder: Beryl Allen
Owners: Jose Junareyes and Jorge Condel
1 GR3; 1 GR4; (both in Puerto Rico)

CH. YANA'S ERIK THE RED VIKING, m. - WB-547161; Ch. 1971
(Ch. S-K-Mo's Charney Korsar ex Eu-Mor's Yana)
Breeder-Owner: Ralph O. Patt
1 GR1; 1 GR2; 2 GR3; 2 GR4

CH. YETI'S CHARDONNAY OF SELITO, b. - WC-556942; Ch. 1975
(Ch. Overlook's Nanook ex Yeti's Torun Danu)
Breeders: Robert A. and Joy G. Messinger
Owners: Joy Messinger and Lisa VanderMay
2 GR4

CH. YETI'S RED CHILI OF SNORIDGE, m. - WB-714914; Ch. 1973
(Ch. Snoridge's Rusty Nail of Yeti ex Ch. Marlytuk's Georgie Girl)
Breeders: Robert and Joy Messinger and Walter Shanks
Owner: Dr. Cynthia Nist
1 GR2; 1 GR3;
1 Specialty BOB
2 champion offspring

CH. ZODIAC'S SIR IKABOD OF INDIGO, m. - WC-985791; Ch. 1976
(Ch. Fra-Mar's Nikolai Diavol ex Monadnock's Red Bear of Zodiac)
Breeders: Leslie and Daniel Haggard
Owners: David and Sheila Qualls
2 GR3

CH. ZORKA'S FANCEE, m. - WC-659072; Ch. 1976
(Ch. Wintersett Bo Gentry ex Zorka's Filka)
Breeders: Lawrence and Helen Mazek
Owner: Judy Salaba
1 GR2; 1 GR4

In the immediate weeks following the closeout of this list, while we were checking proofs, some added impressive wins. Ch. Dudley's Varska was Best in Show at the 1977 North Shore in June (bringing his overall total in the United States and Canada to 8 Bests in Show), and followed with win of the Group at Buffalo in July. Ch. Innisfree's Sierra Cinnar added three Group placements including a First at Wallkill. Ch. Deerlake's Frosty Kazan was Best Working at Kankakee in July.

And what a splash was made by Ch. Fra Mar's Rayle Diavol! Following upon his back-to-back wins of the Working Groups at Macon and Atlanta in April, Rayle won the Group at Shenandoah Valley on June 12, was Best in Show at Paducah on June 18 and Best Working at So. Missouri the next day, and then won three Groups in three days at Jacksonville, Clearwater and Tampa Bay on July 8, 9 and 10. Whelped December 26, 1974 (by Ch. Rey Tarsu del Serro ex Fra Mar's Cherry Blossom), Rayle was bred by Marie Wamser and is owned by Carolyn Kolseth Pietrack.

Ch. Eu Mor's Tadzhik Tango, two time Specialty winner. Bred and owned by Eunice Moreno.

Excellence runs in families. Ch. Eu Mor's Zhulek of Siber (bred by Eunice Moreno; co-owned by Eunice Moreno and Lynne Witkin) winning the stud dog class at Western Reserve Kennel Club with his two sons: Ch. Eu Mor's Tadzhik Tango and Ch. Fra-Mar's Nicholai Diavol (the latter owned by Leslie and Daniel Haggard).

179

Racing enthusiasm starts early.

Ethan Russell, age 7, and Ch. Baron of Karnovanda CD racing in the 100-yard dash. Until the age of 12, Juniors race in the one-dog division. Then, until the age of 16, they use three dogs. At 16, they automatically enter the five-dog division, often winning over the adult five doggers.

6

Racing

by Lorna Coppinger

AT THE TURN of the century there were no sled dog races and there was no such thing as an AKC-registered Siberian Husky. By 1910, however, the competitive spirit of the Alaskan "dog-punchers" had spawned several long sled dog races, and the first "huskies" had been imported from Siberia. Intensified by the successes of the fast, hardy and attractive new "Siberian Huskies" in the All-Alaska Sweepstakes races, sled dog racing events became annual occurrences in Alaska.

During the next two decades, sled dog racing as an organized sport leaped from Nome to Fairbanks and Anchorage, set down in Manitoba and Quebec, and hit the lower 48 states first in Idaho and California, and then in New England and New York. It is fair to say that much of the popularity of sled dog racing is due to the appeal of the Siberian Husky, even though the Siberian was never (in the strictest sense) bred as a racing dog. Despite the frequent appearances of special breeds of dogs for racing—for example, the crossbred huskies and hounds which dominate some racing trails—the influence of the purebred Siberian Husky is never far removed. When sled dog racing took hold in Europe in the 1960s, the strikingly beautiful Siberian was the primary reason.

In 1946 Anchorage's Earl Norris challenged local dog team owners to a 17½-mile exhibition race. Alaskan dog teams in those days consisted mostly of crossbred freighting dogs, the Siberian Husky of Nome racing fame having gone to New England. There the breed was established, and did not figure importantly again in Alaska until Earl and Natalie Norris began to promote the breed with offspring of some dogs Natalie brought with her from New York and New England just after World War II. Any of the original Siberian Husky genes still left in Alaska were dominated by mixed breeding with the Alaskan freighting dogs, especially the malamute.

Best wishes Lorna
Roger & Ch. Tucker
1969 Tok, Alaska

Roger Peitano, two time winner of the SHCA racing trophy, with his outstanding lead dog, Ch. Tucker, after winning at Tok, Alaska, 1969.

Dale Raitto of Fitzwilliam, NH, competing in the three-dog Junior division.

Jake Butler of Gulkana beat Earl Norris in that first race, but the drivers and everybody else were inspired to plan for another big race the next year. Five dog teams entered the 1947 race, a race destined to become the World Championship Fur Rendezvous Sled Dog Race, one of the most important in the world. Earl Norris was again behind Butler going into the last lap of the 1947 contest, but he pushed his team and himself as hard as he could, running up hills, pedalling on the flat, and slowly, very slowly, he gained on Butler's team. Approaching the finish line, exhausted, Norris managed to pass the leader, and he took the checkered flag first, the winner by 18 hard-fought seconds.

The thrills of the races and the romantic spectacle of a twin line of sled dogs strung out over the snow, running in unison, ensured the future of the sport. The number of organized sled dog clubs in the world was doubled by 1953 with the addition of the Alaskan Sled Dog and Racing Association in Anchorage and the Alaskan Dog Mushers' Association in Fairbanks. Still extant from their pre-war racing schedules were the New England Sled Dog Club and the American Dog Mushers' Association in Idaho. It is doubtful that any of the participants in the early races could have predicted what would happen in the post-war years, but by 1975 there were well over a hundred sled dog clubs worldwide. Each club holds at least one race during the season, and some have schedules of ten or more. Each winter weekend dozens of races are held not only in Alaska, but in New England, most of the northerly states (including some less northerly ones, like Virginia and Missouri), Canada and Europe.

Growing Appeal of the Sport

Sled dogs, like cross-country skis, have ceased to belong primarily to professionals and a few enthusiastic racers. More people, with more leisure time, with an appreciation for working with dogs and with a competitive bent, are training and racing teams of from one to sixteen sled dogs. Whole families quickly get involved, and, again as with cross-country skiing, the degree of family fun and accomplishment is hard to beat. Driving a team does not take a lot of equipment or experience in order to have fun. One dog, one sled, one kid, will suffice to approximate the spirit of mushing across the snow-swept tundra. The dog does not even have to be a Siberian Husky, although the popularity of this spirited, intelligent dog is responsible for introducing many people to a little-known sport.

Once hooked on the sport—and this is usually accomplished by participating in a race or two—the beginning driver starts to look around closely at the other racing dogs, at their harnesses, and at the sleek, tough racing sleds. He pesters the more experienced drivers with his inexperienced questions. Somehow, out on the trail during the race, his team didn't look or feel like the smooth-running assemblages of the top drivers. But an occasional burst of speed or coordination will give him heart and more determination to excel. So he trains harder, he races, thinks, reads, talks, and trains some more. He is learning, and he is hooked.

It seems as though the dogs are hooked, too, for there is nothing so noisy as a sled dog waiting to be harnessed and hitched into the team. The Siberian Husky, especially, loves to run, and many an owner has been amazed at the instinct of his pet Siberian to lean into his collar and pull. Just as hounds will spend days chasing rabbit scents far from home, or retrievers will make up all kinds of excuses for splashing into the nearest water, so do sled dog breeds exhibit a natural superiority on the racing trail.

A major cohesive factor in the world of sled dog racing is the International Sled Dog Racing Association. Based on some thoughtful ideas expressed by Mrs. Elizabeth Nansen of Ottawa to J. Malcolm McDougall of Ste. Agathe des Monts, and filtered through such people as Bill Wilson of Maine, the international organization has been growing steadily since its inception in 1966. The activities of ISDRA, as it is known, are dedicated to the sport of sled dog racing on a worldwide basis by promoting public interest, encouraging cooperation between clubs, and assisting in the standardization of rules and race management procedures. Each section of the United States, Canada and Europe is represented by an area director and several at-large directors, and dozens of members serve on committees which study and make recommendations on everything from animal welfare to an Olympic race. Weight-pulls and long-distance cross-country races are attracting owners of just one or two sled dogs, and ISDRA seeks advice and data so that the achievements of dogs in Alaska will be comparable to those in New England or Europe.

ISDRA has also developed a championship point system, so that drivers in widely separated races can compare their efforts, and a grand champion be determined each year. An organized race must meet certain requirements in order to be fully sanctioned by ISDRA, and drivers competing in sanctioned races accumulate points according to their finishing position, the length of the trail, the number of competitors in the race, and the size of the purse. Only four races a year may be used toward the point championship. The gold, silver and bronze medals awarded each spring have rapidly become symbols of a prestigious achievement in sled dog racing, with two of the sport's best drivers sharing the unlimited class gold medals over the past five years. George Attla, the handicapped Alaskan, has won it three times, and Roland Lombard of Massachusetts, ''the grand old man'' of modern mushing, twice. Limited class teams are recognized by ISDRA, also, with separate medals being awarded in seven-, five- and three-dog maximum classes. The first limited class winner (seven dogs) was Judy Allen of Iowa, with her registered Natomah Kennels team.

One of the strongest appeals of sled dog racing is this ability to accommodate racers of all ages and abilities. Anyone who can put together a team, drive it successfully around a course and finish within a reasonable length of time, can be a sled dog racer. Clubs usually break down their classes into senior professional and senior amateur, and junior, most often amateur, although Canada has some professional races for youngsters. Within each of these categories there can be a further breakdown, into teams of unlimited size and those limited as to the maximum number of dogs. At present the A class is generally unlimited, the B class limited to seven dogs, and the C to five dogs. Three- and one-dog classes usually belong to the youngest mushers. "Unlimited" does not mean that a team can be as long as a driver wants, for the judge can limit a team to whatever he thinks a driver can handle, and a twenty-five-dog team would be much too long for most racing trails. Since a team is only as fast as its slowest dog, and since each additional dog is a potential problem, unlimited class teams tend to number around 12 to 16 dogs.

Another appeal of sled dog racing is the increased drama provided by the practice of running two or sometimes three heats on successive days, the total shortest time serving to designate the winner. In the bigger professional races with purses of thousands of dollars, day money is paid to the top three finishers in each day's heat. This can complicate the strategies of the drivers, for Sunday's day money is more than Saturday's, and although first place day money is an incentive, winning the first prize for the whole race is really why most of the teams are there. All in all, consistency is more valuable than one burst of speed. In 1962, for example, Jean Bryar did not win any heats in the Women's North American Championship at Fairbanks, but her elapsed time was less than anyone else's and she won the race. Bergman Kokrine had done the same thing in the 1939 running of the Livengood Sweepstakes, precursor races to the North American Championships. He ran such a consistent and fast 30 miles a day for three days that although he was beaten each day, he still won the race. Further, although 1972 Laconia World Champion Lloyd Slocum of Maine set a new record for the 18-mile trail on the third day of the 1973 championship, he was not able to make up the long two and one-half minutes he had lost to Dick Moulton on the first day. Moulton beat Slocum by 6 seconds over the 54-mile run.

Racing in Alaska

The sled dog racing season extends from the first cold mornings of early fall to the last cold mornings of late spring. In cool climates, training can extend through the summer. Preliminary training races begin in Alaska in November, with one-day heats, most likely with wheeled rigs instead of sleds. Through December and into January the snow falls, the trails get longer and the dogs stronger, and in villages all over the state the local dog driving clubs hold contests to help get the village teams in shape for the championships. Members of clubs like the Aurora Dog Mushers' Club in Wasilla, the Bethel Sled Dog

Committee, and the new Nome Kennel Club, drive, train and compete for weeks before they are ready for the official preliminaries of the big races. By the second weekend in February everyone is ready for the Women's World Championship in Anchorage, three 12-mile heats and a $1,500 purse. Also held that week is the Junior World Championship, and in Nome, the Women's, the Limited Class, and the Junior Races. The ISDRA-santioned World Championship Fur Rendezvous Race is held at the end of the third week in February, with perhaps two dozen teams from all over Alaska and one or two from Canada and the south 48 racing in three 27.3-mile heats for a $12,000 purse. Nome holds its Businessmen's, Limited and more Junior races, and Tok its Limited Race of Champions that week.

The Alaska State Championship, which used to be held at Anchorage before that city dubbed its race the World Championship in 1960, is now held between Kenai and Soldotna at the end of February, and in Tok, near the Yukon border, is the Women's Race of Champions. Many of the teams in these races are working up to one of the most interesting races of all, the North American Championship at Fairbanks towards the end of March. Before then, however, the Junior Race of Champions is held at Tok, and, in Anchorage, anywhere between two and four dozen daring dog teams will be leaving for the 1,049-mile Iditarod Trail Race to Nome. While they are beginning their trek northwest, the Junior and the Women's North American Championships will be run at Fairbanks.

Although Alaskan races are usually dominated by Alaskans, Jean Bryar of New Hampshire won the famed Women's North American six times between 1962 and 1974. In Anchorage, Doc Lombard of Massachusetts holds eight wins since 1963, and in the North American he has been victorious six times. The three heats of the North American are of 20, 20 and 30 miles, and it is that last extra ten miles on the third day that tests all the training and proficiency of dogs and drivers. At stake is some $9,000 in prize money.

Also that long weekend the seven-dog limited North American championship is held, and the Alaskan racing season is just about completed. Over in Tok the Race of Champions is held during the last weekend of March, or the first of April, and it often lures mushers heading home to Canada or the lower United States, if they can coax themselves into two more days of 20-miles-a-day by dog team.

Meanwhile, if the weather has not been too bad through the passes of the Alaska Range or along the Yukon River, most of the drivers in the Iditarod Trail Race will have made it to Nome. The first running of this longest sled dog race in 1973 took the winner, Dick Wilmarth of Red Devil, 20 days. Two years later the weather was perfect and Emmitt Peters of Ruby made it to Nome and the $15,000 first prize in fourteen and a half days.

On January 28, 1975, at 11 a.m., fifty years to the minute later than the original life-saving serum run started to Nome, Joe Redington, Sr., left Nenana for the fiftieth anniversary commemorative run. This new running honored

186

Paul Koehler driving an early Alakazan team.

William Shearer's team in Jaffrey, New Hampshire.

the men and the sled dogs who did so much to impress upon the outside world the importance of the sled dog in Alaska. The heritage of the dog team still pervades this unusual state, and the modern mushers are still aware of the dependence of Alaska on its dogs. Even more than that, the new excitement and hero-worship generated by the best dogs and drivers are sending more Alaskans back to their dog teams. They are having second thoughts about the loyalty and warmth of the snowmobile.

Racing in the "lower 48"

In the rest of the United States, in Canada and Europe, a profile of sled dog racing resembles that of Alaska. Sled dog clubs hold training and equipment seminars, early fun runs, and gradually ease into the longer competitions. There are local club races almost every winter weekend, there are local and regional championships, and each area has at least one major, big purse race, which attracts the best mushers from other regions. Each area, too, has a style and a flair originating in the customs and preferences of its people.

The New England Sled Dog Club, slowly evolving from its decades of somewhat eclectic tradition, now accommodates the needs of over 300 members. It is difficult for one club to satisfy all the drivers, from the serious professional to the littlest junior, especially with upwards of 100 dog teams showing up for a race. The New England club has changed greatly from its early years, when a close group of maybe a dozen mushers traveled around New England putting on weekend races and staying in the old Yankee inns. That the club has adapted well is evident from its healthy program. The senior professional racers are able to gain enough experience to do well in the biggest championship races, even venturing out of state to challenge top professionals from other areas. The junior program is full of enthusiastic youngsters, some barely able to see their dog over the handlebar of the sled. In between are the biggest classes, the five- and seven-dog teams, where the recreational sled dog racer has a chance to prove that his breeding, training or feeding programs are working better this week than they were last.

There are other clubs in New England, for example the Down East Sled Dog Club in Maine and the Green Mountain Mushers in Vermont. They put on perhaps one or two special races each year. A new cross-country club, the Northeast Overlanders, has held several successful long races of thirty-plus miles a day for two days, and is looking forward to a "little Iditarod," a 700-mile trek across northern Vermont and New Hampshire into the Maine wilderness and back. Also in New England is the venerable Lakes Region Sled Dog Club, which runs the annual, prestigious World Championship Sled Dog Derby in Laconia. The 18-mile trail is a hard one, with some long uphills and many turns, and the weather is often a major factor. Teams from Canada are

Dr. Roland Lombard, probably the greatest of living dog drivers.

Discipline, dedication and the desire to win—Dr. Lombard in action.

Carol Rice's outstanding matched team.

A Monadnock team working in deep snow.

always present, and in any given year the competition can include a top team from the Midwest, the far West, or even Alaska. The first racer to win the Laconia cup after World War II was Dr. Charles Belford, with a team of Siberian Huskies.

The original Siberian Huskies are still evident in New England. Descendants of Seppala's Siberians can be seen at any race, and each year a trophy is awarded by Lorna Demidoff for Monadnock Kennels to the all-Siberian team which makes the fastest time in the opening race of the season. In recent years Howard Drown of Athol, Massachusetts, with his predominantly gray team, and Carol Rice of Hubbardston, Massachusetts, with her beautifully-matched black and white purebreds, have been taking home the big silver Monadnock cup. Charlie Posey and the late Roland Bowles, both of New Hampshire, have also won this cup.

Many of the sled dog clubs emerging in the 1960s found it convenient to base their constitutions and rules on those of the New England club, which in turn reflects a lot of the original Nome Kennel Club experience. One of the earliest of these new clubs is the Canadian-American Sledders, of New York, a club distinguished not only by the great energy it gave to modern sled dog racing but also by its hosting, in 1966, of the first organizational meeting of the brand-new International Sled Dog Racing Association. New York now has several other sled dog clubs and two of their races, at Speculator and Lassellsville, have attracted the top teams due to the professional way in which the races are run.

In the mid-Atlantic states, races are sponsored mainly by the Mid-Atlantic Sled Dog Racing Association, a consortium of five smaller clubs whose members live in New York, New Jersey, Delaware, Pennsylvania, Maryland and Virginia. MASDRA members race mostly with wheeled rigs, snow being scarce, but their enthusiasm and dedication to their sport is undiminished by the lack of deep drifts. Their annual Mint Julep Classic, sponsored by Virginia's Mason-Dixon Sled Dog and Racing Association, offers modest cash prizes and trophies but is the highlight of the season. Siberians predominate in this region, and fanciers of the sprightly Samoyed have also put together fine teams.

In the Midwest, where there is a tradition of northwoods freighting with dog teams dating back to the Nineteenth Century, two major clubs, the Great Lakes Sled Dog Association and the North Star Sled Dog Club, fill the cold winters with dog race after dog race. Several important races have developed, at Ely and Bemidji, Minnesota, and Kalkaska, Michigan. Purses are consistently good, and the best teams from the rest of the United States, Canada and Alaska are drawn to these professional contests. Limited and junior classes are supported in the Midwest with great expertise. In Newberry, Michigan, an annual cross-country race of 120 miles attracts more mushers every year. This race is run Scandinavian style, that is, with the mushers on skis and all their camping equipment on the sled (with the exception of some dog food which may be cached ahead of time). Midwesterners are also enthusiastic about weight-pulling contests for.single dogs.

The Far West has a long tradition on the sled dog trails, too, and in spite of the great distances between races, spirit is high and so is team and driver quality. California, Colorado, Idaho, Oregon, Utah, Washington and Wyoming all have at least one championship race and many local races. The Glacier Country Mushers sponsor contests in Idaho, Montana and Wyoming, and also in British Columbia and Alberta. Purses are good, several races are sanctioned by ISDRA, and lots of drivers participate in lots of classes, including weight pulls and ski-joring. The beaches of Oregon provide hard, flat, year-round excellent running conditions for wheeled rig races with the "Oregon Dune Mushers." The Sierra Nevada Dog Drivers run a few good races in northern California, and the California State Championship at Truckee is a descendant of the earliest races held in California during the 1920s.

Outstanding in the sled dog world in terms of local color were the demonstrations and races held at the annual Christmas markets high in the mountain towns of Colorado. The Christmas markets, instigated by Europeans, according to European tradition, attracted Yuletide shoppers with their handcrafted gifts and Old World atmosphere. The Siberian sled dogs, decked out in brightly colored harnessed with pom poms, bells and holly attached, pulled children, adults and Santa Clauses on sleds.

The Rocky Mountain Sled Dog Club has been the guiding force behind sled dogs and racing in Colorado since 1961. Siberians and a few Samoyeds, plus the ubiquitous Alaskan Husky, prevail. The Rocky Mountain Open Championship in Dillon, two 14.4-mile heats with a $6,000 purse and sanctioned by ISDRA, attracts the top teams from the Midwest and Far West, and in 1975 Alaska's great champion George Attla came to race and finished second to Iowa's Merv Hilpipre.

Racing in Canada

The pattern of sled dog racing circuits within regions is mirrored in Canada, from Quebec, where Arthur Walden's Eastern International Dog-sled Derby was run beginning in 1923, to the Northwest Territories, where the tradition of freighting with sled dogs is still visible in the 50-mile, three-day race at Yellowknife. Local races in Quebec are dominated by the so-called "Quebec hound," a racy-looking crossbred hound-husky that Canadians have favored ever since Emile St. Godard won so many championships in the 1920s. Siberian teams are well represented, however, as Seppala won the race once and

Barry Eton's team at Lake Chocorua, New Hampshire.

Yeso Pac racing team.

placed second twice, and during the 1950s J. Malcolm McDougall and William Shearer did well with Siberian teams.

Ontario has a full circuit of sled dog races, most with purses of $1,000 or more. The big race here is the Towers International Derby, two 13-mile heats for an international array of drivers competing for a $3,000 purse. The Nugget Classic, held in conjunction with the senior race, is a favorite of the juniors. The International Dog Derby at Ottawa has been run for several decades, and was the site of the first foreign victories of some Siberian Husky teams during the 1940s. Although usually won by crossbred teams, the race hosted an upset in 1949 when Bill Shearer and his Siberians beat a Canadian crossbred hound team by 40 seconds.

Canada's four western provinces are expanding their junior programs, and three- to five-dog teams are popular. Racing their dogs is relatively novel to the prairie province drivers, for long-distance freighting has been their style. In fact, the longest of the three World Championships is held here, at The Pas, Manitoba. Three 50-mile heats are run mostly by Canadians, for the course is a bit long for shorter heat-trained racing teams from the south. This race is characterized also by a mass start on the Saskatchewan River, guaranteed pandemonium until the fastest teams can edge ahead before the river narrows. Siberian Huskies from New England took the top three places at The Pas in 1958, as Roland Lombard's team and two teams belonging to Keith and Jean Bryar stopped there on their way to Alaska.

Also in Manitoba, but attracting drivers from the lower 48, the Canadian National Sled Dog Classic in Winnipeg is sanctioned by ISDRA. A $5,000 purse and a well-groomed, fast 17-mile trail make this race growing in popularity. In British Columbia a racing circuit is developing where the clubs try to allot prize money to all finishers if they can. Travel expenses here, as everywhere else, are great, and a piece of the purse at least helps to defray the cost to the mushers. In Vernon, B.C., another practical prize is added to the cash: one thousand pounds of dog food.

The big races in Canada's Far West, the annual Sourdough Rendezvous at Whitehorse, Yukon, and the Caribou Carnival at Yellowknife, NWT, probably evince the most traditional gold-rush atmosphere of any sled dog event. As with so many of the best race weekends, these contests are part of longer mid-winter celebrations in the tradition of Anchorage's Fur Rendezvous—a chance for the miners, prospectors, fur traders and trappers to shake off some cabin fever or the lonelies and whoop it up in town for a while. The Sourdough course stretches out onto the Yukon River and through the bush for 15 miles, and is run in three heats. The course at Yellowknife is 50 miles long, for three days. It crosses part of Great Slave Lake, and a windier course anywhere would be hard to find.

In the 1974 Yellowknife race Herb Brade of Vanderhoof, B.C., entered a team of registered Siberian Huskies and encountered skepticism from other drivers who reacted much as the mushers of 1909 had reacted to William Goosak's "little" huskies from Siberia. Although Brade's team had finished second in the Sourdough Rendezvous and first in the two-day, 30-mile race at Fort Smith, NWT, apparently no one remembered that the Siberian Husky has been bred expressly for consistent speed over a long distance. By the start of the third heat at Yellowknife, Brade was in a respectable fifth place, his team had run the second heat ten minutes faster than the first, and his team of "short-legged little dogs, ha ha" was still ready to go. Running with a sled wider than normal, Brade kept his team on the hard-packed snow beside the trail and led for most of the third heat. His time for the last day was 25½ minutes faster than his second day's time, and he finished in a laugh-silencing third place for the race.

Racing in Europe

The whirlwind of sled dog racing did not really hit Europe until the 1960s, when the Swiss Club for Northern Dogs eliminated crossbred dogs from shows and breeding programs. Thomas Althaus, a Swiss exchange student at the University of Colorado, took a Siberian Husky pup back to Switzerland with him and began to spread the word about racing with these handsome animals. In 1965 the first Swiss Sled Dog Camp was held, with enthusiasts learning about dogs, equipment and race courses as it was done in North America. As the sport developed, two major philosophies about sled dogs surfaced. The owners of the first Siberians imported to Europe, dogs like Winnie of Whalom, Savdajaure's Paavo and Arctica of Baltic (Althaus' pup), favored limiting the racing teams to purebred northern dogs only, in order to improve the natural talents of a particular breed. Others appreciated that any dog which can excel in harness ought to be allowed to compete. The European northern breed clubs have opened up one or two classes for all breeds or crossbreds, but classes made up of all Siberians or Samoyeds or Malamutes are the most popular. The Trail Club of Europe has no such limitations on the racing dogs, and runs open races in Switzerland, Germany and Austria.

In addition to this dichotomy, another clearly defined style of racing exists in Europe. While central Europe has happily adopted the "Nome style" of racing, advised by Alaskans such as Earl Norris, with whom they have had close contact, and by ISDRA, northern Europe, in particular Scandinavia, has its own heritage of traveling with dogs. For generations Scandinavians have harnessed a dog or two to a small sled, carrying their camping equipment, and skied alongside, for pleasure. The *trekkhundclub* or sled dog club also organized the sled-doggers as "ambulances" to help rescue injured recreational cross-country skiers on weekends. The dogs here were generally hunting dogs, as that is what the people had, but in recent years, with the growing Siberian Husky population, these northern dogs are more in evidence. Scandinavian-style races, with perhaps up to three dogs pulling a loaded sled, the

Different strokes for different folks. On facing page, top to bottom: Jean Bryar, Keith Bryar and Jim Briggs. On this page: Charles Belford and Roland Bowles.

Bottlenecks.

"driver" skiing behind and at least one overnight camp required, remain popular in these northern countries. It has spread to central Europe, and even to the midwest United States, just as the American style of racing has captured the fancies of many Scandinavians. Strict quarantine laws in Scandinavian countries prohibit easy border crossing with dogs, so it is likely that the regional differences will remain.

The Siberian's Aptitude for Racing

Except for Europe, the professional races everywhere are dominated today by the crossbred Alaskan Husky, a result of the breeding of the best, the fastest and the hardiest sled dogs available in any particular area. The Siberian Husky influence is visible in these long-legged, rangy dogs, but so are the genes of anything from hound to sheep dog to greyhound to wolf.

The difference between drivers breeding crossbreds and those favoring purebreds is simply a matter of philosophy. Both are striving for speed, endurance and responsiveness, but one is interested in the "ultimate" racing dog and works with different breeds or types, trying to incorporate the speed from one breed and the stamina from another into a superior hybrid racing dog. Art and Dorothy Christensen of Oregon, for example, developed what they call the "Chilkoot Husky" from an Alaskan Husky male and a setter-greyhound female. The other musher is enamoured of a particular breed, fascinated by trying to arrive at an "ultimate" racing dog within the constraints of a gene pool already disposed to produce dogs which can run far and fast. The success of breeders like Milton and Eva Seeley, Charles and Kit MacInnes, Art and Judy Allen, Bill Shearer, Doug Bard, Jim Keller, J. Malcolm McDougall, Roland Bowles, Tony Landry, Lorna Demidoff and Don McFaul, and the early racing teams of Roland and Louise Lombard, Earl and Natalie Norris, Alex and Charlie Belford, and Keith and Jean Bryar, attest to the fact that the Siberian Husky has and does hold its own in the sport of sled dog racing.

Not only do Siberians excel on the racing trails, but most Siberian Husky racers also show their dogs. Many a team has sported a show champion, and in Alaska Champion Bonzo of Anadyr, CD, led the Norris Siberians in major Alaskan races, and Champion Tyndrum's Oslo, CDX, was a familiar sight at the head of the MacInnes team during the 1950s. The Norris Siberians were based on Chinook Kennels stock, and the MacInnes dogs, on Monadnock ancestors.

The modern sport of sled dog racing may be only 68 years old, but it is one of the most exciting, enthralling, engrossing sports around. The role of the Siberian in its development is major, and there is no question that this multi-talented breed will continue to exert a significant influence on sled dog racing.

WHAT IT'S LIKE TO DRIVE
A TEAM OF RACING SIBERIANS
AT 19.5 MILES PER HOUR

History was made and an exciting racing story resulted when in 1975, over an almost dangerously fast trail at Priest Lake, Idaho, Lee Muller and his team of registered Siberians ran an 11.7-mile heat at the breath-taking speed of 19.5 miles an hour. Exact tenths of miles or tenths of seconds notwithstanding, no one can seriously suggest that Lee Muller's account of what it is like to ride a sled behind a team of streaking Siberians is anything but thrilling. While crossbred racing dogs tend to have names like Yapper, Bozo, Streak, Flash or Nellie, Muller's dogs had purebred names: Natomah's Nemat (called Mat), Kimtah's Kiowa of Snoshu (Ki), Natomah's Soo Ne Yaw (Spook), Teesa of Smo-Ki-Luk, Shasta of Anadyr, Lobo of Igluk, and Tunyuk of Smo-Ki-Luk. *Northern Dog News*, a monthly publication which features articles on all aspects of northern dogs, published Lee Muller's account of his record-setting race, and it is included here with their permission:

"My usual training methods produce a kind of Fast Freight Dog Team when applied to Siberian Huskies. Good enough speed, the inherited endurance and the blind, stubborn, cussed sense of pace have always shown up with the Siberians we've trained. Maybe they trained me to accept these qualities (or a lack of same).

"In any case, we accepted these attributes and worked with them, along with a fairly rigid control to build a steady, controllable team. This may lack the excitement of spirited sprints and uncontrolled surprises, but it seemed safe and, in most cases, satisfying.

"All the above is true up until Priest Lake (1975) and the point of all this. I was asked if I'd do a first person impression of running a dog team averaging 19.5 miles per hour.

"Driving to Priest Lake is a long boring trip and I'm not sure why we always go. The people in Idaho are great and really behind Mick Booth. Mick puts out one of the best trails with terrain to interest every driver. The timing is perfect. I just never do well at Priest Lake. Lloyd Slocum believes that the dogs sense your feelings. I believe it, because every year, my dogs get as uptight as I do at Priest.

"Well, here we are at the trail site Friday evening. It sure looks fast. Mushers are telling us that Mick finally got an okay from Ma Nature and arranged

200

for deep snow, followed by a couple of days of rain and finished off with below freezing temperatures. Good ol' Mick! Hope he didn't overdo it.

"Been running eight dogs in Open all season but one went out at the finish of Diamond Lake. Don't think he's in shape to try this 20 miles so I guess I'll drop to seven-dog Super B. Besides, I've never taken my dogs 20 miles and besides I, etc., etc.

"Out at the course early Saturday, and see many mushers I hadn't seen since last season. One good thing about running Super B. Sure not uptight. Dogs all made the trip in excellent spirits and are eager to be hooked up to run. We are second out and dogs are a little less controllable. That's good to see for a change. Maxine starts the count down and I tell Kiowa and Mat to get ready. The whole team gets up and starts leaning into the harnesses. I yell, "All right" and the dogs almost leave me in the chute. Maybe I can get 4 or 5 miles out of them at this speed and then let them settle into their normal pace. You can see Mick has put some serpentine turns across the airport to break up that mile long straight away. Almost lose the sled. The trail is a lot slicker than I first thought. Better pay a little more attention to working the sled. Into the woods and the trail seems more controllable. A short pitch up a hill and the dogs slow down some so I'll hop off and run up. Damn! Drag myself back onto the runners. Faster than I thought. Catch and pass a team. Looks like he's having more trouble than I am. Dogs should be starting to ease down into their normal lope soon. At least before the halfway point. Still haven't had time to enjoy the scenery or really sit back and enjoy the team working so well.

"Steep up and down hills coming up and a couple of very sharp curves. Sure wishing I'd put in my short tug line for the two wheelers. They're beginning to get pulled around very badly. The dogs start up the first long grade of the course. This should slow them down some. Nope, more curves and downhills. Seems like most of this trail is downhill! Round a slight turn and here's the toboggan run. Incoherent and fragmented thoughts are all that's left. Like, if I had one wish in the world right now, I'd ask for a magic genie to put the brakes on. Squat down and throw both feet under the sled. Doesn't help. I've glissaded off glaciers with more control than this. Rack the sled over hard as possible and look at the runners almost hitting the berm. Sure could go over the high side on this one. Glance at Tunyuk and Lobo, my two wheelers. They're both leaning at a 35 degree angle, throwing snow as they pull to the inside. This was probably the most beautiful sight of the week to me. I can't figure out if these two wheelers are super smart or just pull the inside curve because it's shorter.

"Soon we're in a long straight stretch and I can see another team ahead. Just squat down and admire the Idaho scenery for awhile and let the dogs do their own thing. Crash! A snow-covered log across the trail almost knocks me off the runners. I think I'll wait on the Idaho scenery until I can get a guided tour on a bus!

"Come up on the team and I can see it's Mick. His hands are clenched on the sled as tight as mine. (His comment after the race—'I'd rather run out of gas in my airplane as ride that fast behind a dog team again.') Mick shouts a few pleasantries at me as the team goes by. Up ahead, the spotters are pointing out a left hand turn. Can't really see how sharp it is because of the berm height. The command "haw" is closely followed by a three word shout not usually found in racing manuals. The leaders are past my left shoulder before I'm onto the turn. Rack the sled hard and yell at those big fuzzy-butt wheelers again. Sure don't want to repeat that turn again.

"Trail is easier now but the dogs are still running very fast. Short down hill and a swing dog decided it is time to take a dump. Down Shasta goes and she's drug for 50 or 60 feet. Can't react fast enough, but she gets back on her feet and her tug is tight. Great.

"Soon we're back on the main trail. Look at my watch and we've been going for close to 30 minutes.

"This section of trail is very short and sharp curves and hills. Round a blind corner and start up a steep hill. Suddenly the hair on the back of my neck raises and the mind-chilling cry of 'Hika-Deeka-Dakka' is roaring through the timber. Down the hill comes Art Christensen at 85 mph in Mexican overdrive. His Chilkoots have their ears planed like airfoils to hold them down to the trail for traction. The shock wave of passing is similar to a Mo-ped and semi-truck passing on a narrow highway. Thanks to the spotters, Art was informed of the possibility of meeting a team in this section. All of a sudden I can see spotters ahead. I didn't think any more spotters were along the trail until the airport strip. But this is the airport and only a mile or so to go. The dogs know it too and really work. The half-mile marker flicks by and suddenly we're home. The dogs happy and dodging the marking crew, and then it's a short lope to the truck. The dogs are barking and jumping around the truck, but it takes me 15 minutes to get the hair off my face from kissing those silly Siberians."

The official timer of the race, Maxine Ramey, reported Lee Muller's time at 36 minutes flat for the 11.7-mile course, an average of 19.5 miles an hour. On Sunday a snowfall the night before had slowed the course down considerably, but the Siberians apparently weren't aware of it. Their total elapsed time for the whole 23.4 miles was 1 hour, 15 minutes, 50 seconds, an average of 18.51 miles and a limited class win in the U.S. Pacific Coast Championship for Lee Muller and his Siberian Huskies.

7

The Siberian in Obedience

OBEDIENCE COMPETITION as we know it today did not exist in America prior to 1934. There did exist a few trials geared to certain working breeds, but the emphasis was on aggressiveness rather than companionship. All this changed in 1934 when Mrs. Whitehouse Walker, a Poodle breeder from Westchester County, New York, grew tired of hearing that bench show dogs were beautiful but essentially stupid and traveled to England to study their Obedience programs which, she had heard, were oriented toward companionship rather than aggression. Upon her return, she set up an Obedience class in Bedford Village, New York, with the idea of proving that not only could any breed be trained in the rudiments of companionship, but that the training could be done by the owner, himself, and did not require the special attention of a professional dog trainer. After two years of hard work the American Kennel Club accepted her program, and Obedience trials received official sanction.

This was in 1936, two years before the organization of the Siberian Husky Club of America and five years before a Siberian named King walked into the ring and proved that even a strong-willed clown of a sled dog from Siberia could earn a Companion Dog degree. It was another five years, however, before his example was emulated. In fact, 1946 saw two Siberians achieve their C.D.'s. One was a dog named Ivan Alyeska Kolymski who, like King before him, went no further in his training than the Companion Dog degree. The other was Chornyi of Kabkol who, in the Siberian world, was to become to the Obedience ring what Togo had been to the trail or what Pando was to become to the conformation ring.

Whelped in 1945, Chornyi came to live with Richard and Virginia Garrett of Washington, D.C. in April of 1946. Trained and handled exclusively by Mr. Garrett, Chornyi earned his Companion Dog (C.D.) title in December of that year, his Companion Dog Excellent (C.D.X.) degree in September of 1947, his bench show championship in December of 1947, his Utility Dog

(U.D.) title in April, 1948, and his Tracking degree in April of 1949, making him the first Siberian to go beyond the C.D. and one of the few Siberians to this day to have earned the coveted U.D.T. title. Chornyi lived until 1959, during which time his training was put to use by entertaining children in hospitals and schools and by aiding police on several occasions that required his remarkable tracking ability.

No doubt largely because of the example of Chornyi and the Garretts, other Siberian owners began working their dogs in Obedience. But enthusiasm did not catch on overnight. By 1950 there were only about ten Siberians with Companion Dog degrees, and through the 1950s only another 16 entered the ranks. But in 1955 a Siberian owned by Beth Murphy and bred by Monadnock Kennels named Alaskan Twilight of Long's Peak did earn a perfect score of 200 points in a trial, and in 1960 Dr. Brillhart's Ice Chips of Marex earned the coveted "Dog World" award for outstanding performances in Obedience with scores of 197, 197½ and 197, so that gradually the Siberian came to be considered a legitimate contender in the field.

Advanced titles, however, were still rare in the breed and by 1960 only two dogs other than Chornyi had earned C.D.X. degrees, and none had progressed further. In 1960, however, the Garretts again entered the scene, this time with a champion bitch they had acquired from Louise Foley and James Whitfield to replace Chornyi after his death. Her name was Ch. Chuchi of Tinker Mountain, and she proceeded to earn her C.D. in October of 1960, her C.D.X. in October 1961, and in September of 1963 became the second Siberian to attain the U.D. She then became the second Siberian to attain a U.D.T. degree. This was in October 1965.

Although the Garretts never owned another Siberian, their contribution to the advancement of the breed in Obedience is probably unrivalled. Not only did their example serve as an inspiration to would-be Obedience contenders all over the country, but as active members of the All Breed Training Club at Rock Creek, Maryland, of which Mr. Garrett was president for many years, both maintained their interest in Siberians and helped many Siberian owners get started in this highly challenging and rewarding field. And it is no doubt largely due to their efforts and example that by the end of 1972 there were some 400 Siberians with Companion Dog Titles, almost 50 holding C.D.X.'s, over a dozen with Utility Dog degrees and three with Tracking degrees. Of these three, however, only Chornyi and Chuchi held the U.D.T. title.

The Siberian's Aptitude for Obedience

Despite the Siberian's undeniable record in the field of Obedience, there has always been a certain reluctance on the part of many Siberian owners and breeders to enter the field. Some racing drivers argue that Obedience training

Ch. Chornyi of Kabkol, UDT.

Chornyi in action.

Ch. Chuchi of Tinker Mountain, UDT.

suppresses some of the initiative and drive in their leaders. There have, however, been a number of excellent leaders who were also Obedience title-holders. It is probably true that among the fastest teams in the world, there are few Obedience title-holders, but then this elite group of dogs is so small that generalization is rendered ridiculous. It is also argued by some breeders that Obedience training may sufficiently suppress a dog's animation and hinder him in the conformation ring. This argument, however, is almost certainly unfounded, providing the training in both areas has been adequate and that the experience has been a happy one. In fact, Obedience training has often been employed to bring out the best in a young dog that, for one reason or other, has not had proper socialization in puppyhood, thus making him a better contender in the conformation ring.

With the possible exception, then, of the person interested in developing a very, very top flight racing team, in which case there is little time left for anything else, it is the general consensus that Obedience training is a great asset to any Siberian owner. For the owner of large numbers of Siberians, it is an excellent method of socialization and may be used as further preparation for the conformation ring. For the sled dog enthusiast, it has a number of advantages, ease in harnessing and reliability on the trail when unexpected situations arise being two of the more obvious. But it is the owner of the individual pet, or the owner of several dogs who values a close relationship with his animals, who probably gains the most from Obedience. In the case of the unruly puppy who seems determined to run the household, it is a basic necessity. But even owners who have enjoyed long, comfortable, close relationships with their pet Siberians have been amazed to discover how much closer they felt to their animals after an Obedience course. For at its best, Obedience training is not merely a matter of learning a routine; it is an exercise in increasing communication, an exercise which is not over with a training class or the completion of a degree, but continues at home until the end of a dog's life as a constant process of renewing and refining the bonds of companionship between dog and master. A well-trained dog is a happy dog, a dog who has the security of knowing what is expected of him and who has the opportunity of partaking in the pleasure of pleasing his owners—an opportunity, strange as it may seem, that is not always afforded the average pet. For under even the rowdiest, most strong-willed, stubborn exteriors, there lurks the inherent desire to please.

Tapping this desire, however, is not always an easy task, especially in a breed like the Siberian — renowned for his clownishness, his independence, and according to his detractors, his stubbornness. According to Don Carlough, one of the top Obedience trainers in the breed today, however, the Siberian is not so much stubborn as he is easily bored. The challenge in training him, then, becomes not so much a matter of getting the idea across as it is a matter of making the proposition interesting enough to merit the cooperation of this somewhat supercilious canine who is apt to find much of human behavior a little silly and of very fleeting interest. Getting a Siberian to perform a

Ch. Eumor's Kiev, UD continuing the tradition.

given exercise once is no great feat; getting him to perform the same exercise two or three times without adding his own comic variations, however, is quite another matter.

Hints on Training the Siberian for Obedience

The purpose of this chapter is not to set forth a step-by-step guide to Obedience training. There are numerous books on the subject, and Obedience training classes are held by most all breed clubs across the country. These books and classes are invaluable to anyone interested because no matter how many dogs one has trained, one never learns everything there is to know about the field. The purpose of the following, then, is to set forth some guidelines that will be helpful in training your Siberian in Obedience, or even if you simply want to have a well-mannered house pet.

In the first place, one should acquire a good specimen of the breed. It is true that the Obedience ring allows dogs to compete who would be disqualified in the conformation ring, such as over-sized dogs or those that have been altered. This should never be taken as an excuse, however, for either purchasing or breeding inferior specimens. One should seek a litter that exhibits the same conformation to the standard one looks for if buying a show dog. The personality of a given puppy, however, may be of slightly greater importance in selecting a future Obedience contender than in selecting a potential bench show dog; for while the more dominant bowl-you-over puppy with proper handling can become a very flashy show dog, he is not the best bet for Obedience—especially if he is to be the first dog the family has owned. Having become accustomed to asserting his will over his littermates, he will be slower to subordinate his desires to those of his new owner and will always have a tendency to be more unruly. By the same token, one should avoid the shy, withdrawn puppy, as he will always have a tendency to find new places and situations frightening and distracting. By far the best puppy for the Obedience ring is the one who approaches a stranger in a cautious but friendly manner, who is affectionate but not overpowering. True, some people have had success in working with puppies with more extreme temperaments, but puppies exhibiting more moderate behavior are certainly the easiest to work with.

In naming a puppy, a certain amount of care should be taken in selecting both a fairly unique name and one that neither rhymes nor alliterates with any of the standard Obedience commands. The uniqueness of the name becomes important in that a dog performing in one ring is not distracted by having his name being called in another. And avoiding names like ''Neal'' which rhymes with ''heel'' or ''Star,'' which begins like ''stay,'' avoids much confusion.

Although formal Obedience training does not usually take place until a puppy is five or six months old, there are a number of things that can be taught

The proper heeling position, demonstrated by Doncar's Snow Valley Flicka, UD, with owner Don Carlough handling.

John Holad with Ch. Savdajaure's Kunuk show two of the heeling positions to avoid—at left, heeling in forging position and at right, heeling at lagging position.

earlier. First, of course, is housebreaking. This is most effectively accomplished without the intermediate step of paper training. If a puppy is confined to a small area, such as his crate, and taken outside to the same spot after sleeping and eating and before and after playing, housebreaking can be accomplished very quickly. And gradually, as long as there are no accidents, he can be allowed greater and greater freedom in the house. Paper training simply serves to complicate the issue by first teaching the puppy to use the paper and then later discouraging him from doing what he has been taught.

It is also helpful during these early weeks to teach the puppy not to jump up on people, not to bite, not to steal food and to ride calmly in the car. Jumping up is always a difficult problem with Siberians, as they are by nature, extremely exuberant. It is a habit that it is best to break early; do this by pushing your palms downward and kneeing the puppy in the chest while saying firmly, "No jumping!" and then playing with him and giving lots of praise. Do not say "Down." With the puppy who bites, even in play, one should grasp and shake the muzzle firmly while saying "No biting!" and then providing a great deal of praise. Discouraging food stealing can be effectively accomplished in a few sessions by deliberately placing food on the table and reprimanding the puppy whenever he takes it. Teaching a puppy to ride calmly in a car with you is most easily done by having a second person keep the puppy on a lead and, with praise and reprimand, encourage him to remain quiet.

By this point the puppy should also be learning to walk on a leash. This is most painlessly accomplished by fastening a buckle collar on him and allowing him to drag the lead around for a few minutes every day. Later, the other end of the lead can be picked up and, by way of gentle tugs and jerks and lots of praise, the puppy can then be taught to walk with his trainer.

It is at about this point that formal Obedience training can be initiated, for not only has the puppy become well-mannered enough to have around, but he has also learned to pay attention. In other words, the channels of communications between dog and master have been established. Before starting formal training, however, there are a few things one must always remember. First, such training requires a great deal of time and patience, and one should not undertake such a program without an honest self-assessment of one's capabilities. Second, never train when one is in a bad mood. Always give a lot of praise. And last, be creative: remember that the Siberian is more easily bored than most breeds and thus his trainer must always be adding new exercises and be on the lookout for different ways to capture the dog's interest.

Rewarding as Obedience work is, it is not without its harrowing moments. In fact, among those intrepid enough to enter a Siberian in the field, it is occasionally professed that there are few moments that are anything else. Dedication and determination are, of course, essential to the Obedience trainer; but of equal importance is that quality which, even among the most tight-lipped Obedience handlers, is always conspicuous — a sense of humor. Without this quality the Obedience enthusiast is lost, especially if his breed happens to be

Stand for Examination—dog must stand-stay while judge examines dog. Modeled by Don Carlough with Doncar's Snow Valley Flicka, UD.

Dog sitting in front during the recall. Dog has come on first call, sits straight, within reaching distance.

Stay signal. Used when leaving dog for recall or group exercises.

the Siberian Husky. The following article by Wes Meador gives a fairly vivid indication as to why this is so.

THE TERROR OF TANACROSS
by Wes Meador

In April of 1973, my wife Debbie and I entered a new and exciting phase of our careers as dog fanciers and Obedience enthusiasts — we purchased our first Siberian Husky. At the time, we were training for a local commercial school, plus being members of a training club, and so were exposed to 100 to 150 dogs a week in our capacity as instructors. We, therefore, felt that we had a pretty good notion of how to deal with any type of dog, even though we had never been actively involved in training a Siberian. As it turned out, we were sadly mistaken as Tosha developed into the most exasperating canine friend I have ever had!

The training techniques we were using at the time were really geared to Shepherds, Dobermans, etc., and as we found out, not truly effective on the dynamic Siberian Husky. I was training our only remaining Shepherd in Open work when we got Tosha, and as a result let her have free run of the place, so to speak, until she was about seven months of age. We felt, through past experience, that the best age to start a dog was between five and seven months old, with collar and leash breaking starting two weeks earlier. So we started Tosha in on this routine and everything went fine through puppy training until we hit formal training; then PFFFT!

It wasn't that she resisted the training — it was more that she thought it was a big bore. She'd look at me as if to say, ''I've been running around the backyard for the last five months just having a great time, not bothering anybody, minding my own business, and then you have to go all masculine and dominant on me. I mean, *really!* I could abide it when you put that heavy thing on my neck, and did I complain when you made me drag that dumb piece of leather around, with it always hanging between my legs and me stepping on it and tripping and that sort of junk? But this business of jerking on me, and yelling at me, and making ugly faces. . . . well, that really is a bit much, don't you think?''

Shortly after we started our daily tug-of-war (her going her way, and me going mine) she began a little psychological warfare of her own. Holes mysteriously started appearing in the backyard, at first in out-of-the-way places, then all over. Our backyard had a windbreak of young poplars which started disappearing — chewed off at the stump. You'd have thought she was a beaver the way she felled those trees. One of our daughter's rabbits turned up missing; then my wife's yews were chewed up, and at $12 a whack that was a low blow! By this time our erstwhile lovely backyard had begun to take on the appearance of a scene from Dante's Inferno, but when one of my beloved col-

Figure Eight—dog and handler heeling around two persons (posts) without sniffing or jumping on them. John Holad and Ch. Savdajaure's Kunuk CDX. Posts: Peggy Grant and Anna Mae Forsberg.

Drop on Recall. In Open, the dog is left for recall. The handler calls dog and then must drop him on judge's command. Don Carlough and Doncar's Snow Valley Flicka, UD, demonstrate.

Retrieve over solid jump. Handler throws dumbbell over jump and sends dog after it; dog must jump hurdle, pick up dumbbell and return over hurdle.

Directed retrieve—signal to go out and retrieve glove.

Directed retrieve. Dog returning to handler with glove.

Directed retrieve. Dog sitting in front with glove after retrieve.

214

lection of science fiction classics, which I had indiscreetly left on the chaise lounge, turned up in pieces. . . . well, brother, the battle was joined! The challenge had been issued! The gauntlet had been smacked in my face, not once, not twice, but over and over again!

I was just a little peeved by this time, so with my backbone stiffened, and my heart filled with firm resolve, Tosha and I began training in earnest. It didn't take her very long to realize that I was deadly serious about this (in her mind) nonsense and that I was a lot bigger and stronger than she. So we came to an understanding—she would be a good little girl and not do all those naughty things she did so well, and I wouldn't dismember her, piece by piece.

When she was nine months old, or thereabouts, we got a little copper male, thinking it probably would help for Tosha to have a playmate to keep her out of mischief. Besides, he was so beautiful, and such a good pedigree, etc. Oh, brother! She didn't like this new addition one little bit. But she was smarter this time; no direct retaliation — just very subtle, insidious little things when we weren't looking. Like "accidently" knocking over the plaster horse we picked up in Mexico City, or . . . I can't go on. And, all this time, I had been taking her to fun matches and she was doing beautifully, the little stinker! So, we decided to start showing her, because if she was in a show, she couldn't be in the backyard at the same time, right?

By the time the first show came, I thought she was really ready — she had scored 199½ in a fun match the week before and had been working very well with no backyard blitzkriegs for a week or so. I thought we were over the hump, but little did I realize.

In we went, our first show together, both of us excited and alert, tails wagging, ears up, and eyes bright. Everything went nicely until the Recall. When I called her, she just sat there — tail wagging, ears up, eyes bright, and disqualified. Well, it was her first show . . .

The next shows were a weekend double-tailer in Kansas City. At the first one she was doing very well all through the preliminary exercises; then came the Recall. I had considered the possibility that I might have been a little harsh when I had called her before, so I was all prepared to call her in a happy, cheerful, and very probably, silly tone of voice, so as to take no chances. Anyway, as I turned to await the judge's command, she sat there happy and alert again, the very picture of an obedient dog. My hopes were up. She looked so eager, I just knew she was going to come zooming when I called her! I looked at the judge and in a clear, resonant voice he said, "Call your dog". Tosha came flying in, perfect sit and everything — but the dummy had come when the *judge* had spoken, before I could call her. Disqualified!

The next show was the killer! She went through the exercises like a baby through a diaper. I was elated! I was ecstatic! I was happier than heck! If she had more than two points off in all the exercises, I was going to eat my leash. The group exercises were coming up and she had NEVER failed in them, never! The long sit went by without incident. On the long down she lay on her side and went to sleep, and I thought we had it made. Then it happened! A Miniature Poodle broke and went over to her. She started sniffing, and when the steward came over to get the Poodle, she broke and very jauntily followed him away. I was crushed! A near perfect score down the old drainola. But it could have happened to anybody, right? Yech!

After moping in my room for a week, I decided something had to be done — I didn't know what, but SOMETHING; my heart couldn't take much more (not to mention my liver, kidneys, and bladder, too.) So I took Tosha up to my study, put her on my lap, and explained to her that if a little girl doggie wanted to grow up to be a big mamma doggie, then she shouldn't do things that gave her master coronary attacks, or apoplexy, or hissy-fits — it just didn't make sense! All right, I know this isn't the way a rational man is supposed to act, but I couldn't think of anything else to do. At least, nothing she would have survived. And would you believe, she qualified her next three shows, placing fifth, fourth, and first in Novice B!

All facetiousness aside, we have found that the Siberian Husky, as opposed to the "established" Obedience breeds (Doberman, Shepherd, Sheltie, Golden Retriever, etc.) must start training as a pup. They are of hardier constitution and temperament, and are much more difficult to train after they have begun to assert their independence. The male (he's no longer little) of Debbie's started his training at three and a half months and achieved his C.D. title at *seven months and two days*, placing in Group his last time out. He is the most lovable and gentle dog I have ever had the good fortune to be associated with, and Tosha, despite all the trials and tribulations we have experienced, has become at 16 months of age, an exciting and (at times) brilliant performer. The big difference between the two is in the attitude with which they approach Obedience work. Tymber has never balked at anything we have tried to teach him, while Tosha's Obedience career has been marked by an almost terminal case of stubborness. Even recently, while learning exercises for Open work, she would approach each one with an attitude of "Well, let's see if you *really* want me to do this stuff." My response to this attitude has been known to make strong men quake and send children screaming for their mothers. Tymber, on the other hand, reacts to a disapproving voice and has never had to have been physically disciplined. I believe this difference is directly attributable to their ages when starting training.

Siberian Huskies are fantastic animals, both in conformation and Obedience, and the problems I had were my fault for using the wrong techniques and timetable. The Siberian is not the humble, devoted dog that the German Shepherd or Golden Retriever is, nor does he possess the high-strung and dependent nature of the Sheltie or Poodle. Siberians are unique unto themselves: proud, intelligent, independent, and gentle. I believe that the next decade will see the Siberian Husky established right alongside the German Shepherd, Doberman, Sheltie, etc., as a top Obedience breed, and I for one, plan to be right

216

Signal exercise. Left, hand signal to heel. Right, hand signal to stand dog.

Signal exercise. Hand signal to down dog from stand position.

Signal exercise. Hand signal to sit dog from a down position.

Scent discrimination—dog seeking out article which handler has touched. Dog must do this twice—once with leather article and once with metal article.

out there with the trembly knees and aching ulcers doing my best to see it happen.

So, if you're tired of the humdrum, uneventful, ordinary type of life, then start training your Siberian at, say about twelve months; but if you have a history of coronary trouble, or are subject to gastro-intestinal problems, then I wouldn't advise it.

Don Carlough, with Doncar's Snow Valley Flicka UD, demonstrating action of a scent hurdle relay race at the SHCA National Specialty at Keene, N. H.

Ch. Belka of Monadnock II, elegant lady and a racing leader—winner of the 1950 National Specialty. Owned by Monadnock Kennels.

Tanya of Monadnock, 1951 National Specialty winner.

8

Showing Your Siberian

ODAY the Siberian Husky is more popular than ever. Because of his intelligence, beauty, tractibility, and wonderfully gregarious nature, he is to be found in homes throughout the United States, Canada, and Europe where he serves a housepet as well as in his original capacity as sled dog, both on pleasure teams and in active competition. In recent years, he has also made great inroads in the field of Obedience, a field he was not bred for but in which he has shown a great capacity to excel. But the area which, dog for dog, probably exerts the greatest influence on the progression of the breed is the conformation ring. Thus, it is helpful for even the most casual pet owner to have some idea of the basis and procedures of a dog show.

To many people who have never seen one, or who have attended one only briefly without fully understanding the procedures, a dog show may seem nothing more than a canine beauty contest — an absurd pageantry of displaced egos, painted toenails and coiffured pom-poms, the judging of which amounts to little more than the whim of the day.

As with most negative observations, there is at least a figment of truth in this picture. Today more and more people show their dogs purely as a sport, and many are not, themselves, breeders. Consequently, winning becomes the central object, an object which, without the basic notion of a breed's continuous improvement, is essentially meaningless. Also with competition greater today than it has ever been, there is an increased emphasis on showmanship, baiting, and, in some breeds, greater emphasis placed upon the kind of grooming designed to drastically alter the dog's natural appearance. Like all institutions, dog shows have their flaws, and these superficialities are what have made dog shows, like garden clubs, the objects of facile and supercilious jibes by the uninformed.

On the other hand, at its basic level, the dog show is the very foundation of purebred dogs. It is there that the best specimens of a breed are brought together for comparison, where breeders meet and exchange information and

Ch. Otchki of Monadnock, CD, a racing leader and the National Specialty winner in 1949, '52, '53 and '54. Owned by Monadnock Kennels.

Ch. Monadnock's Nina, first Siberian bitch to place in the Group, National Specialty winner of 1955, and dam of Ch. Monadnock's Pando.

make future breeding arrangements, where all that makes a breed a breed — namely type, temperament and soundness — are kept alive, and where virtually the future of a breed is decided. So as long as breed clubs strive to maintain meaningful standards for their breeds, dog shows are good for dogs.

It might, of course, be questioned what, in this day and age, is the value of maintaining purebred dogs in the first place. By way of justification, it can only be pointed out that, not only is the purebred dog one of man's most ingenious inventions, a link with the life and ingenuity of our historical past, he is, in a more radical sense, a link with that which is primal in all of us — the beauty, dignity, grace and simply proffered affection that, in an increasingly cold and mechanical age, acts as a touchstone to what, at heart, we still are. He is an integral part of our heritage and, as such, deserves preservation and protection.

What Makes A Winner?

The basis upon which dogs are judged in the show ring is what is known as *the standard*. The standard of any breed is set forward by members of its breed club and represents an idealization of what that breed should look like — in terms of physical appearance and structure — and act like — in terms of temperament. In evolving this standard, two factors are always kept in mind: 1) the original function of the dog, and 2) given the original function and natural tendency of the breed in terms of appearance, what is most pleasing to the eye.

Broadly speaking, *type* is what makes a breed a breed: those aspects of appearance such as coat, skull structure, ear type and set, and general physical proportions that differentiate one breed from another. *Soundness* refers to the basic skeletal and muscular structure of the dog and varies little from breed to breed. Cowhocks, for instance, are frowned upon in all breeds. *Temperament* is the third consideration in an assessment of a dog and, since it is really a subdivision of *type*, varies from breed to breed according to the function for which the dog was bred.

These are the aspects of a breed, then, that a judge must weigh and consider before choosing a winner. This is why to a novice the show ring can be such a confusing place. He may see a dog that he feels is obviously the most beautiful — meaning it fits his general idea of what the breed should look like — not even receive a ribbon. What he may not have noticed is that something in the dog's structure is unsound, having a bad front or rear, or he may be unsound in a place only the judge would notice, having a bad bite or insufficient muscle mass.

The next mistake made by the person at ringside is not usually made by the novice but by the person who has learned something about structure. He considers only the soundness of the dogs and is surprised or feels slightly superior

223

Ch. Monadnock's Pando and Ch. Monadnock's Belka taking Best of Breed and Best of Opposite Sex at the 1958 National Specialty. Judge, Mrs. Milton Seeley.

Ch. Monadnock's Pando taking a Group first. Pando was the winner of 1958, 1959 and 1960 National Specialties.

Ninaki of Monadnock, at right, owned by Mr. and Mrs. R.J. Williams, winning Best of Breed at 1960 Specialty under Mrs. Seeley. Ch. Monadnock's King, at left, was Best of Opposite Sex. King won 1962 Specialty at International.

Yeso Pac Kennels' Ch. Monadnock's Prince Igor, winner of the 1961 National Specialty.

if the judge picks a dog with some fairly obvious structural fault. What he has forgotten is that the judge must find what he feels is the best blend of type and soundness in the ring that day, and the dog that the viewer felt was the most faultless may have borne only a vague resemblance to the breed standard as to type. Every dog, no matter how good, has some fault. The key to judging, however, is not the ability to ferret out a fault, but the ability to recognize aspects of a dog that are truly superior and weigh those against the superior aspects of his competitors. Negative judging, that is judging that is based solely upon eliminating a dog from consideration when a weakness in structure is discovered, will normally result in a sound but generally mediocre dog receiving the ribbon. It should be remembered that occasionally even a mongrel is sound, and that if you lose type, you've essentially lost a breed.

The process of viewing the judging from ringside is made more complicated by the fact each judge varies somewhat in the balance he seeks between type and soundness, that different dogs show differently on different days, and that evidences of temperament problems, such as growling or shying away when being examined, may go unnoticed by everyone except the judge. So it is best to be wary of experts at ringside, for although one can learn a great deal from people's comments, no one else sees what the judge sees. And even disregarding that fact, it is a rare spectator who actually knows more than the judge. Opinions come cheaply in the dog world, but the true acquisition of knowledge, as in any field, is a long and arduous process.

Training for the Show Ring

Training a dog for the conformation ring, while not as difficult as training one for the Obedience ring, is not as easy as it might seem and requires a reasonable amount of time, energy and patience. Furthermore, since dog and handler operate as a team in the ring, a certain amount of time is necessarily spent in training oneself to adapt to the various peculiarities of a given animal, as each dog will react somewhat differently to different stimuli.

Basically training can be broken down into two phases: 1) familiarization or initiation, and 2) actual ring training. The first phase can start as early as six or eight weeks, although it is not absolutely essential that it begin this early. However, much of what makes a dog stand out in the ring is that extra spark of interest, the fact that he is enjoying what he is doing, and this quality is usually more easily instilled in puppyhood.

During the initiation period there are basically three things the puppy should be familiarized with: his crate, his collar and lead, and people. Often upon attending their first dog show, people are alarmed at the sight of hundreds of caged animals. Animals, however, do not seem to suffer the same kind or degree of claustrophobia as humans. In fact, left to their own devices, dogs, like other animals in the wild, will intentionally seek out small, secure

Ch. Foxhaunt's Tovarisch CD, winner of the 1962 National Specialty. Owned by Betsy Korbonski.

Ch. Savdajaure's Cognac, winner of 1963 and 1964 National Specialties. Also winner of 3 Group firsts. Owned by the Forsbergs.

Ch. Monadnock's Rurik of Nanook, a 1964 National Specialty winner. Sire of 12 champions. Owned by Frank and Phyllis Brayton.

places in which to rest or sleep. For this reason, if a puppy is encouraged to sleep in his crate if he is a house dog, or to spend a few hours each week in it if he is a kennel dog, the crate becomes home and the place he feels safest, especially among the clamor and bustle of a dog show.

Leash breaking is also a vital part of this early training for, although a dog can be readily trained to grudgingly move on a lead, he will not move with the freedom and assurance necessary for proper ring deportment unless he is thoroughly familiar with, and unintimidated by, the lead. For this reason a puppy should be encouraged to walk on the lead a few minutes a day at the earliest possible age. Tidbits are a helpful means of encouragement during these practice sessions which should be kept short and fun. It is also best to practice somewhere other than the puppy's backyard, since he will be likely to find the sessions more appealing in somewhat less familiar surroundings, it being only logical that if sessions are held in an environment where he normally experiences complete freedom, he will only find the lead an unpleasant infringement on that freedom.

Having the practice sessions outside of the puppy's normal domain also furthers his socialization, the third aspect of early training. From the time a puppy is three weeks of age, he should be exposed to as much human contact as possible, getting used to being touched and played with. And from the time that he can walk on a lead, he should be exposed to as many people and environments as possible. Shopping centers are excellent for familiarizing a puppy with the noise and hubbub of human behavior, especially if he has any tendency toward shyness.

After the puppy has been familiarized with his crate, his lead, and people, it is time for more directed training. He should become accustomed to moving in the various patterns required in the show ring: the up and back, the ''L,'' the triangle, and, although it is used less frequently, the ''T.'' He should also get used to circling the ring counter-clockwise. Although for the most part a dog is gaited on the left of the handler, ring decorum requires that the dog always be kept between the handler and the judge. Thus, it will be noted that in order to perform the ''L'' or the ''T'' patterns, it is necessary to change hands. Consequently it is useful to train a puppy to gait on either side of his handler, the lead always being held in the hand nearest the dog. ''Honoring the judge'' a formality that involves making a small circle in front of the judge before moving if the judge is standing on the handler's right, should also be practiced. This formality is also in the interest of giving the judge an unobstructed view of the dog from the time he begins a pattern until he finishes it. It should not, however, be overdone. One should always bear in mind that the judge is working to a strict time-table and cannot afford to have his time wasted by handlers who insist on moving their dogs in large, leisurely circles while honoring the judge. And, of course, there is no reason to go through the formality when it is possible to move the dog in the prescribed pattern without obscuring the judge's view of him.

228

Ch. Kronprinz of Kazan, a great team dog, winner of the 1965 National Specialty, Best of Breed at Westminster 1966 and a Group winner. Owned by the Koehlers.

Ch. Czar Nicholas, winner of the 1966 National Specialty. Owned by Dichoda Kennels.

229

Ch. Dichoda's Yukon Red, National Specialty winner—1968 and 1969. Owned by Dichoda Kennels.

Foxhaunt's Suggen, National Specialty winner—1969. Owned by Mr. and Mrs. R.J. Williams.

230

Ch. Marlytuk's Red Sun of Kiska, National Specialty winner
1970 and 1971. Owned by Marguerite F. Grant.

Am. Bermudian and Can. Ch. Innisfree's King Karl, National
Specialty winner 1970. Owned by John B. and Lila M. Weir.

Ch. Wolfden's Copper Bullet, National Specialty winner 1973. Bred by Beryl Allen, and now co-owned by Mrs. Allen and Dr. Gabriel Mayer.

Ch. Yeti's Red Chili of Snoridge, National Specialty winner of 1975. Owned by Drs. R.T. and C.R. Nist.

It is also at this point that the puppy should be learning to stand for examination, to be felt over by someone other than his handler from head to tail. This examination also includes checking the puppy's bite and, if it is a male, feeling for testicles. He should also be getting used to being set up, that is having his legs placed in a show pose. Since the Siberian is considered one of the "natural" breeds, it is preferrable that a dog be trained to walk into a show pose, using bait if necessary, and not be set up by the handler. However, no matter how sound and how well-trained the dog is, there will be times when one foot or another is out of position, and it will be necessary to reset it in a hurry. So since Siberians are more rambunctious than many breeds, it is helpful to have a puppy get used to having his legs placed as early as possible. In doing this, it is better to place a front leg by taking it just below the elbow and the back leg at the stifle joint or just below, as this affords greater control than if the leg is held further down. However one should guard against over handling for, as the judge William Kendrick once remarked, no handler can show a dog as well as the dog can show himself. The handler's job is merely to make sure that the dog shows himself to best advantage, and a handler who is constantly fussing with his dog only distracts the judge and draws attention to himself and away from the dog.

This second stage of training is made much easier by enrolling in one of the handling classes that are held periodically by local all-breed clubs. This not only is a useful place to get constructive criticism, it also exposes a puppy to many other dogs. Furthermore, it is one place to learn about upcoming fun matches and matches sanctioned by the American Kennel Club. These matches are run very much like a regular dog show, except that there are no championship points awarded and the entry fees are minimal. And they are by far the best places to give a puppy ring experience.

Structure of the Dog Show

During the time that one is training a puppy, it is useful to attend at least one all-breed point show to get some idea of ring procedure and to watch some of the better handlers. The structure of the classes is really quite simple and can be followed in the catalogue that is sold on the grounds. Briefly this is the procedure:

First, second, third and fourth prize ribbons are awarded in each of the following classes, Puppy Dogs, Novice Dogs, Bred-by-Exhibitor Dogs, American Bred Dogs, and Open Dogs. The winners of all the classes then compete for the "Winners Dog" ribbon and the "Reserve Winners Dog" ribbon. The Winners Dog is the only one eligible to receive championship points, the number of which varies according to the number of entries.

The same procedure is then followed for bitches until a "Winners Bitch" and "Reserve Winners Bitch" are determined.

At this point the "Winners Dog" and "Winners Bitch" re-enter the ring with any "Specials," that is, dogs who have already completed their championships, to compete for the "Best-of-Breed" award. After this award is given the judge then awards the "Best of Opposite Sex" ribbon to the specimen he feels is the best from among those of the opposite sex from his "Best-of-Breed" winner. He then awards his "Best-of Winners" ribbon to either the "Winners Dog" or "Winners Bitch," depending on which he feels is better.

The winner of the "Best-of-Breed" award is then eligible to go on to compete in the Working Group, the winner of which then goes on to compete for "Best-in-Show."

Ch. McCracken's Aladin, only the third white to finish in the history of the breed - the first finishing soon after the breed was recognized, and the second in 1963. Aladin is pictured finishing at Chicago International April 1977 under Mrs. Demidoff, with Dorothy McNulty handling. Bred by Mr. and Mrs. T. McCracken (Canada), he is owned by Dr. and Mrs. Alan H. Snell of Kansas. Mrs. Demidoff noted that he is one of the few whites she has ever seen with black pigmentation - most whites have liver pigmentation.

9

Official AKC Standard of the Siberian Husky —with Authors' Commentary

WE HAVE ALREADY NOTED that *the standard* is the basis upon which dogs are judged in the conformation ring. In actual fact, of course, dogs in the breed ring are judged comparatively, one against the other, and the standard merely sets the guidelines for this comparison. Assumably in a good class, there will be a number of dogs that conform to the basic tenets set by the standard. The judge then must resort to a comparison of the more indefinable areas of canine aesthetics such as carriage and bearing, perhaps looking for what the noted judge William Kendrick is fond of calling "the look of eagles." Or he may resort to the more technical areas of structure and pick, among a number of well moving, well balanced dogs, what he feels is the very best moving specimen.

This kind of latitude in choosing a winner is what makes a dog show, and it is precisely this latitude that is written into every breed standard. They are written, after all, in words, which are necessarily open to interpretation, and they are written only to the level of technical knowledge available to its composers at a given time. Most breed clubs strive to keep their standards as clear and up to date as possible. But this is a more difficult task than it might at first seem. For instance, most of the early standards were written by horsemen who, when using a phrase like "a cleverly built hunter," had a precise idea of what this connoted. But to generations who came after them who were not horsemen, a phrase like this might seem vague and not very useful. Another problem is simply that the connotations of certain phrases may be different in

235

Visualization of the SIBERIAN HUSKY standard.

SKULL medium size, in proportion to body; slightly rounded on top; tapering gradually from widest point to eyes

EYES almond-shaped; moderately spaced; set trifle oblique; expression keen, friendly, interested, mischievous. Color brown or blue—one of each or parti-color acceptable

STOP well defined

NOSE black in gray, tan or black dogs; liver in copper dogs; may be flesh-colored in white dogs; pink-streaked acceptable

MUZZLE medium long; from nose to stop about equal from stop to occiput; tapering gradually to nose; lips well-pigmented, close-fitting; scissors bite

CHEST deep, strong, not too broad

FORELEGS straight, well-muscled; substantial bone, but not heavy; strong pasterns

FEET oval, medium size, compact; well furred between toes and pads (trimming for neatness permitted); pads tough, thickly cushioned

SIZE: (At withers): Dogs, 21" to 23½"; Bitches, 20" to 22". Weight in proportion to height: Dogs, 45 to 60 lbs.; Bitches, 35 to 50 lbs.

APPEARANCE: Medium size, moderately compact well-furred dog of power and grace; body proportions reflect speed and endurance; firm, well-developed, never coarse.

EARS medium size, triangular, close-fitting, set high on head; thick, well-furred; erect, slightly arched, with slightly rounded tips straight up.

NECK medium length; arched; carried erect when standing, extended when moving

SHOULDERS powerful, well laid back, approximate 45° angle

BACK: Length medium; strong; topline level; loins taut, lean; croup slopes away from spine at angle

RIBS well-sprung, deep

DISQUALIFICATIONS: Dogs over 23½"; Bitches over 22".

TAIL, well-furred brush, set on just below level of topline; when up, does not curl to either side of body, or snap flat against back; in repose, trailing tail is normal

HINDQUARTERS well-muscled, powerful. Stifles well-bent. Hind legs (rear view) parallel, moderately spaced. Dewclaws to be removed.

COLORS: All colors allowed

DOUBLE COAT: Undercoat soft, dense, sufficiently long to support outercoat. Outercoat straight, smooth-lying, medium in length, well-furred appearance but not obscuring clean-cut outline different parts of the world. Thus, many breed standards in England ask for a "straight front," meaning, not a straight shoulder when viewed from the side as we would tend to interpret it, but a parallel positioning of the front legs when viewed from the front.

Added to these problems is the fact that initially a standard evolves merely as a description of the few available specimens of that breed, without too much consideration for what is perhaps ideal. For instance, the Siberian standard once asked for rather large "not too compact" feet and a "rather short" neck. Later it was decided that the somewhat splayed foot found in many of the early specimens was perhaps more coincidental than functional and that the more compact foot required by most breeds was more desirable. Also, when it was found how important the neck was for the proper maintenance of balance when moving, the phrase "rather short" was changed to "medium in length."

There are then two kinds of vagueness found in any given breed standard. The first is simply the result of the ambiguity of language or the limits of knowledge and is, for the most part, unintentional. The second is the intentional leeway left for interpretation. Because the Siberian came to this country very recently as a still functioning working dog, and because "naturalness" has always been an important quality to his fanciers, the emphasis in the standard has always been on function. Consequently, the Siberian Husky standard is what might be called a fairly loose standard, its emphasis being placed upon soundness and the basic requisite of type, without undue emphasis on coat color, markings, eye color, or even the precise structure of the skull. However, there is a standard, and although judging is necessarily comparative, and although any breed is subject to certain changes in fashion, it would be wrong to assume too much leeway in interpretation. The following analysis of the standard is intended, then, to clarify some of the ambiguity and to define some of the limits of interpretation.

Current AKC Standard for the Siberian Husky
(Approved November 9, 1971)

General Appearance—The Siberian Husky is a medium-sized working dog, quick and light on his feet and free and graceful in action. His moderately compact and well-furred body, erect ears and brush tail suggest his Northern heritage. His characteristic gait is smooth and seemingly effortless. He performs his original function in harness most capably, carrying a light load at moderate speed over great distances. His body proportions and form reflect this basic balance of power, speed and endurance. The males of the Siberian Husky breed are masculine but never coarse; the bitches are feminine but without weakness of structure. In proper condition, with muscle firm and well-developed, the Siberian Husky does not carry excess weight.

Comment: Underlying this simple description is a prescription for moderation that would please even the staunchest Aristotelian. In the space of several sentences we find that the Siberian is "medium-sized," "moderately compact," reflects a "balance of power, speed and endurance," that males are "masculine but never coarse" and bitches "feminine without weakness," and that neither should carry excess weight. We find, also, the reason for this prescription: that the original function of the Siberian was to carry a "light load at moderate speed over great distances." This is a tremendously important phrase in coming to an understanding of the conformation of the Siberian for, although he has gained much recognition for his accomplishments in the area of Arctic and Antarctic exploration as well as in the field of sled dog racing, he was intended neither as a heavy draft animal nor a sprinter. He was bred to pull light loads often as much as one hundred miles in a single day, a job that required a dog that was "quick and light on his feet and free and graceful in action." Anything clumsy or heavy in movement would be unable to maintain the pace required of these dogs; anything too refined would lack the necessary pulling power and stamina.

Head:

Skull—Of medium size and in proportion to the body; slightly rounded on top and tapering gradually from the widest point to the eyes. *Faults*—Head clumsy or heavy; head too finely chiseled.

Muzzle—Of medium length; that is, the distance from the tip of the nose to the stop is equal to the distance from the stop to the occiput. The stop is well-defined and the bridge of the nose is straight from the stop to the tip. The muzzle is of medium width, tapering gradually to the nose, with the tip neither pointed nor square. The lips are well-pigmented and close fitting; teeth closing in a scissors bite. *Faults*—Muzzle either too snipy or too coarse; muzzle too short or too long; insufficient stop; any bite other than scissors.

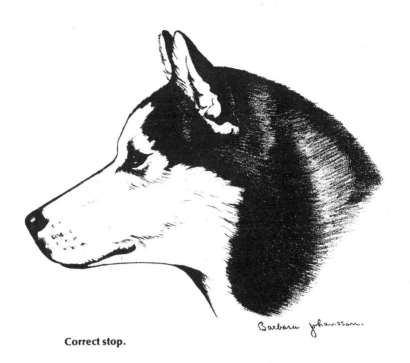

Correct stop.

Not enough stop.

Correct ear set.

Barbara Johansson.

Ears set too wide.

Barbara Johansson.

240

Ears—Of medium size, triangular in shape, close fitting and set high on the head. They are thick, well-furred, slightly arched at the back, and strongly erect, with slightly rounded tips pointing straight up. *Faults*—Ears too large in proportion to the head; too wide-set; not strongly erect.

Eyes—Almond shaped, moderately spaced and set a trifle obliquely. The expression is keen, but friendly; interested and even mischievous. Eyes may be brown or blue in color; one of each or parti-colored are acceptable. *Faults*—Eyes set too obliquely; set too close together.

Nose—Black in gray, tan or black dogs; liver in copper dogs; may be flesh-colored in pure white dogs. The pink-streaked "snow nose" is acceptable.

Comment: Along with coat type and the general size and proportion of the body, the head is the primary indicator of *type* in a breed and thus is an important factor in the assessment of any purebred dog. It has been argued that heads are basically a matter of aesthetic whim and have little to do with the actual functioning capability of a breed. This is, of course, not altogether true. A Siberian, for instance, would be hard pressed to survive in an Arctic climate with anything but a well-furred ear, and an argument could probably be made that the smaller ear, as opposed to that of the German Shepherd, would be less vulnerable to cold. The erect ear is also more generally efficient than the lop ear and less prone to infection. It has further been hypothosised by Richard and Alice Fiennes in their book, *The Natural History of Dogs*, that the well-defined stop called for in the Siberian standard allows for the maximum development of the frontal sinuses which trap exhaled warmed air, thereby forming a warm cushion over the delicate tissues of the eyes and forebrain and also helping warm the cold inhaled air as it passes along the nasal passages. The requirement for close-fitting lips would also be necessary for survival in sub-zero temperatures, one of the things noted by the earliest fanciers of the breed being the dogs' ability to work with their mouths closed thereby avoiding frostbite of the lungs. The scissors bite is also the most efficient for tearing and eating and, perhaps more importantly, for severing the umbilical cord during whelping. The medium size head, like the medium length of neck that is called for later in the standard, is optimal for endurance, the head and neck performing a vital function in the maintenance of balance and the movement of the front assembly. Since it can probably be further argued that the almond shaped eye that is called for by the standard is the one most easily protected between the frontal bones and zygomatic arch (cheek bone), it being the eye most frequently found among wild Canidae, this leaves only the slightly oblique eye set and very high ear set called for by the standard in the realm of simple aesthetic preference. But since these characteristics were found on the majority of early specimens, and since they are among the characteristics distinguishing the Siberian from his cousins, the Malamute, Samoyed and the now no longer recognized Eskimo, requiring their maintenance seems eminently justifiable.

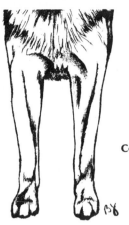

Correct front.

Front too narrow.

Front too wide.

Unfortunately there is something of a tendency in the dog world to think of heads as being merely a matter of fashion, without a great deal of regard either for the guidelines set by the standard or for the premises upon which these guidelines are based. It is true that the specifications set for the Siberian head are looser than in many breed standards, allowing the existence of various kinds of looks. This variety, especially when emphasized by the variety of facial markings, has always been one of the most appealing aspects of the breed. However, a large, domed head with round eyes, wide ear set, and a short, abruptly set-on muzzle is no more typical of the Siberian than a small, shallow, snipey one, no matter how impressive it may appear. Part of the problem in this respect may arise from the fact that, although a heavy head and short muzzle are specifically faulted, there is no mention in the standard of the proper depth of skull or muzzle. The standard does ask for an expression that is "keen, but friendly; interested and even mischievous." A skull and/or muzzle showing extreme depth may of often appear regal or impressive, but will seldom appear keen, friendly or mischievous.

Body:

Neck—Medium in length, arched and carried proudly erect when dog is standing. When moving at a trot, the neck is extended so that the head is carried slightly forward. *Faults*—Neck too short and thick; neck too long.

Shoulders—The shoulder blade is well laid back at an approximate angle of 45 degrees to the ground. The upper arm angles slightly backward from point of shoulder to elbow, and is never perpendicular to the ground. The muscles and ligaments holding the shoulder to the rib cage are firm and well-developed. *Faults*—Straight shoulders; loose shoulders.

Chest—Deep and strong, but not too broad, with the deepest point being just behind and level with the elbows. The ribs are well-sprung from the spine but flattened on the sides to allow for freedom of action. *Faults*—Chest too broad; "barrel ribs"; ribs too flat or weak.

Back—The back is straight and strong, with a level topline from withers to croup. It is of medium length, neither cobby nor slack from excessive length. The loin is taut and lean, narrower than the rib cage, and with slight tuck-up. The croup slopes away from the spine at an angle, but never so steeply as to restrict the rearward thrust of the hind legs. In profile, the length of the body from the point of the shoulder to the rear point of the croup is slightly longer than the height of the body from the ground to the top of the withers. *Faults*—Weak or slack back; roached back; sloping topline.

Comment: The foregoing description deals primarily with the standing, or static, dog. However, since no dog was bred to stand still, the requirements given here imply the animal in motion, and there is perhaps no better indicator as to how a standing animal is likely to move than the set of his shoulder blades.

The standard asks for the blade to be set at an angle of 45 degrees to the ground when viewed in profile. This is the optimal angle when the heel pad is set directly under the center of the shoulder blade and not when the feet are any further forward, as is sometimes the case in the show ring when the front is "dropped" into position by the handler. This is why it is also asked that the upper arm angle backward to the elbow and not be perpendicular to the ground, since a straight shouldered dog can be made to give the appearance of having more shoulder layback by bringing the front legs forward, thus rotating the shoulder blade backward. The result, however, will be to bring the upper arm perpendicular to the ground. The ideal angle formed by the blade and the upper arm is 90 degrees. This allows maximum shock absorbency when the dog is moving and also, in conjunction with the 45 degree set of the shoulder, allows maximum reach and follow-through. Unfortunately, few specimens of any breed exhibit this ideal degree of shoulder layback. Nevertheless, not only does this shoulder offer maximum efficiency when moving, it also indicates a great deal about the rest of the dog since all the parts of the body are interrelated.

The neck, for instance, is absolutely essential to proper movement since many of the muscles activating the front assembly are connected to it. Thus, not only should it be of medium length and arched for maximum endurance, it should be set firmly into the body. That is to say, it should join the topline as far back as possible and slope into it gently. It should not join the topline abruptly as will be the case with a straight shouldered dog. It should also be carried forward somewhat when the dog is moving, propelling him in the direction of travel. If the shoulder is too steep, however, the dog is forced to move with head and neck more erect, thus causing an up and down movement with much waste of energy.

A straight shoulder will also cause a relatively longer back, since it places the withers further forward, thus increasing the tendency toward a weak or slack back. It also causes the withers to be substantially higher than the croup producing a sloping topline while the standard asks for a level topline. Actually, what is looked for is the *appearance* of a level topline, or more precisely, a level back, that portion of the topline from just behind the withers to just in front of the croup. This *apparently* level topline will actually be slightly higher at the withers than at the croup. Furthermore, after sloping down from the withers and running parallel to the ground over the midsection of the dog, the spine arches slightly in front of the croup to support the slight tuck-up called for by the standard. This arch is crucial for strength and endurance as this section of the spine connects the front and rear of the animal, delivering the momentum from the thrust of the rear leg forward, and supporting many of the muscles that activate both front and rear assemblies. Regardless of these minor deviations in the spine, however, the visual impression should be basically that of a level topline, since this allows the transfer of mementum from the

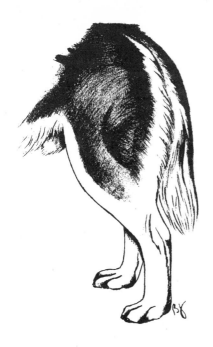

Correct angulation.

Stifles are too straight.

rear to the front to be most directly in the line of travel, thus providing the greatest efficiency and endurance of movement.

The slightly sloping croup called for by the standard is also necessary for the most efficient transfer of energy from the rear leg to the spinal column. In this respect, a croup angle of about 30 degrees to the line of the back is the one that most closely meets the demand for a balance of power, speed, and endurance.

Where endurance is required, a deep chest is of utmost importance since it houses the heart and lungs. A broad chest also provides sufficient room for these vital organs but impedes the follow-through of the front legs: thus the request for a deep chest with ribs well-sprung but flat on the sides. It is also important that the chest depth be maintained well back along the body, producing a fairly short loin, or coupling, as a rib cage that begins its upward sweep toward the loin too quickly decreases heart and lung capacity. Again, because of the interrelation of these parts, a dog exhibiting good depth of chest, with ribs well-sprung but flattened on the sides and a fairly short loin will normally exhibit good layback of shoulder.

Throughout this discussion, shoulder layback has been emphasized, not only as an indicator of how a standing dog is likely to move, but as a clue to how the rest of the body is put together. The standard further specifies that the muscles and ligaments holding the shoulder blade to the ribcage be firm and well-developed. This request is again in the interest of endurance and is more apt to be complied with in specimens exhibiting good shoulder layback since a well laid back shoulder allows for a longer, larger bone which, in turn, allows the formation of larger and longer muscles and ligaments adhering to it. Nevertheless, a shoulder blade is only as good as it functions, and a dog that exhibits good layback of shoulder but who fails to exhibit good reach and follow-through in the forequarters should be more severely penalized than a specimen who exhibits a straight shoulder but uses what he has to better advantage. The request for the strong muscles and ligaments attaching the shoulder blade to the chest, for instance, should never be taken as justification for a dog's moving from the elbow without the rotation of the shoulder blade and the full swing of the upper arm.

Legs and Feet:

Forelegs—When standing and viewed from the front, the legs are moderately spaced, parallel and straight, with elbows close to the body and turned neither in nor out. Viewed from the side, pasterns are slightly slanted, with pastern joint strong, but flexible. Bone is substantial but never heavy. Length of the leg from elbow to ground is slightly more than the distance from the elbow to the top of withers. Dewclaws on forelegs may be removed. *Faults*—Weak pasterns; too heavy bone; too narrow or too wide in the front; out at the elbows.

Hindquarters—When standing and viewed from the rear, the hind legs are moderately spaced and parallel. The upper thighs are well-muscled and powerful, the stifles well-bent, the hock joint well-defined and set low to the ground. Dewclaws, if any, are to be removed. **Faults**—Straight stifles, cowhocks, too narrow or too wide in the rear.

Feet—Oval in shape, but not long. The paws are medium size, compact and well-furred between the toes and pads. The pads are tough and thickly cushioned. The paws neither turn in nor out when dog is in natural stance. **Faults**—Soft or splayed toes; paws too large and clumsy; paws too small and delicate; toeing in or out.

Comment: Like those for the body, the requirements for the legs and feet, although describing the standing animal, are based upon the necessities of movement. The moderate spacing of the front legs, for instance, is optimal for an animal that is to have both speed and endurance. A wide front caused by too broad a chest or too thick muscling will lack smoothness of action and endurance. A narrow front will be caused either by an insufficient breadth of chest or a shoulder that is steep and sits too far forward. In either case the potential for endurance is limited. The request for slightly slanted, flexible pasterns is also in the interest of smoothness of action, endurance and speed. A straighter pastern with a straighter shoulder is effective on a heavy freighting animal such as the Malamute. The slightly slanted pastern, however, especially in conjunction with a well laid back shoulder increases shock absorbency and speed as well as producing better static, or standing, balance. This request for a slanted pastern, however, should not be taken to mean a broken-down pastern. In other words, the bend should actually come in the bones just above or just below the pastern joint and not be in the joint itself.

The request for medium bone in the leg is again a request for that balance of speed, power and endurance. But since the phrase ''substantial but never heavy'' is necessarily comparative, it perhaps deserves some clarification. Although the bones on various breeds vary somewhat in shape, the bone on a Siberian is considerably lighter than that of a Malamute, slightly lighter than a Golden Retriever's, slightly heavier than a Collie's, and about equivalent to that of a Boxer or Doberman Pinscher.

The length of leg, slightly longer than the depth of body, is again optimal for speed and endurance. Anything longer implies the sprinter, and anything shorter would be too slow and plodding.

The hindquarters of a dog generate power. The fastest four-legged animals are rather high on the hock, this producing the greatest amount of thrust. The rabbit and kangaroo are extreme examples of this. However, a low set hock joint requires less muscular activity and, thus, is more enduring.

The actual stifle-bend is produced by the angle at which the upper and lower thigh bones meet, and this will vary somewhat according to the relative lengths of these bones. What is of utmost importance, however, is not so much the precise degree of bend but that there be good depth of thigh when viewed from the side, and this depth depends largely on the angle at which the

Correct rear.

Rear too narrow.

Cow-hocked.

248

upper thigh is joined to the pelvis. Normally, where this angle is approximately 90 degrees to the desired 30 degree slope of the croup, the depth of thigh is sufficient to generate good power.

The request for moderate size and durability is again made in the description of the typical Siberian foot, and because feet are so fundamental to the function of any working dog, any weakness or clumsiness in this quarter should be penalized. It should be noted, however, that most dogs with good fronts toe out very, very slightly in front. In fact, a dog whose toes point dead ahead when he is standing often tends to toe in when moving. Any marked toeing out, however, is a decided fault and is usually accompanied by a narrow front. The toes of the rear feet, however, should point straight ahead.

Tail—The well-furred tail of fox-brush shape is set on just below the level of the topline, and is usually carried over the back in a graceful sickle curve when the dog is at attention. When carried up, the tail does not curl to either side of the body, nor does it snap flat against the back. A trailing tail is normal for the dog when working or in repose. Hair on the tail is of medium length and approximately the same length on top, sides and bottom, giving the appearance of a round brush. **Faults**—A snapped or tightly curled tail; highly plumed tail; tail set too low or too high.

Comment: The comment is occasionally heard at ringside, "A dog doesn't run on his tail." Overlooking the tail set and carriage in one's assessment of a dog, however, is rather like overlooking the last chapter of a novel. Few good novels have bad last chapters and few mediocre ones have particularly good endings. This is because the success or failure of a last chapter is largely dependent on what has come before. And, if anything, this is truer of dogs than of novels, for the novelist might just be lucky enough to come up with a brilliant enough finale to momentarily transform in the reader's mind the mediocrity that has come before. Such sleight-of-hand, however, rarely takes place ih nature, as the bones and muscles of the body are intimately interrelated and not subject to good days and bad days, as are the workings of a writer's mind.

The demands made for the tail, then, are intimately related to the demands made for the more obviously functional parts of the body. The set of the tail, for instance, is dependent on the angle of the croup, a slightly sloping croup placing the base of the tail just below the level of the topline. The tail carriage, on the other hand, indicates a great deal about the condition of the muscles along the spine, a tightly snapped tail or tail deviating to one side or the other being caused by poor muscling. And since these muscles that control the tail carriage are also influential in propelling the dog, it is unlikely that muscles that are inefficient for the one job will be any more efficient for the other.

The tail is thus much more than decoration. Rather it is a kind of critique on what has come before. So, although it is true that a dog does not run on his tail, it is equally true that a dog who runs well will normally exhibit a good tail set and carriage.

The distinctive tail shape and carriage of the Siberian also has its basis in function, for we are told that not only was this thick brush necessary for covering the dogs' noses while sleeping in sub-zero temperatures, but that the distinctive over the back or straight trailing carriage was less apt to get tangled in the harnesses, and that many dogs of cross breeding had to have their tails docked to avoid this problem. The request for the even brush shape rather than a heavily plumed tail is simply consistent with the medium length coat that is requested later in the standard.

Gait—The Siberian Husky's characteristic gait is smooth and seemingly effortless. He is quick and light on his feet, and when in the show ring should be gaited on a loose lead at a moderately fast trot, exhibiting good reach in the forequarters and good drive in the hindquarters. When viewed from the front to rear, while moving at a walk the Siberian Husky does not single-track, but as the speed increases the legs gradually angle inward until the pads are falling on a line directly under the longitudinal center of the body. As the pad marks converge, the forelegs and hind legs are carried straight forward, with neither elbows nor stifles turned in or out. Each hind leg moves in the path of the foreleg on the same side. While the dog is gaiting, the topline remains firm and level. **Faults**—Short, prancing or choppy gait, lumbering or rolling gait; crossing; crabbing.

Comment: With the exception of a few stipulations made in the interests of type and refinement, everything in the standard so far has led up to this demand for "smooth and seemingly effortless" movement. Since movement has been mentioned throughout, however, there are really only a couple of things that should be pointed out here. The primary one is that this is where the phrase "the whole equals the sum of the parts" is particularly relevant, since, basically, the moving dog is the whole dog. Consequently, a dog who has exhibited a well-bent stifle but a somewhat steep shoulder will likely show this discrepancy when moving. Balance is the key to movement, in other words, and a dog who is slightly under-angulated, but balanced, front and rear, will likely move better than, and is thus preferable to, a dog who is extreme in one quarter or another. The request for single-tracking and for the rear legs to follow in the line of the front is in the interest of efficiency. A dog who is more angulated in the rear than in the front, for instance, is likely to crab, especially if he has a short stiff back. In other words, he will tend to move diagonally to the line of travel, placing his rear feet to one side or the other of his forefeet in order to avoid having his rear feet actually hit his front feet. Short, prancing, or choppy gaits are usually caused by insufficient angulation or straight pasterns, and since this causes the dog to bob up and down

Correct tail at attention.

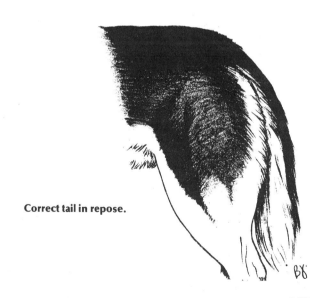

Correct tail in repose.

rather than move directly in the line of travel, he is apt to be slower and tire more quickly. A lumbering or rolling gait is caused by a dog's inability to single-track properly, either because of an inherited weakness in structure or poor muscle tone. Often overweight dogs exhibit this tendency, and puppies often tend to roll somewhat before they develop adequate muscles and coordination. Since this type of movement also produces motion in a direction outside the line of travel, it is less than efficient. The same is true of any movement of the legs other than directly forward to a point directly under the longitudinal center of the body.

The only other point that should be made about proper Siberian movement is that it is dangerous to read beyond the standard. Occasionally the comment is heard at ringside. "That dog looks like he could pull a sled." Too often this comment is made in reference to a heavily boned, heavily muscled dog who, when simply being gaited, already looks like he is pulling a 200 pound load. Remember that the standard asks for a balance of power, speed and endurance and that this balance will be reflected in a dog who is "light and quick on his feet" and whose "gait is smooth and seemingly effortless."

> Coat—The coat of the Siberian Husky is double and medium in length, giving a well-furred appearance, but is never so long as to obscure the clean-cut outline of the dog. The undercoat is soft and dense and of sufficient length to support the outer coat. The guard hairs of the outer coat are straight and somewhat smooth-lying, never harsh nor standing straight off from the body. It should be noted that the absence of the undercoat during the shedding season is normal. Trimming of the whiskers and fur between the toes and around the feet to present a neater appearance is permissible. Trimming of the fur on any other part of the dog is not to be condoned and should be severely penalized. *Faults*—Long, rough or shaggy coat; texture too harsh or too silky; trimming of the coat, except as permitted above.

Comment: The Siberian coat is unique among Arctic breeds because of its medium length, both the Malamute and the Samoyed having a somewhat longer, shaggier coat. The reason for this difference lies primarily in the difference in the climates in which these dogs were originally bred. In the case of the Siberian, the specific conditions of climate and terrain found in his homeland made the formation of ice balls in a long coat an ever present danger. Thus, consciously or unconsciously, the Chukchi developed a coat on their dogs that could both withstand the Arctic cold and prevent the formation of ice balls. And it is for this reason that the long, shaggy, or coarse coat is specifically faulted by the standard. Nevertheless, there does exist a certain range of coat length, probably from about one inch to three inches, that is considered typically Siberian so long as the outline of the dog remains unobscured and the texture is correct.

Incorrect tail—excessive plumage.

**Incorrect tail—
curled to one side of body.**

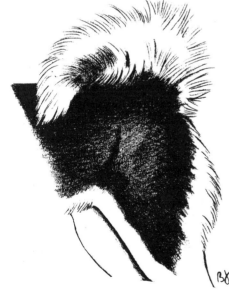

**Incorrect tail—
snapped flat to back.**

Trimming is faulted, except of the whiskers and feet, in an attempt to maintain "naturalness" in the breed.

Color—All colors from black to pure white are allowed. A variety of markings on the head is common, including many striking patterns not found in other breeds.

Comment: It is also in the interest of naturalness that any color of coat or variation of marking is allowed. On the other hand, simply because something is allowed does not mean it is preferred. This particularly is true of asymmetrically marked dogs, sometimes called piebald or pintos. They have always existed in the breed and there is nothing wrong with them as Siberians. However, it is a general rule of canine aesthetics that symmetry is usually more attractive than asymmetry, meaning that in order for a piebald or asymmetrically marked dog to win, he must be sounder and exhibit better type than anything in the ring with him at that time. This is simply because a dog who is equal to the piebald in every other way but who is also symmetrical has that one point in his favor. Occasionally the argument is heard that judges are biased against piebalds, the implication being that judges should have a preference for the asymmetrical simply because it is allowed. This not to say, of course, that a beautiful piebald could not walk into the ring tomorrow who, because of some striking pattern of markings, might be more appealing than all the more symmetrically marked dogs. But since, as a rule, breeders do not intentionally breed for asymmetry, this seems unlikely.

Temperament—The characteristic temperament of the Siberian Husky is friendly and gentle, but also alert and outgoing. He does not display the possessive qualities of the guard dog, nor is he overly suspicious of strangers or aggressive with other dogs. Some measure of reserve and dignity may be expected in the mature dog. His intelligence, tractability, and eager disposition make him an agreeable companion and willing worker.

Comment: Temperament is of utmost importance in a Siberian Husky. An aggressive dog is not a team dog, and since the Siberian is a sled dog, any sign of aggression toward other dogs should be severly penalized. It has been pointed out in defense of more aggressive dogs that the majority of the early Chukchi teams were neutered, except for the lead dog. Evidence, however, points strongly to the viewpoint that these dogs were neutered, not to avoid fighting, but because a neutered dog, having a more retarded metabolism, requires relatively less food. It also insured that only the best dogs were active in breeding.

254

Size—*Height*—Dogs, 21 to 23½ inches at the withers. Bitches, 20 to 22 inches at the withers. *Weight*—Dogs, 45 to 60 pounds. Bitches, 35 to 50 pounds. Weight is in proportion to height. The measurements mentioned above represent the extreme height and weight limits, with no preference given to either extreme. **Disqualification**—Dogs over 23½ inches and bitches over 22 inches.

Comment: Size is as integral a feature of the Siberian as coat texture or ear set and just as important to his functionality. A dog smaller than that called for by the standard will lack the necessary strength to be a good sled dog, while one larger will lack the speed and endurance. So again it is the mean that is required with absolutely no preference given to either extreme set by the standard. This is important to realize even though in a large class it is often the larger specimens that stand out immediately simply because of their size. However, a dog standing 23½ inches at the shoulder is in no way preferable on a team to one who stands 22. It should be remembered that Togo weighed only 48 pounds. It is also interesting to note that as a possible by-product of this insistence upon the maintainance of medium size, Siberian fanciers have so far avoided many of the problems found in breeds where greater size is preferable, problems such as hip dysplasia and osteochodritis that remain relatively rare in this breed.

Summary—The most important breed characteristics of the Siberian Husky are medium size, moderate bone, well-balanced proportions, ease and freedom of movement, proper coat, pleasing head and ears, correct tail, and good disposition. Any appearance of excessive bone or weight, constricted or clumsy gait, or long, rough coat should be penalized. The Siberian Husky never appears so heavy or coarse as to suggest a freighting animal; nor is he so light and fragile as to suggest a sprint-racing animal. In both sexes the Siberian Husky gives the appearance of being capable of great endurance. In addition to the faults already noted, obvious structural faults common to all breeds are as undesirable in the Siberian Husky as in any other breed, even though they are not specifically mentioned herein.

DISQUALIFICATION
Dogs over 23½ inches and bitches over 22 inches.

Short Seeley and friends.

256

10

Owning a Siberian

SINCE the average dog remains with a family longer than they own their car, and, in many cases, longer than they own their house, it is ironic and not a little sad that the consideration given to selecting a pet is often less than that given to selecting a new pair of shoes. With the pet population increasing at an alarming rate, and with it the number of unwanted pets as well as the amount of legislation and sentiment levied against pets, this trend of casual acquisition imperils the entire canine population. If the tradition of man-dog relationships is to continue, then, it can only be hoped that acquiring a family pet will more and more be approached with the same careful consideration one gives to bringing a child into the world, for the commitment of time, money and affection over a ten to fifteen year period is not that dissimilar.

Some of the best reasons *not* to acquire a pet are the casual "it might be nice to have a dog about the place," or "the kids want one," or worst of all, "it will teach the kids responsibility." In regard to the latter, although there is nothing more appealing than a child-dog relationship, it is totally unfair to expect a child to take the full responsibility for caring for an animal; he will only grow up to resent it as a chore. And by the same token, there is nothing more perverse than to bring a young puppy into the house to have his tail pulled and eyes poked under the pretext of teaching a child responsibility or the value of life or whatever.

What the Siberian is not—

Providing one really is committed to acquiring a dog, however, one of the great advantages of purchasing a purebred dog is that one has a pretty good idea what the cuddly eight-week-old puppy will grow up to be, not only in terms of size and general appearance, but in terms of temperament. Each breed has been developed to perform certain functions. But no breed is of the proper size or disposition to suit *every* family's particular needs. Since

257

The fascination that sled dogs have held for the dog fancy is apparent in this picture of a demonstration by Roland Bowles' team that stole the show at Cheshire KC in 1961.

throughout this text we have devoted ourselves to the positive aspects of the Siberian, it is only fair to note here some of the negative considerations.

First of all, the Siberian has none of the protective instincts or even the inclination to bark found in good watch dogs. He is utterly democratic in his affection and will normally greet the burglar as happily as he would his family. He has an insatiable desire to run and has no "traffic sense" and should be kept in a fenced yard or pen or on a leash at all times. He is very energetic and can be extremely destructive if left in a house alone for periods of time. This is especially true of puppies. Even outside, many love to dig holes. And last, but not least, the Siberian has a very thick coat which, although normally odorless and non-allergenic, does come out once or twice a year in enormous quantities.

If, on the other hand, one is willing to put up with these drawbacks in order to own what we in the breed feel is the most affable and beautiful of all breeds, then the following chapter on the selection and care of the Siberian by Kathleen Kanzler should prove useful.

11

Selection, Care and Maintenance of the Siberian Husky

by Kathleen Kanzler

So YOU WANT a Siberian Husky puppy! This chapter will explain how to make the new family member more joy than trial. All puppies are appealing but the most appealing puppy is not necessarily the best one for you. First you must decide whether you want a family pet, or a dog to show in conformation shows or for Obedience. You may decide that you want a foundation bitch to start your own kennel.

If you are looking for a show or breeding animal, obtain the best available. The Siberian Husky Club of America publishes a breeders' directory that may help you locate the puppy you want. Local veterinarians and persons active in other breeds may be of help in directing you to a reputable breeder. Do not limit your search to your local area. Dogs may be shipped safely and economically from most areas of the country by air. Bargain hunting in the dog world is a mistake; one gets what one pays for, and if a top quality show dog is required, one should obtain the best regardless of price.

After initial inquiries let you know what is available and the general price range, use common sense in deciding on a breeder to buy from. If you want a show dog the seller should have some credentials that qualify him to recognize a show puppy. How actively do they show dogs? What qualities did the sire and dam of this litter have that made the breeder feel this would be a successful litter?

A puddle of Synordik puppies—just a few weeks old. Breeder, Dr. Cynthia Nist.

Feeding time at Monadnock.

Choosing the Right Puppy

A dog is a responsibility that a buyer takes on for the life of the dog. Such a long-time commitment should not be entered into casually.

Siberians should be friendly and relatively tractable in a situation familiar to them. Certainly, excuses should be made for the dog just brought in from a kennel run. After he has had time to express his joy at being a "people" dog again, he should settle down and act civilized. If he runs around constantly crying and being a nuisance and a firm tone of voice does not calm him down he may be hyperactive and a poor choice. Try and see the parents of a dog you are interested in buying and determining what kind of temperament they have. We will assume they have good dispositions or they would not have been bred. However, if one or both parents is hyperactive — always on the go, difficult to calm down — their offspring may have inherited this tendency. A hyperactive Siberian is very difficult to live with. Its tendency to "self destruct" can take much of the joy out of living with a Siberian.

A sweet, quiet type female is often much the best choice for a family of young children, especially if the woman involved is a small, rather quiet person. The aggressive, into everything, knock it over and eat it puppy is the natural eye catcher in a litter and has great appeal. This puppy is better placed with a strong no nonsense type family that has, ideally, coped with a dog before.

When choosing a puppy, either for show or pet, its appearance as well as temperament should appeal to you. However, remember that eye color and coat color are superficial and are not the qualities upon which Siberian Huskies are judged. Be wary of the breeder who sets different prices simply on the basis of eye color or coat color, and when one is choosing a puppy these factors should be the last consideration.

The most reliable way to buy a Siberian is to contact a breeder in whom you have confidence and rely on his judgment. There are many variables that go into selecting a puppy, both for pet or show. The breeder knows his puppies and their ancestors and the character traits and physical characteristics that are apt to be produced in his line of dogs.

The uniformity of a litter gives some indication of the range of genetic variables, and the smaller that range, the greater will be the tendency of a given puppy to produce offspring similar to himself. It may be that the litter under consideration is a repeat breeding of the parents. The overall quality of the previous litter may influence your decision. Again, the breeder's selection may be the best choice. The breeder is familiar with the tendencies of his own lines. In selecting a show dog, the pedigree and overall consistency of the litter are factors that should weigh as highly or higher than the appearance of a given puppy. Show dogs are breeding stock, and the chances of a single beautiful puppy in an otherwise mediocre litter producing offspring as good as himself are very slim.

Some considerations that may be successful in choosing a Siberian for quality are provided in the following paragraphs.

A puppy whose front feet turn out to the sides at seven weeks probably won't have a proper front as an adult. A puppy with a snap tail probably will always have a bad tail. Tails on Siberians may turn into snap tails as late as four to six months of age. The mouth on a Siberian puppy should show a scissors bite. In some individuals, the alignment of the teeth may change during the growth period, but if the bite was correct as a puppy, it is realistic to hope that the mouth may be proper as an adult. Ear set on a puppy should be high on the head and hopefully not too large.

Growth Pattern of the Siberian:

This may be the place to attempt to explain the growth pattern of Siberians.

A newborn puppy weighs about one pound. At ten weeks the puppy may weigh fifteen pounds. Keep in mind that this young animal will go through many stages of growth. Depending on the family characteristics of the puppy he may obtain most of his height by about eight months. Very possibly this fast growing puppy will be awkward, gangly, and may be high in the rear; in fact, may appear to have excess skin that rolls when he moves rapidly. Ears, depending again on family characteristics, may be large in this juvenile stage. Some ears that look hopeless do come around in the adult dog and appear smaller than they once did.

Some of these fast growing puppies are loose, move sloppily with large feet, heads and ears; their bodies lack depth in the rib and brisket area. Generally it is males that go through the most difficult adolescence.

If you have one of the above type of dog, be realistic in your expectations. This is not the type of animal that should be shown as a puppy. Wait on this dog until he is about two years old before you start showing him. In actuality he may be three before he is mature.

Another common growth pattern is the puppy that grows evenly throughout most of his first year. Hopefully, this puppy has a full coat that covers some of its immaturity. He looks "all of a piece," a miniature Siberian. These pups are great fun as they usually do well at puppy matches and bring favorable comments from friends. This type of puppy may appear small at seven or eight months. Usually they will go into a growth spurt around a year of age. This type of dog will continue to grow slowly through his second year.

Both types of dogs will mature through their third year. Do not be impatient with the development of your young dogs. If a basic soundness and quality is apparent, time should produce a good Siberian. A male usually is not mature enough to pick up the points before he is two years old. A female often is ready by eighteen months.

262

Curious by nature.

The Right Start

When you finally purchase this well considered puppy some type of guarantee of good health should accompany the bill of sale. Once having brought the puppy home, it is important to have him examined by a good veterinarian. His advice, along with a complete book on dog care, will prove invaluable throughout the dog's life.

If the puppy is to be a house pet, never to be shown or bred, it is highly advisable to have it either spayed or neutered. Many problems are alleviated by this simple surgery which has virtually no effect on the dog's personality. A basic obedience course is extremely helpful if the puppy is to become a well adjusted member of the family.

Puppies love to chew, great care should be taken in removing all items from his reach that might be harmful. Bones, contrary to popular opinion, are dangerous for dogs as they may break and cause damage to the stomach lining and intestines. The most suitable toys are rawhide chew toys that are digested when eaten. Rubber balls and squeak toys if used at all, should only be brought out for supervised play.

Housing Your Siberian

Ideal housing for your Siberian would involve the purchase of a portable chain link dog run. This pen, approximately six feet wide by twelve feet long by six feet high is adequate, set on concrete or concrete patio blocks, and will provide a safe, comfortable home for your active Siberian throughout his lifetime. The initial investment is offset by protection of your property from your own furry ''jaws.'' A chewed sofa or shoes will soon add up to the price of a pen. The other rationale is the safety of this lovable Indian that knows no fear of cars.

Often people say that my dog is to be a ''house dog!'' A house dog needs a secure place to stay when the family members are shopping or away for the day. A pen convenient to an outside door keeps the rest of a nice backyard, nice. The addition of a dog house and a bucket of water provides a complete housing facility for the dog while giving the owner maximum mobility.

The other useful purchase for the puppy is a collapsible wire dog crate. The puppy may be fed in his crate to get him used to being in it. It is a very useful tool in housebreaking your puppy. Putting the puppy in his crate at bedtime in your bedroom will keep him from being lonesome and howling. If you are a light sleeper he will let you know when he has to go out to relieve himself. He will fuss before he dirties his cage. His instinct is not to mess where he sleeps.

The cage may be used in the car for short or long trips. The dog is safe in the car and the windows may be left open without fear of the dog escaping. Traveling to ''non-doggy'' friends or relatives' homes is possible if the dog is

The kiss—a classic by any standard. Ch. Monadnock's Pando and Ch. Monadnock's Belka demonstrate the social affability that makes Siberian Huskies such a delight to their owners.

265

kept in his crate, except for exercising during the visit. Babies are prepared for by the purchase of a crib and playpen. Puppies are live, lively young beings that need some facilities for their confinement.

Feeding Your Siberian

Modern commercial dog foods are generally well researched and well balanced diets. Siberians in particular, utilize a low bulk dog food more effectively than some of the high bulk popular diets manufactured for some of the less energetic breeds. A dry, bite-sized highly palatible feed made mostly of chicken has seemed to work very well for Siberians of all ages. However, never feed raw chicken.

One of the continuing problems in raising Siberian puppies has been loose stools. Assuming that any parasite problems are being controlled, many puppies continue to have loose, unformed stools during their early rapid growth period. This syndrome often makes housebreaking chaotic and produces near desperation in new owners. If the puppy is gaining weight steadily, has a healthy coat, and lively attitude, it is probably just a feeding problem.

Whole milk and most table scraps are not recommended for growing puppies. These additions often upset the delicate balance of the puppy's digestion. A complete, dry type dog food, preferably, the chicken based feed, is usually the answer in reaching a balance between large food needs in the fast growing puppy and his digestive capabilities. The addition of vitamins or minerals is seldom necessary in a healthy, parasite-free animal. However, if a puppy is anemic, he should be fed an iron supplement.

Several methods of feeding are acceptable. A few well organized people may find that feeding three to four measured meals a day suits them. Many people find that self feeding or the dry ration works well for them. Free access to food works well for many Siberian puppies' digestion. Small amounts of food often keep a Siberian's digestion working efficiently. Some puppies need to be taken off self feeding at four to six months because they overeat. If your puppy becomes too fat, change to measured meals two or three times a day depending on age.

Often a feeding problem develops when the puppy has gone through his most rapid growth period. He becomes a finicky eater. Often he appears thin and if he is lacking in coat he looks starved. Trips to the veterinarian determine that parasites are not a problem and the dog appears healthy but thin. This is a common syndrome of adolescent Siberians. There is no "cure."

Some things to try: mix dry feed with a small amount of canned meat or table scraps and water. If feeding once a day try two feedings a day. Determine if more exercise might improve appetite. Be aware that some dogs will become tyrannical. They know you are anxious about their eating habits and pick at their food knowing you will open more cans and keep tempting their

The Siberian pup's insatiable desire to run. Quiquern's Commando; at 8 months.

Playtime at Synordik Kennels.

palates with more goodies. Some success is achieved by putting down the dog's food twice a day for ten or fifteen minutes and then picking up any uneaten food and offering nothing between meals. This method may take several days or a week of will power on the owner's part. It is a power struggle, the "Morris the Cat" syndrome.

The mature Siberian (between two and three years of age) is normally a very easy keeper and will carry the proper weight on one feeding a day. A low bulk, high protein diet is preferred even for the older dog.

Grooming Your Siberian

One of the joys of showing a Siberian is the easy transition he can make from the team or the house to the show ring. No elaborate grooming is usually necessary. Sometimes it is difficult to discover just what to do with him to make the most of his natural beauty.

A Siberian in new, tight coat usually can take a warm bath in a mild detergent or Castile shampoo. Rinse until he squeaks. After towel drying, if practical, lay or stand him on a table and brush dry using an electric hair dryer. Aim dryer at area that you are brushing with a pin or slicker brush. The object is not to remove hair but to dry him quickly and to end up with a coat that looks its best. If it is fashionable in your area to trim whiskers, do this with a good quality scissors the day of, or before, the show. Trim as closely as possible for a clean looking profile.

Grooming a Siberian that is blowing his coat or approaching a shedding period is more of a problem. A moment of silent prayer is recommended. An all over bath is not advisable. Washing the dog's legs, chest, face and tail with Castile soap and cool water usually won't accelerate shedding. Again, the dog must be rinsed properly to turn out white. Several products that are mixed with water in a pan and sponged into the white areas or the entire coat if necessary, are useful for the lightly soiled or shedding Siberians. The foam from the solution is used and the soil is rubbed out by toweling the area.

Siberians shedding in their unique patch-like way look better if the worst areas are brushed out with a slicker brush, metal comb and rake. If it is on the hips and sides the absence of hair detracts less from the dog than the bumps and hollows that result from leaving the hair in place.

If the neck, tail and britches are fairly tight, the appearance is usually enhanced by combing out the worst of the body hair. Wash non-shedding areas that need it. Brush lightly to fluff up the coat. Spray sparingly with water or a coat dressing and towel body coat gently to remove dust and make the coat shine. If the dog is still looking patchy, pick tufts out with fingers or end of comb to give the dog a tidy outline.

Stand back and examine the dog. If the middle of his back has shed, rake the shoulder area and over the hips to blend the coat areas and maintain a level

Synordik's "Call Me Ursula".

Ch. Baron of Karnovanda CD and son.

topline. A dog with a shed out mid-back with hair left in shoulder and rear areas appears weak in topline.

Proper grooming of a full coated Siberian will do much to enhance the over all appearance of the dog. A rake, a wooden grooming tool with two rows of nail-like teeth, is a most valuable grooming aid for the Siberian.

Raking through a new coat three times a week from the top of the head through the body and chest areas and two inches down the tail keeps the coat healthy and open. Many dogs can be kept in show coat indefinitely with this method of grooming. Dead hair is removed constantly, allowing the skin to stay clean. The undercoat replaces itself continually without "packing up" and giving the dog the signal to shed. Many dogs' coats are such that with this constant grooming they rarely go into a full shed. With this type of dog, on this type of grooming program, the dog may be shampooed before every show weekend.

A problem-coated dog with dry, harsh hair that will not shed properly, that appears rough and dry should have hair conditioning treatments. Rake through the coat. Wash and rinse the dog thoroughly. Towel dry and apply Clairol Kolesteral conditioner to the coat generously. Apply hot, wet towels for twenty minutes, rinse and dry. Repeat once or twice a week raking the coat daily until the coat is improved. Use conditioner after all regular pre-show baths. This is especially useful on red Siberians. Keep red dogs in covered runs out of the sun to prevent sun bleaching and coat damage.

If your Siberian's toenails are too long cut back to, but not into, the pink quick. To eliminate the problem of a bleeding nail on show day, trim nails at least a day ahead of the show.

The question of chalking the white areas is a matter of opinion. Usually if there is time and the facilities prior to the show to wash the white areas, the results will be more satisfactory. If washing is not practical, chalk with caution. Whitening, even when used for cleaning, that remains in the dog's coat and is apparent to the judge can cause the dog to be disqualified. So brush and lightly "pound" the chalked areas until no chalk "flies."

When preparing the Siberian for showing, an image of a clean, glowing coat, with a trim outline is to be maintained. A show Siberian in new coat is simply a clean, brushed dog. A Siberian shedding or preparing to shed should be groomed cautiously. Clean him as well as possible and remove hair necessary to maintain a proper outline.

Breeding the Siberian

Much of the preceding discussion on buying a puppy has been based upon the dubious assumption that a person knows from the outset if he is interested in a single house pet, a show dog or breeding stock. This, of course, is seldom the case. Much more common is the person who, after having a pet Siberian for a period of time, decides he is sufficiently interested in the breed to start exhibiting and breeding. And such a decision usually raises the question of whether or not to breed the dog already in one's possession or to go out and buy another.

Because Siberian breeders seem to be, by and large, somewhat less stuffy in placing their top quality puppies than many owners of other breeds, it is very possible that, if one has purchased his dog from a top quality kennel, the dog may be of the calibre to breed. On the other hand, one of the most difficult adjustments to make in becoming a breeder is to divorce one's sentimental attachment for a given animal from one's overall interest in the betterment of the breed. But this kind of objectivity is especially crucial in a breed that, like the Siberian Husky, has mushroomed so rapidly in popularity for, unless great care is taken in breeding only the best available specimens, there is the ever present danger that the breed as a whole will degenerate. But not only does one do a disservice to the breed in breeding a mediocre specimen, in the long run one does a disservice to oneself, for the money spent in trying to upgrade one's stock, if it is founded upon a mediocre specimen, will be far greater than the money that is necessary to invest in obtaining a top quality specimen to begin with; and even after years of frustration and careful breeding, the results are not likely to be as good as could have been attained in the first generation if one were using only first rate specimens.

So if one is considering breeding a dog, it is important to ascertain if he is of high enough quality, and the decision should be based, not only upon one's own appraisal after a careful reading of the standard and attending a number of shows, but upon the opinion of a number of qualified breeders.

Lastly, of course, one should consider whether one has the time, money, and facilities to have a litter of puppies. The time spent whelping and rearing puppies is extensive; the return on the litter will generally be far less than the amount spent; and one should have facilities to adequately accommodate five or six dogs until they are six months or so of age as buyers may be scarce.

And for all of the above reasons, under no circumstances should one consider breeding a dog for such vague reasons as "it might be interesting to have a litter," or "it would be educational for the chilren," or "we might make some money." Among good breeders, there is no such thing as a "casual" breeder. There are breeders who breed more frequently or less, who maintain larger or smaller numbers of dogs, but each breeding is approached with seriousness, a definite sense of the purpose of a specific breeding, and a knowledge that the frustrations will always outnumber the successes.

Once armed with the proper motivation and the bitch of quality, there are some practical considerations when breeding dogs.

The bitch should be X-rayed and certified free of hip dysplasia. Also her eyes should be checked by a canine opthomalogist and certified free of hereditary eye diseases. The stud should be selected and his owner should have had the dog's hips and eyes checked. The stud's owner should be informed when the bitch is due in season. When the bitch comes in season the stud's owner should be informed immediately. Shipping or arrival details should be arranged for the bitch to arrive, usually, by the tenth day. The bitch should have been checked for parasites and wormed if necessary. Generally breedings will take place between the eleventh and fourteenth days. Two breedings are usual. One breeding may be agreed upon in the case of the older or extremely popular stud dog. The stud fee is due when the bitch is bred and ready to be returned to the owner. Delayed payment or a stud puppy (usually the choice puppy of the litter) should be agreed upon in preliminary discussions. This agreement should be in writing and signed by both parties.

The stud owner's responsibility include safe, maximum security housing for the bitch in his care. When a male is put up as a public stud, his owner should have educated himself in the mechanics of training and managing a stud dog. All stud services should be supervised for the safety of the dog and bitch. The bitch's owner should have confidence that his bitch will be bred. This is not accomplished in a well ordered manner by putting the two dogs together and letting "nature take its course." Each breed has its breeding peculiarities. Siberian females may be willing partners until the male breeds and ties her. Often she will decide this is not at all what she wants. Screaming is the usual reaction. Often she will struggle, attempt to bite, throw herself on the ground and turn into a whirling dervish. This is where the stud owner needs to be aware and prepared. Two people are needed, one to hold the bitch and support her and the other to work with the stud. The bitch, if she is an unknown quantity, should be muzzled. A humane muzzle is a wire basket that fits over the muzzle. This does not cut the bitch's air supply, as a bandage type may.

It is of paramount importance to keep any breeding under control. The bitch must be held steady and on her feet. The stud is the partner most likely to be injured in a breeding. Do not let him fall or roll over.

The bitch should be watched for the rest of her season as she may be bred to another dog before she goes out of season.

Whelping

Upon her return home it is wise to have the bitch checked for parasites about three weeks into whelp. She may maintain her usual level of exercise, generally, as long as she wishes. She will tend to slow herself down at about six weeks into whelp. Her food should be increased from four weeks in whelp.

The matter of proper housing for the bitch and puppies should be dealt with early. It is unrealistic to approach a Siberian litter without a good secure pen. A portable dog pen with a whelping box or dog house is ideal. If the puppies are to be born in the house, set up an exercise pen or some other arrangement that will confine the bitch to the spot you have chosen for her. She should be put in her whelping area at least a week before her due date as she needs this time to become acclimated and she may deliver her puppies from the 58th to the 63rd day, or even a few days later.

The bitch probably will not settle down the morning of the 63rd day and deliver her puppies by evening. She may be anxious, restless, whining on and off for several days. This is not labor. She is not in trouble. Bitches ordinarily do not eat the day they whelp. True labor usually sees the bitch digging her newspapers, panting heavily and having contractions. When real pushing contractions begin a puppy should be delivered in about fifteen minutes. If the bitch is really pushing, trying to expel a puppy, do not let her go more than one hour before getting veterinary assistance. After an examination the veterinarian may be able to determine that the puppy is correctly placed in the birth canal and a pituitary shot that produces stronger contractions may deliver the puppy.

Siberian bitches as a breed, are good, natural whelpers. Many of the problems that people get into at whelping time are brought on by their own anxieties. If the bitch does not have a dark, smelly discharge and is not obviously ill with an elevated temperature, she is probably all right. Some bitches make quite a production of getting down to business. One thing that helps is if the owners will treat her matter-of-factly, observing her but not talking baby talk and overly sympathizing with her condition. It is fact that some very spoiled house pets simply will not start into labor. As soon as they are uncomfortable they cry and quit. Be prepared for a couple days of pre-labor. This activity gets everyone into a fever pitch and one must resist the impulse to take her to the veterinarian and tell him to do something.

Siberians are as prone to whelping after the 63rd day as they are before that time. It is not the moment for panic if the due date arrives and she is showing no signs of labor. Larger litters may come earlier. Small litters may be very comfortable where they are and if the bitch is showing no signs of discomfort, be patient. Most textbooks say the 66th day is a cut off date for waiting. Certainly have her checked by the veterinarian, and if he sees no problem, you may decide to wait a couple more days. Many Caesarian sections can be avoided if the breeder has patience.

One note, if a section is done, the puppies must be with the mother when she wakes up. Owners tend to feel so sorry for her that the pups are kept away and introduced to her when she is fully awake. Since she did not go through the birth process she may not have the natural, maternal instincts she would have had if she had delivered normally. It is preferable to put the pups on to nurse while she is still groggy although supervision is a must in case the bitch should try to bite one of the puppies. But this way any initial discomfort is out of the way before she is fully conscious.

A temperature check is a useful tool for determining approximate whelping time. A temperature check several times a day when you think she is close to whelping may give you an indication of progress. A dog's normal temperature is 101 degrees. This usually drops a degree or more as whelping time approaches. This check may be useful if you must be away for the day and are uncertain whether she should be left alone. In this chapter we are talking about Siberians in particular of course, but the basis of the chapter is simply good animal management.

Supervised whelping is a necessary part of dog breeding. The bitch may not attend to her first puppy, particularly in a first litter, with the needed speed. She may nose it and seem confused about her role. This is the time to get involved. Remove the membrane from the face of the puppy with speed. Your fingernails will do. Wipe his face and the inside of his mouth. Remove the rest of the membrane from the puppy. Often the after-birth is still inside the bitch so the cord is holding the puppy closely to the mother. Gently pull the cord until one or two inches is outside the bitch and cut the cord leaving at least one inch or one and one half inches attached to the puppy. Time is critical when you are delivering a puppy. Pick it up with its head down to let any fluids drain from the mouth and lungs. Rub vigorously with a towel, wiping out its mouth often. The puppy should be crying and squirming. Do not be afraid to handle it. You probably will not be too rough. Pats and soft rubbing are out of order when you are trying to get a puppy introduced to life. If the puppy's nose is blue and he is not breathing properly give artificial respiration or mouth to mouth. The pup may have fluid in his lungs. Rough him up, stick your finger down his throat, any action that will force him to rid himself of excess fluid and begin breathing. When the puppy is separated from the umbilical cord he must begin breathing on his own.

During a normal whelping the puppies may follow each other by fifteen minutes to one hour. An interval of two hours is not cause for alarm if the bitch seems free of distress. In large litters a bitch may settle down with several puppies, cleaning and nursing them and rest for as long as three to four hours before she gets on with the business of producing the rest of the litter.

Some bitches have their entire litter in two hours, some take all day. As each puppy is born, wait and see if the bitch is willing to take care of the puppy herself. If it is crying and moving and she seems to have the situation under control, observe, do not interfere. If the bitch thrashes around the pen a great deal as she prepares to deliver another puppy, remove the first pups and dry them off and place in a box with a towel and a heating pad set on low.

Many bitches will be happy with one puppy with them and allow you to keep the rest warm and dry until all the puppies are delivered. Keep dry newspapers in the whelping box so the puppies do not become chilled. Puppies at this time need to be kept at a temperature of 90 degrees, so it is important not to let them stay wet and cold.

As the bitch's stomach flattens you try and guess how many more puppies are to come. The bitch that is finished whelping will tend to look for a comfortable place to settle and encourage however many puppies she has with her

Phyllis Brayton (Dichoda Kennels), current president of the Siberian Husky Club of America, with her first Siberian Husky puppy, Dingo Dmitri of Kabkol, 1946.

to nurse. She then tends to lick and clean them. This is a sign that she may indeed be finished. Take her outside to exercise on a leash. She may be reluctant to leave her new family. The reason for exercising her on a leash is that she may very well have another puppy while she is outside.

Take this opportunity to clean her whelping area and put a thick layer of clean newspaper down in her pen. When the bitch is installed in her clean quarters with her litter of puppies, offer her water and food. Within twelve hours, it is a good idea to take her to the veterinarian for a check up. He may want to give her a pituitary shot to clean out any retained after-births and to stimulate milk production.

Bertram and Katherine Hulen's Petya of Monadnock, who charmed Capitol Hill during the 1940s and 1950s.

Ch. Kodiikuska de Sforza CDX and owner Antonio Zarlenga. Kodii saved his master's life by rousing him to the danger of escaping gas.

12

Heroes, Mascots and Something Called Character

It is traditional in breed books to at one point recount some of the unusual or heroic acts performed by dogs of the breed. But since for countless centuries, the Siberian has played such an integral part in the human struggle for survival, it seems almost pointless to single out individual acts of canine heroism.

Nor has this quality been lost. The incredible rise in popularity of the Siberian over recent decades has been largely attributable to his ability to adapt to the role of house pet—a role that requires somewhat different behavior patterns from those of the sled dog, yet which, from time to time, elicits responses that can be as heroic, in their own way, as those of a working sled dog.

Such was the case when Kodiikuska de Sforza, CDX smelled gas escaping in his owner's house on a fall night in 1966 and managed to rouse his master, Tony Zarlenga, and, by continual yipping and prodding, was able to get the almost unconscious man out of the house in time to save his life. Such was also the case with Czar of Monadnock who, seeing his owner, Charles Rizzo, held at gunpoint by an intruder, leaped at the man's throat and was shot. Although the bullet was lodged too close to the spinal column to risk removal, Czar survived and was nominated for an ASPCA award.

Perhaps less spectacular, but certainly no less noteworthy, have been the number of Siberians trained as seeing eye dogs. Among these is a bitch named Mischa living in the Midwest who, like clockwork, awakens her mistress at 6 A.M. every morning and accompanies her to the factory where she works. There she lies patiently until quitting time and the journey home. Her only failing, it is reported, is that, like many humans, it takes her three days to adjust to the time change when daylight saving begins in April and ends in October.

Like many breeds, in its rise to popularity the Siberian has enjoyed a certain vogue with celebrities. President Herbert Hoover was the proud owner of one of the earliest Siberian Huskies, a dog named Yukon bred by Julian Hurley in Alaska in 1929.* A decade later, Petya of Monadnock, owned by correspondent Bertram Hulen and his wife (long-time Siberian Husky Club *Newsletter* editor), enjoyed great popularity in Washington, D.C. and was even the subject of an on-the-street interview by a young newspaper woman named Jacqueline Bouvier. Carole Lombard also owned a Siberian, as did Clara Bow—who spent her last reclusive years with the dog as her constant companion.

And from the time that the school children of New York City contributed their pennies for the statue of Balto erected in Central Park after the famed Serum Run, the Siberian has enjoyed a special popularity with the young. Pando, of course, was the long-time mascot of the Monadnock Regional High School whose yearbook is still called the *Pandorian*. Nalegaksoa II of Peary, call-name King, bred by Yeso Pac Kennels, served for many years as the mascot of the Robert E. Peary High School in Rockville, Maryland, and not only attended athletic events but was even handled in the show ring by members of the student body, winning numerous ribbons and trophies, all of which were proudly displayed at the school. When a handsome black and white Siberian appeared in a family group one year in the National Geographic Society's Christmas brochure, it created a mild flutter in the Siberian Husky world until the identity of the "borrowed dog" was established as that of King.

It is an established tradition for the University of Connecticut at Storrs to have its Siberian Husky mascot present at athletic contests. This mascot is unique in that he must be white and his name is always Jonathan. At this writing, it is Jonathan IV who holds this esteemed position.

Northeastern University in Boston has also had a series of Siberian mascots, all named Yukon. The student body is strongly devoted to these mascots, and one year a bronze statue was commissioned of the reigning Yukon. A tradition quickly arose of rubbing the statue's nose for luck before examinations, and Yukon's nose brightens with each passing year.

It is easy to see, then, that in somewhat over a half a century, the breed we call the Siberian Husky has come a long way: it is many miles and many life styles away from the ice packs of the Arctic Ocean to the football fields of Massachusetts, or from the Chukchi village to a living room in Florida. And with the popularity of the breed soaring dangerously high, it can only be hoped that it has not come too far too fast, for it would be a terrible irony if the very adaptability of the Siberian should be his downfall.

*Yukon by Northern Light Star ex Alaska Silver Moon, was listed in the AKC Stud Register of February 1931 as being owned by Lou Henry Hoover, the President's wife.

278

"Yukon", mascot of Northeastern University, Boston.

Ch. Monadnock's Belka being trained for Seeing Eye work.

279

Christmas cheer.

It is undeniable that the Siberian of today is not the same dog that arrived scruffy and half starved in the villages of Alaska. Yet it is the pride of the fancy that he is not far removed. Beyond the greater consistency of markings and refinement of features and furnishings, there lies the same affable clownishness, the same insolence, the same rakish nobility and the same indomitable exuberance that allowed his forebears to survive the harshest of all possible environments. Today, although he lives in what is perhaps the softest of all environments in human history, it is this same combination of qualities—which for want of a better word we call character—that constitutes the heritage and tradition of the Siberian Husky, a tradition which has allowed him to outlive at least one human tradition and enter another.

The following essay by Betsy Korbonski, reprinted from the April, 1972 issue of the Siberian Husky Club of America's *Newsletter,* is about tradition, about the powers of rejuvenation found in tradition, and, most of all, it is about character.

CALL IT CHARACTER
by Betsy Korbonski

A gentle wind ruffles the fur on the old dog's shoulder. His magnificent coat is dense, seemingly depthless—no sign of shedding yet, though the santana winds have blown through most of March. My fingers touch it lightly, letting the early-morning sun filter through its varied shadings of grey, black and white. Age has frosted over the old dog's once velvet-black ears, but his fur is vibrant, indestructible. He is still the most beautiful of all my dogs. Even in death.

A truck has pulled off Sunset Boulevard onto the empty service station lot. It is Easter Sunday, and the service station is closed. A metal door slams, I hear muffled steps, and someone is standing beside me.

"How did it happen?"

I look toward the questioner, and through him. He is all darkness; his face, his clothes, his boots and hat, all one color, a sooty brown. He reminds me of the chimney sweeps of Europe; they too stopped to admire the old dog, an eye-catcher wherever he went.

In Europe they say a chimney sweep so early brings good luck all day. But this dark apparition brings no such omen. Finally I manage an answer: "He was old. I don't know how. It doesn't matter."

"I'm sorry," he says gently. "Somebody already reported it."

Only now I place him. "You're from Animal Rescue."

"You'll want the collar," he says, searching for it in the depths of the dog's mane.

"If I hadn't found him first"—I am crying now—"would I have known?"

"Yes, we always call if there's a tag on."

So I help with the loading and start to leave. Some reflex halts me, and I reach in my pocketbook for a dollar bill. "Here, take this"—I hand it to him—"after all, you did have to come out Easter morning."

"Thanks, Thanks a lot." And he is gone. Did he have a face, that soft-spoken phantom? I can remember only the darkness of that first impression.

My two young daughters are in the back yard planning our Easter egg hunt. They know I have been out looking for the dog, so I call them with a deliberate edge to my voice. "Holly and Ellen, I have something to tell you."

Ellen is six. She stops in mid-stride and faces me directly. "Tavi's dead," she says tensely.

"Yes."

She squares her jaw, expressionless, and continues her passage across the yard, where she squats to stroke the puppy.

Holly, who is eight, has heard us and now she is sobbing. Her tears flow splendidly—she really looks beautiful when she weeps, not blotchy like most of us. Suddenly, she stops and points at me accusingly: "Mommie, you're not crying!"

"I did," I say shakily. "But all alone, and now I'm finished. He had a good life. He lived the way he wanted to live, and he died the way he wanted to die. What more can you do for a dog?"

"Ellen!" She is merciless. "Why aren't *you* crying?"

"I don't know," Ellen moans helplessly.

"That's all right, Ellen," I sympathize. "I could always cry over my dogs. But when my mother died, I couldn't cry."

She looks at me doubtfully. "Not at all?"

"Not for a long time. And then only because some stupid salesgirl was rude to me. Then I thought I'd never stop."

Holly looks at the two of us in despair and retreats into a long, low lament.

But we must be done with this for now, I tell them firmly. The neighbor children will come soon for the Easter egg hunt. The show must go on.

The puppy is chewing a daffodil, but I walk past him to Baika, his dam and the old dog's granddaughter. She looks like a scrawny coyote just now, having lost her coat once the puppies were weaned. I grasp what is left of her ruff and look deep into her gentle brown eyes. "Tavi's dead, Baika." But she is only a dog, she does not understand. And tonight, as we take our bedtime walk she will be looking for him; she will get excited when she thinks she sees him nosing about a garbage can; then when it turns out to be a strange dog, she will walk past aloof and unseeing. And probably, as long as the puppy remains with us, she will not miss him at all. She will sleep on his rug by my bed and be queen.

Queen? She was supposed to be his consort, too. But by the time she was old enough, he was too old. He never fully recovered from the shock of his failure. His placid nature disappeared, he became so nervous and destructive that for two months I had to keep him on tranquillizers. My husband, otherwise less in tune with the vagaries of canine mentality, had shuddered in sympathy.

My husband comes up to retrieve the puppy who is rooting out the Easter eggs as fast as I hide them, "Well," he grumbles, "*now* I suppose you'll want to keep Archie."

Keep Archie? It hadn't occurred to me. He is the last of the litter, the only puppy I haven't been able to pronounce a possible show prospect. "Some

"Paws across the water." Ch. Foxhaunt's Tovarisch, the first AKC-registered Siberian Husky to travel behind the Iron Curtain, is seen in front of the Stalin Palace of Culture in Warsaw in 1966. Below, making friends with a Pole.

people may be coming over later today to look at him," I say, wondering privately if indeed they actually will, since the past weeks of advertising have taught me that most of those who promise to come seldom do. If they do, they will buy him, and at *my* price. Of this much I am confident. They only want a "pet" and now that the puppy, the only one left unsold, has been brought into the house, he is made to their order, the epitome of the bouncy, friendly puppy.

Archie wriggles free of my husband's grasp and dashes off with an Easter egg. Ah, yes, he's cute all right. Well built, lovely coat, nice strong high-set ears. But really he *is* small. And that little pink spot above his nose does detract from the over-all symmetry. Yet I cannot bring myself to sell him at "pet" prices. He does have something, quality, I guess I'd call it. Of course, nothing to compare with the old dog.

Tavi. Say it broadly, Tah-vi, a soft sound, a sweet dog, so stubborn but so sweet.

Tavi with the laughing eyes.

Tavi with the ice-blue laughing eyes.

Tavi with the mask of Marcel Marceau, the grin of Mephistopheles, and, on cue, the voice of Chanticleer.

Tavi, now the elegant New Yorker, browsing through the litter in Riverside Park, captivating our landlord, and crowing for our fellow apartment-dwellers as the elevator made its laborious way up to the eighth floor.

Tavi, now the leisured Californian, lying beneath our jacaranda tree, bestrewn and bedecked with daisies and geraniums offered to him lovingly by our once-toddling two-year-old as to some benign far-northern deity. Yelping to come indoors when the long-awaited rains began. And creeping from my side during our Sunday-night bedtime walk with the stealth of a cat, lest the chinkle of his collar warn me of his intent to hide among the neighborhood garbage cans placed along the curb for the Monday-morning trash collection.

Tavi, Mr. Continental, charming *our* way across Czechoslovakia and Poland, where he joined us during my professor-husband's sabbatical year abroad, and where his insouciant disregard for international boundaries could have landed us all in jail in East Germany had he not somehow touched the chord that made potential one-worlders out of the most calloused border guards.

Tavi. Answered also to his real name, Tovarisch. In Russian it means "comrade," but in the lands lying near modern Russia it means fellow Communist, so it was politic to stick to the diminutive, which in time acquired a wealth of Slavic suffixes; Tavchik, Tavichku, Tovarish-chik. A free spirit, a true communist; what was thine was his, especially if you were eating it.

A show dog, too, ranking among the best. When wind and weather were right, he bore himself like a champion and in time became one; oh yes, he beat them all—once or twice. But never often enough to be taken for granted. He could acquire the stance of a dairyman's dog and the gait of a plowhorse if the day was hot, or the wind brought the scent of snow—from the *other* side of the mountains.

And in Obedience competition, too, his performance fetched many a trophy and the best scores of any dog I have trained. Also the worst. For it was never more than a "performance"—a roll of the eye as we entered the ring to suggest, "Shall we show 'em today?" Or that malicious gleam which I learned to dread: "Thought you had me figured, didn't you?" as, with the finesse that only a fully trained dog could muster, he executed a perfect retrieve-and-finish—in front of the *judge!*

And as if dedicated to the task of proving that Obedience training does not break a dog's spirit, he remained steadfastly disobedient to the end, when, chafing perhaps under the regimentation of the nephritic's diet, which could never satiate his appetite for garbage—or lusting after the scent of some far-away female, which his arthritic spine would never have allowed him to mount—he barged past me through the half-open door and vanished into the night. Well, he has done his thing.

Archie lies curled in a tight, miserable little ball. He has just vomited up a collection of brightly tinted Easter-egg shells. My husband, commiserating with him, says grudgingly, "Well, if you want to keep Archie, you have my permission."

But my husband had been counting the days till we were back to only one dog! He chuckles sheepishly. "I guess I've gotten used to having two dogs."

I glower over toward the puppy. "Archie." Even the nickname taunts me. It was meant as a joke, short for Anarchist, in tribute to the jolly irreverence of his breed. But "Archie?" You whippersnapper, you. You cull. You *runt!*

("But he's *not* a runt," my veterinarian told me indignantly, "A runt is deficient in some way. But *look* at him! And the pink spot will go away.")

Archie rouses himself, his beady dark eyes intent upon an errant jellybean.

You do not have those ice-blue laughing eyes, little one. You do not grin like Mephistopheles, nor crow like Chanticleer. You do not have that look of majestic insolence that was the hallmark of your magnificent forebear. There may be things about you I like as well, even better, but you will never be as utterly ingratiating, nor yet as infuriating. For you are not he. You will not take his place.

The people who have promised to look at Archie that afternoon do not come.

At night I lock him up in the pantry, newspapers spread near the door. Probably he will howl all night, his first quite alone. Probably he will chew up the wires of the washing machine, and mess all over the floor. Then my husband will change his mind anyway.

He whines twice and is silent. Next morning I find him standing in sleepy dignity upon the newspapers, a puddle of gargantuan proportions slowly forming about his feet.

I go out with him into the early-morning sunshine. He spots a mockingbird and his sturdy nine-week-old frame goes taut. In his stance, and in the arch of his neck he is all male. His shoulder slopes strongly; his chest is deep. His feet have grown during the night.

So something has rubbed off onto him, it seems.

A gentle wind ruffles his fur, and off he frisks, heedless of the mantle which has fallen about his shoulders.

The king is dead.

Long live the king!

Long live the King! "Archie" (Ch. Tovarin's Merry Anarchist), handled by owner Betsy Korbonski, winning the National Specialty, 1974. Judge, Donald Booxbaum.

Ch. Monadnock's Stiva of Markova, owned by John and Margaret Falkowski.

IN A BOOK of this sort, it is not always possible to thank all the people who have helped in one way or another. For this we are sorry. However, we would like to especially thank the following people and organizations:

L. Stewart Cochrane, for his flattering Foreword.

The Siberian Husky Club of America, for permission to use Barbara Johansson's conformation drawings and the article by Betsy Korbonski that appears in Chapter 12.

Betsy Korbonski, again for the use of her article.

Robert Crane, for providing *all* of the information contained in Chapter 2.

Elizabeth Nansen, for clarifying details in Chapter 3.

Alice Watt, editor of *Siberian Husky News,* for providing the statistics used in "Top Winning Siberians of the 1970s" in Chapter 5.

Lorna Coppinger, for writing Chapter 6.

Wes Meador, for permission to use his article in Chapter 7.

Rachel Page Elliott, for advice on the presentation of Chapter 9.

Kathleen Kanzler, for writing Chapter 11.

Anna Mae Forsberg, for providing various historical information.

And *Peggy Koehler,* for advice and encouragement beyond the call of duty.

We would also like to thank everyone who provided photographs and information and to apologize to those of you who, for reasons of space and format, could not be included. We would also like to thank Lynne and Wes Kemp for the work they did duplicating these photographs, thereby insuring their preservation.